BIG HORN OUTDOOR

WOOD PELLET GRILL &

SMOKER COOKBOOK 2021

300 DELICIOUS, EASY & HEALTHY RECIPES FOR EVERYONE

AROUND THE WORLD

KARIN MASON

CONTENTS

INTRODUCTION

How the BIG HORN OUTDOOR Wood Pellet Grill Works

Essentially, pellet grills are high-performing outdoor cookers that combine elements from smokers, ovens and charcoal or gas grills. They run on 100 per cent hardwood pellets and can provide direct and indirect heat to your grilling.

The hardwood pellets are poured into a storage container, or hopper, in the grill that moves them into a cooking chamber. Through combustion, the pellets ignite and heat the cooking chamber. Fans bring in air which is dispersed throughout the cooking area. You'll want to be sure you can position your grill near an electrical outlet, as these functions are powered by electricity.

Much like an oven, these grills are capable of tracking precise temperatures. You can control these digitally or with a dial to ensure your food is cooked just the way you want.

Wood pellet grills pack a big flavour and allow users better temperature management than traditional grills. You also have the added benefit of choosing the wood you use to grill with — a factor that can impact flavour, cooking time, and maintenance.

Five Significant Reasons to Choose the BIG HORN OUTDOOR Wood Pellet Grill

1. TASTE

If the taste of your food is one of the most important reasons that you grill, then BBQ pellets should be your first choice. They provide a much better flavor than charcoal, especially when charcoal burners use lighter fluid to start then coals. When you grill with wood pellets, you give your food a strong, smoky flavor. There is also a lower chance of overcooking using a wood pellet grill, and it locks more of the natural moisture into the meat or fish.

Americans are very familiar with the taste and flavor of charcoal. However, when given a chance to barbecue with wood pellets, they find the food is delicious and tender, and it's hard to beat that wonderful flavor.

2. CONVENIENCE AND EASE-OF-USE

When you grill with charcoal, it can be a pain to start and once started it requires your constant attention because you don't want your food to burn or the charcoal to flare up too much. When you use a wood pellet grill, you push a button to start then set your temperature where you know it will give you the flavor that you want and the tenderness that you desire. You can leave the grill and prepare other food that you may be serving at your barbecue. A wood pellet grill burns with consistent heat, so you never have to worry about the grill getting too hot or the wood pellets flaring up and burning your meat or fish, making it tough and unpleasant.

3. VERSATILITY

When you buy a wood pellet grill, it's like you're getting a smoker for free. You can use your wood pellet grill to barbecue, grill, roast, bake, smoke, and even sear. That's because the ability of a wood pellet grill to cook your food at a consistent temperature allows you to use all these different methods.

Most charcoal grills will smoke, barbecue, grill, and sear and that's about it. Charcoal grills lack the versatility of a wood pellet grill. This is especially important if you like to experiment with your barbecue and use it for cooking in a variety of ways.

4. SAFETY

With a charcoal grill, even when you're finished grilling, you still need to keep an eye on the hot coals. When you use a wood pellet grill, you simply turn the grill off, and there are no more concerns or wasted fuel.

5. COST

It would be foolish to say that you can't get a charcoal grill for a reasonable price. Small grills sell for as little as $30. But most people prefer larger grills. In the past, wood pellet grills were more expensive than charcoal grills. But with the advances in technology made by wood pellet grills, along with competition, the costs are relatively similar. The actual difference in price depends on which model you choose. For instance, you can buy a pellet grill where you could use your smartphone to control the temperature.

Then there's the question of fuel. Lump charcoal is relatively inexpensive, but if you barbecue frequently, the cost of charcoal adds up quickly. If, on the other hand, you purchase a 20-pound bag of wood pellets, it can last five times longer than a comparable bag of charcoal because wood pellets burn more slowly.

Tips for Making the Most of Your BIG HORN OUTDOOR Wood Pellet Grill

(1) Take time to give your grill behind-the-scenes TLC. A clean smoker grill produces flavorful recipes without any lingering oiliness or staleness. We know cleaning's not exactly as fun as whipping up award-winning ribs or deep dish pizzas. Still, it's a necessary component to owning a smoker grill that's going to serve up mouthwatering meals.

(2) Store your wood pellets properly. Wood pellets that have been exposed to humid conditions won't give you the burn you need. Plus, they'll lose their freshness. So keep your wood pellets safe and dry.

(3) Pick the right wood pellet for the job. Want a nice smoke ring around your beef brisket? Choose cherry wood pellets for a predictable presentation. Want strong smoke flavor that stands out? Choose hickory or apple wood pellets for their intensity.

(4) Remember to cold smoke, too. At low temperatures, you can cold smoke foods like cheese, fish, cream and even butter, infusing them with the flavor of food-grade wood pellets made from hardwoods like pecan and oak. Get creative and go the distance by cold smoking ingredients to liven up your cooking.

Tips and Tricks on Cleaning Your BIG HORN OUTDOOR Wood Pellet Grill

1. Make sure the grill is cold.
2. Place the grill rack and the chimney dome in the hot soapy water.
3. Remove foil from the drip pan and flame reflector and brush off debris; put these parts in the tub only if they're still very dirty after brushing.
4. Remove solids from the grease bucket and place in the tub.
5. Scrub all parts, then air-dry completely.
6. Use the paint stirring stick to clear the grease chute.
7. Use rubber bands to secure the scrubby to the end of the spoon, brush handle or stirring stick and wipe the (often surprisingly disgusting) inside of the chimney.
8. Give the inside of the lid a good scrape with the brush.
9. Vacuum the grill interior and the firepot, being sure to clear the holes in the firepot.
10. Wipe the interior with a scrubby dampened with water or a natural cleaning product.
11. Carefully wipe the temperature probe.
12. Give any stainless steel parts a wipe with stainless steel cleaner.
13. Replace the grease bucket; line it with foil for future easy maintenance.
14. Keep things easy and flavors clean by maintaining your pellet smoker all year. All you'll need: your brass wire brush, a damp rag, and heavy-duty aluminum foil.
15. Run on high for ten minutes, then brush the grates.
16. Switch off and cool the smoker according to your grill's instruction manual.
17. Carefully remove the grease bucket and put it out of the reach of animals.
18. Wipe any drips off the grill exterior with a damp rag.
19. Allow to cool overnight and replace the foil on the drip pan.

VEGETABLES RECIPES

Baked Heirloom Tomato Tart

Servings: 4

Cooking Time: 45 Minutes

Ingredients:

- 1 Whole Puff Pastry Sheet
- 2 Pound heirloom tomatoes, various shapes and sizes
- 1/2 Tablespoon kosher salt
- 1/2 Cup Ricotta Cheese
- 5 Whole eggs
- 1 To Taste salt and pepper
- 1/2 Teaspoon thyme leaves
- 1/2 Teaspoon red pepper flakes
- 4 Sprig thyme

Directions:

1. Supply your smoker with wood pellets and follow the start-up procedure. Preheat the grill, with the lid closed, to 350° F.

2. Place the puff pastry on a parchment lined sheet tray, and make a cut ¾ of the way through the pastry, ½" from the edge.

3. Slice the tomatoes and season with salt. Place on a sheet tray lined with paper towels.

4. In a small bowl combine the ricotta, 4 of the eggs, salt, thyme leaves, red pepper flakes and black pepper. Whisk together until combined. Spread the ricotta mixture over the puff pastry, staying within ½" from the edge.

5. In a small bowl whisk the last egg. Brush the egg wash onto the exposed edges of the pastry.

6. Place the sheet tray directly on the grill grate and bake for 45 minutes, rotating half-way through. Grill: 350 ˚F

7. When the edges are browned and the moisture from the tomatoes has evaporated, remove from the grill and let cool 5-7 minutes before serving. Enjoy!

Green Bean Casserole

Servings: 6

Cooking Time: 25 Minutes

Ingredients:

- 1/2 Stick butter
- 1 Small onion
- 1/2 Cup sliced button mushrooms
- 4 Can green beans, drained
- 2 Can cream of mushroom soup
- 1 Teaspoon Lawry's Seasoned Salt
- pepper
- 1 Can French's Original Crispy Fried Onions
- 1 Cup grated sharp cheddar cheese

Directions:

1. Supply your smoker with wood pellets and follow the start-up procedure. Preheat the grill, with the lid closed, to 375° F.

2. Melt butter in a cast iron skillet and add onions and mushrooms, stirring occasionally until softened.

3. Add drained green beans and cream of mushroom soup and stir gently to combine.

4. Season with seasoned salt and pepper and sprinkle the top with grated cheddar cheese and fried onions.

5. Bake for 25 minutes. Serve warm, enjoy! Grill: 375 ˚F

Baked Garlic Duchess Potatoes

Servings: 8
Cooking Time: 60 Minutes

Ingredients:

- 12 Medium Potatoes, Yukon gold
- salt
- 5 Large Egg Yolk
- 2 Clove garlic, minced
- 1.24 Cup heavy cream
- 3/4 Cup sour cream
- 10 Tablespoon butter, melted
- black pepper

Directions:

1. Place potatoes in a large pot and fill with water. Season with salt. Bring to a boil over medium-high heat.
2. Reduce heat and simmer until a paring knife easily slides through potatoes, about 25 to 35 minutes. Drain and let cool slightly.
3. Supply your smoker with wood pellets and follow the start-up procedure. Preheat the grill, with the lid closed, to 450° F.
4. Whisk together egg yolks, garlic, cream, sour cream, butter, and pepper in a large bowl. Season with salt.
5. Peel potatoes and push flesh through a ricer or a food mill directly into bowl with egg mixture. Fold in the egg mixture being careful not to overmix.
6. Transfer to a 3-quart baking dish and bake until golden brown and slightly puffed, about 30–40 minutes. Enjoy! Grill: 450 ˚F

Bacon Wrapped Corn On The Cob

Servings: 4

Cooking Time: 21 Minutes

Ingredients:

- 4 Whole Corn, ears
- 8 Slices bacon
- 1 Teaspoon freshly ground black pepper
- 1 Teaspoon chili powder
- 1 To Taste Parmesan cheese, grated

Directions:

1. Peel back the corn husks, remove silk strings and rinse corn under cold water.
2. Wrap 2 pieces of bacon around each ear of corn, securing with toothpicks.
3. Dust each ear of corn with some chili powder and cracked black pepper.
4. Supply your smoker with wood pellets and follow the start-up procedure. Preheat the grill, with the lid closed, to 375° F.
5. Place the ears of corn directly on the Traeger and grill for approximately 20 minutes or until the bacon is cooked crisp. Grill: 375 ˚F
6. Take the corn off the Traeger. Carefully remove the toothpicks and season with a little more chili powder and a grating of parmesan cheese, if desired. Serve & enjoy!

Roasted Jalapeno Cheddar Deviled Eggs

Servings: 6
Cooking Time: 30 Minutes

Ingredients:

- 7 Eggs, hard boiled
- 3 Tablespoon mayonnaise
- 1 Teaspoon brown mustard
- 1 Teaspoon apple cider vinegar
- 1 Dash hot sauce
- 1 jalapeño pepper, seeded and minced

- salt and pepper
- 1/2 Cup shredded cheddar cheese
- paprika

Directions:

1. Supply your smoker with wood pellets and follow the start-up procedure. Preheat the grill, with the lid closed, to 180° F.

2. Place your eggs directly on the grill grate and smoke for 30 minutes.

3. Remove from the grill and allow the eggs to cool. Smoking the eggs will give them a slightly yellowed color, but an intense smoky flavor. If a classic white egg is your preference, then skip this step.

4. Slice the eggs lengthwise and scoop the egg yolks directly into a gallon zip top bag.

5. Add the mayo, mustard, vinegar, hot sauce, roasted jalapeños and salt and pepper to the bag.

6. Zip the bag closed and, using your hands, knead all of the ingredients together in the bag until completely smooth.

7. Squeeze the yolk mixture into one corner of the bag and then cut the corner off. Pipe the yolk mixture into the whites.

8. Sprinkle with the finely shredded cheddar or paprika and chill until you are ready to serve. Enjoy!

Roasted Pumpkin Seeds

Servings: 8

Cooking Time: 40 Minutes

Ingredients:

- 1 Whole Pumpkin, seeds
- olive oil or vegetable oil
- Jacobsen Salt Co. Pure Kosher Sea Salt

Directions:

1. As soon as possible after removing the seeds from the pumpkin, rinse pumpkin seeds under cold water in a colander and pick out the pulp and strings.

2. Place the pumpkin seeds in a single layer on an oiled baking sheet, stirring to coat. Supply your smoker with wood pellets and follow the start-up procedure. Preheat the grill, with the lid closed, to 180° F.

3. Place the baking sheet with the seeds on the grill grate, close the lid, and smoke for 20 minutes. Grill: 180 °F

4. Sprinkle your seeds with salt and turn the temperature on your grill up to 325°F. Roast the seeds until toasted, about 20 minutes. Check and stir seeds after the first 10 minutes. Grill: 325 °F

5. Seeds will be brown because they were smoked before being roasted. Enjoy!

Baked Breakfast Mini Quiches

Servings: 8

Cooking Time: 15 Minutes

Ingredients:

- cooking spray
- 1 Tablespoon extra-virgin olive oil
- 1/2 yellow onion, diced
- 3 Cup Spinach, fresh
- 10 eggs
- 4 Ounce shredded cheddar, mozzarella or Swiss cheese
- 1/4 Cup fresh basil
- 1 Teaspoon kosher salt
- 1/2 Teaspoon black pepper

Directions:

1. Spray a 12-cup muffin tin generously with cooking spray.

2. In a small skillet over medium heat, warm the oil. Add the onion and cook, stirring frequently, until softened, about 7 minutes. Add the spinach and cook until wilted, about 1 minute longer.

3. Transfer to a cutting board to cool, then chop the mixture so the spinach if broken up a little.

4. Supply your smoker with wood pellets and follow the start-up procedure. Preheat the grill, with the lid closed, to 350° F.

5. In a large bowl, whisk the eggs until frothy. Add the cooled onions and spinach, cheese, basil, 1 tsp salt and 1/2 tsp pepper. Stir to combine. Divide egg mixture evenly among the muffin cups.

6. Place tray on the grill and bake until the eggs have puffed up, are set, and are beginning to brown, about 18 to 20 minutes. Grill: 350 °F

7. Serve immediately, or allow to cool on a wire rack, then refrigerate in an air tight container for up to 4 days. Enjoy!

Roasted Potato Poutine

Servings: 6
Cooking Time: 40 Minutes

Ingredients:
- 4 Large russet potatoes
- Tablespoon olive oil or vegetable oil
- Prime Rib Rub
- Cup chicken or beef gravy (homemade or jarred)
- 1 1/2 Cup white or yellow cheddar cheese curds
- freshly ground black pepper
- 2 Tablespoon scallions

Directions:
1. Supply your smoker with wood pellets and follow the start-up procedure. Preheat the grill, with the lid closed, to 500° F.

2. Scrub the potatoes and slice into fries, wedges or preferred shape.

3. Put potatoes into a large mixing bowl and coat with oil. Season generously with Traeger Prime Rib rub.

4. Tip the potatoes onto a rimmed baking sheet and spread in a single layer, cut sides down.

5. Roast for 20 minutes, then using a spatula, turn the potatoes to the other cut side. Continue to roast until the potatoes are tender and golden brown, about 15 to 20 minutes more.

6. While potatoes cook, warm the gravy on the stovetop or in a heat-proof saucepan on your Traeger.

7. To assemble the poutine, arrange the potatoes in a large shallow bowl or on a serving platter. Distribute the cheese curds on top. Pour the hot gravy evenly over the potatoes and cheese curds.

8. Season with black pepper and garnish with thinly sliced scallions. Serve immediately. Enjoy!

Roasted Fall Vegetables

Servings: 6
Cooking Time: 30 Minutes

Ingredients:
- 1/2 Pound Potatoes, new
- 2 Tablespoon olive oil
- salt and pepper
- 1/2 Pound Butternut Squash, diced
- 1/2 Pound fresh Brussels sprouts
- 1 Pint mushrooms, sliced

Directions:
1. Supply your smoker with wood pellets and follow the start-up procedure. Preheat the grill, with the lid closed, to 200° F.

2. Toss potatoes and squash with olive oil, salt and pepper and spread out on a sheet tray.

3. Place directly on the grill grate and cook for 15 minutes. Add brussels sprouts and mushrooms and toss to coat.

4. Cook another 15-20 minutes until veggies are lightly browned and cooked through.

5. Adjust seasoning as needed. Enjoy!

Traeger Smoked Coleslaw

Servings: 8
Cooking Time: 20 Minutes

Ingredients:
- 1 Head purple cabbage, shredded
- 1 Head green cabbage, shredded
- 1 Cup shredded carrots
- 2 scallions, thinly sliced
- 1 1/2 Cup mayonnaise
- 1/8 Cup white wine vinegar
- 1 Teaspoon celery seed
- 1 Teaspoon sugar
- salt and pepper

Directions:
1. Supply your smoker with wood pellets and follow the start-up procedure. Preheat the grill, with the lid closed, to 180° F.

2. Spread cabbage and carrots out on a sheet tray and place directly on the grill grates. Smoke for 20 to 25 minutes or until cabbage picks up desired amount of smoke. Grill: 180 °F

3. Remove from grill and transfer to the refrigerator immediately to cool. While cabbage is cooling, make the dressing.

4. For the dressing, combine all ingredients in a small bowl and mix well.

5. Place smoked cabbage and carrots in a large bowl and pour dressing over them. Stir to coat well.

6. Transfer to a serving dish and sprinkle with scallions. Enjoy!

Grilled Ratatouille Salad

Servings: 4
Cooking Time: 25 Minutes

Ingredients:
- 1 Whole sweet potatoes
- 1 Whole red onion, diced
- 1 Whole zucchini
- 1 Whole Squash
- 1 Large Tomato, diced
- vegetable oil
- salt and pepper

Directions:
1. Supply your smoker with wood pellets and follow the start-up procedure. Preheat the grill, with the lid closed, to High heat.

2. Slice all vegetables to a ¼ inch thickness.

3. Lightly brush each vegetable with oil and season with Traeger's Veggie Shake or salt and pepper.

4. Place sweet potato, onion, zucchini, and squash on grill grate and grill for 20 minutes or until tender, turn halfway through.

5. Add tomato slices to the grill during the last 5 minutes of cooking time.

6. For presentation, alternate vegetables while layering them vertically. Enjoy!

Spicy Asian Brussels Sprouts

Servings: 4
Cooking Time: 10 Minutes

Ingredients:
- 2 Cup fresh Brussels sprouts
- 2 Tablespoon vegetable oil
- 1 Tablespoon Asian BBQ Rub

- 1/4 Cup Thai sweet chile sauce

Directions:

1. Supply your smoker with wood pellets and follow the start-up procedure. Preheat the grill, with the lid closed, to 350° F.

2. Spread the halved brussel sprouts in a single layer on a lined cookie sheet. Drizzle with the oil and toss to coat.

3. Sprinkle the brussel sprouts evenly with an Asian BBQ rub and put the cookie sheet on the grill. Close the lid and cook for 7-8 minutes. Grill: 350 °F

4. Toss the brussels sprouts in the Thai Chili Sauce and return to the grill for an additional 3-4 minutes, or until the sprouts are crisp-tender. Grill: 350 °F

5. Serve immediately. Enjoy!

Roasted Red Pepper White Bean Dip

Servings: 4
Cooking Time: 40 Minutes

Ingredients:

- 4 Whole garlic
- 4 Tablespoon extra-virgin olive oil
- 2 Bell Pepper, Red
- 3 Tablespoon Dill Weed, fresh
- 3 Tablespoon chopped flat-leaf parsley
- 2 Can cannellini beans, mashed
- 4 Teaspoon lemon juice
- 1 1/2 Teaspoon salt

Directions:

1. Roasting the garlic and red peppers:

2. Supply your smoker with wood pellets and follow the start-up procedure. Preheat the grill, with the lid closed, to 400° F.

3. Peel away the outside layers of the garlic husk. Cut off the top of the garlic bulb, exposing each of the individual cloves. Drizzle olive oil over the top of the head of garlic and rub it in. Wrap the garlic in foil, completely covering it. Put the head of garlic and the two red peppers (washed and dried) on the Traeger.

4. Roast the garlic for 25-30 minutes and the peppers for about 40 minutes. Rotate the peppers a quarter-turn every 10 minutes until the exterior is blistered and blackened. Grill: 400 °F

5. Pull the peppers off the grill and put them in a bowl. Cover the bowl with plastic wrap and leave them for 15 minutes. The steam will loosen the skins so that they slip off like a drumstick covered in barbecue sauce.

6. Peel off the pepper skin. Cut off the stems and scrape out the seeds and they're ready to use.

7. As for the garlic, let it cool and then pull out the individual cloves as needed.

8. The dip:

9. In a blender put the roasted red peppers, 4 cloves of roasted garlic, dill, parsley, drained and rinsed beans, olive oil, lemon juice and salt.

10. Blend until the dip is smooth and creamy. You may need to scrape down the sides of the blender a couple of times. If it's having difficulty blending or looks too thick add more olive oil or lemon juice. (Add more lemon juice if it tastes like it needs more acid or brightness.) Enjoy!

Christmas Brussel Sprouts

Servings: 6
Cooking Time: 50 Minutes

Ingredients:

- 1/2 Pound thick-cut bacon
- 1 Medium onion, diced

- 2 Pound fresh Brussels sprouts
- 2 Tablespoon olive oil
- salt and pepper

Directions:

1. Supply your smoker with wood pellets and follow the start-up procedure. Preheat the grill, with the lid closed, to 350° F.

2. Place bacon directly on grill grate and cook for 15-20 minutes, or until lightly browned. Remove from grill and set aside on paper towel lined plate.

3. Slice onion in half and then slice into 1/4 inch moons and add to large mixing bowl. Slice brussels sprouts in half lengthwise and add to bowl.

4. Cut reserved bacon into 1/2 inch pieces and add to bowl. Drizzle with olive oil and sprinkle with salt and pepper. Toss to coat and pour into baking pan.

5. Turn the temperature on grill to 375 and place baking pan on grill. Roast for 30 minutes mixing halfway through cooking. Grill: 375 °F

Roasted Vegetable Napoleon

Servings: 4
Cooking Time: 30 Minutes

Ingredients:

- 2 Whole sweet potatoes
- 2 Whole zucchini
- 2 Whole Squash
- 1 Whole red onion
- 2 Whole Bell Pepper, Red
- salt and pepper

Directions:

1. Supply your smoker with wood pellets and follow the start-up procedure. Preheat the grill, with the lid closed, to High heat.

2. Salt and pepper all vegetables and grill them on both sides. Begin with the peppers and onions as they will take a little longer to cook. Grill: 450 °F

Roasted New Potatoes

Servings: 4
Cooking Time: 25 Minutes

Ingredients:

- 2 Pound small new potatoes
- 3 Tablespoon butter, melted
- 2 Tablespoon olive oil
- 2 Tablespoon whole mustard seeds
- salt and pepper
- 2 Tablespoon freshly minced chives
- 2 Tablespoon freshly minced parsley

Directions:

1. Place potatoes in a colander and rinse with cold water. Dry on paper towels and transfer to a rimmed baking sheet large enough to hold them in a single layer.

2. Drizzle the potatoes with butter and olive oil, then sprinkle them with the mustard seeds. Season with salt and pepper.

3. Supply your smoker with wood pellets and follow the start-up procedure. Preheat the grill, with the lid closed, to 400° F.

4. Place the baking sheet with the potatoes on the grill grate. Roast for about 25 minutes shaking the pan once or twice, until potatoes are tender and the skins are slightly wrinkled. Grill: 400 °F

5. Transfer potatoes to a bowl or platter. Top with fresh chives and parsley. Enjoy!

Grilled Broccoli Rabe

Servings: 4

Cooking Time: 10 Minutes

Ingredients:

- 4 Tablespoon extra-virgin olive oil
- 4 Bunch broccoli rabe or broccolini
- kosher salt
- 1 lemon, halved

Directions:

1. Supply your smoker with wood pellets and follow the start-up procedure. Preheat the grill, with the lid closed, to 450° F.

2. On a platter or in a mixing bowl, drizzle the olive oil over the broccoli rabe. Use your hands to mix thoroughly, coating the vegetables evenly with the oil. Season with sea salt.

3. Place the broccoli rabe in one layer directly on the lowest grill grate. Close the lid and cook for 5 to 10 minutes. You want there to be some color and slight char on the first side. Flip and cook for a few more minutes. Grill: 450 ˚F

4. Transfer the broccoli rabe to a serving platter and squeeze the juice of half a lemon evenly over the top.

5. Serve with more lemon wedges on the side. Enjoy!

Smoked Mushrooms

Servings: 4

Cooking Time: 45 Minutes

Ingredients:

- Pound Mushrooms, fresh
- 1/2 Cup apple cider vinegar
- 1/2 Cup soy sauce
- 1 Teaspoon Blackened Saskatchewan Rub

Directions:

1. Clean mushrooms and place in a large Ziploc bag. Add apple cider vinegar, soy sauce and rub.

2. Mix well and allow to marinate in the refrigerator for at least 2 hours.

3. Supply your smoker with wood pellets and follow the start-up procedure. Preheat the grill, with the lid closed, to 350° F.

4. Place cast iron skillet inside grill for 20 minutes to warm up.

5. Add the mushrooms and marinade slowly into the cast iron skillet.

6. Cook uncovered for 15 minutes, then cover the skillet and cook another 30 minutes until mushrooms are tender. Grill: 350 ˚F

7. Remove skillet from grill and let mushrooms cool down for 5 minutes before serving. Enjoy!

Traeger Baked Potato Torte

Servings: 6

Cooking Time: 25 Minutes

Ingredients:

- 6 Yukon Gold potatoes, sliced 1/4 inch thick
- 2 Stick butter, melted
- 3 Clove garlic, crushed
- 2 Tablespoon rosemary, chopped
- 1 Cup Parmesan cheese, grated
- salt and pepper

Directions:

1. Supply your smoker with wood pellets and follow the start-up procedure. Preheat the grill, with the lid closed, to 375° F.

2. While the Traeger is heating up, peel and slice the potatoes (make sure to put them in water so they will not oxidize). Melt the butter and combine it with the crushed garlic.

3. Grease a 12" cast iron pan with butter and start to layer the torte. The layers should go as

follows, potatoes, butter garlic mixture, rosemary, parmesan, continue layering to the top of the pan, about 4 to 5 layers.

4. Place the pan in the Traeger and bake for 20 to 25 minutes, or until the potatoes are fully cooked. If the top of the torte starts to darken before it is finished cooking, reduce the heat to 325°F. Serve hot and enjoy! Grill: 375 °F

Potluck Salad With Smoked Cornbread

Servings: 6
Cooking Time: 45 Minutes

Ingredients:

- 1 cup all-purpose flour
- 1 cup yellow cornmeal
- 1 tablespoon sugar
- 2 teaspoons baking powder
- 1 teaspoon salt
- 1 cup milk
- 1 egg, beaten, at room temperature
- 4 tablespoons (½ stick) unsalted butter, melted and cooled
- Nonstick cooking spray or butter, for greasing
- ½ cup milk
- ½ cup sour cream
- 2 tablespoons dry ranch dressing mix
- 1 pound bacon, cooked and crumbled
- 3 tomatoes, chopped
- 1 bell pepper, chopped
- 1 cucumber, seeded and chopped
- 2 stalks celery, chopped (about 1 cup)
- ½ cup chopped scallions

Directions:

1. For the cornbread:
2. In a medium bowl, combine the flour, cornmeal, sugar, baking powder, and salt.

3. In a small bowl, whisk together the milk and egg. Pour in the butter, then slowly fold this mixture into the dry ingredients.

4. Supply your smoker with wood pellets and follow the start-up procedure. Preheat, with the lid closed, to 375°F.

5. Coat a cast iron skillet with cooking spray or butter.

6. Pour the batter into the skillet, place on the grill grate, close the lid, and smoke for 35 to 45 minutes, or until the cornbread is browned and pulls away from the side of the skillet.

7. Remove the cornbread from the grill and let cool, then coarsely crumble.

8. For the salad:

9. In a small bowl, whisk together the milk, sour cream, and ranch dressing mix.

10. In a medium bowl, combine the crumbled bacon, tomatoes, bell pepper, cucumber, celery, and scallions.

11. In a large serving bowl, layer half of the crumbled cornbread, half of the bacon-veggie mixture, and half of the dressing. Toss lightly.

12. Repeat the layering with the remaining cornbread, bacon-veggie mixture, and dressing. Toss again.

13. Refrigerate the salad for at least 1 hour. Serve cold.

Roasted Sheet Pan Vegetables

Servings: 4
Cooking Time: 25 Minutes

Ingredients:

- 1 Small head purple cauliflower, stemmed and cut into 2 inch florets
- 1 Small head yellow cauliflower, stemmed and cut into 2 inch florets

- 4 Cup butternut squash
- 2 Cup oyster or shiitake mushrooms, rinsed and sliced
- 3 Tablespoon olive oil
- 2 Teaspoon kosher salt
- freshly ground black pepper
- 1/4 Cup chopped flat-leaf parsley

Directions:

1. Supply your smoker with wood pellets and follow the start-up procedure. Preheat the grill, with the lid closed, to 450° F.

2. In a large mixing bowl, combine all of the vegetables. Drizzle olive oil over the top, along with kosher salt and a generous grinding of black pepper.

3. Using your hands, toss the vegetables until they are evenly coated.

4. Spread out onto 1 or 2 half sheet pans or baking sheets, ensuring there is a little space between the veggies. (If they are too crowded, the vegetables will steam instead of roast and you won't get that crispy texture.)

5. Place the sheet pans on the grill and cook for 15 minutes. Open and stir, then close the lid and continue to cook until the vegetables are brown around the edges, about 5 to 15 minutes longer. Grill: 450 °F

6. Toss with parsley and serve immediately. The vegetables are also delicious at room temperature. Enjoy!

Traeger Grilled Whole Corn

Servings: 4
Cooking Time: 25 Minutes

Ingredients:

- 3 green onions
- 6 Tablespoon butter, softened
- 1 Teaspoon chile powder
- 1 Teaspoon toasted sesame seeds
- 4 ears corn, in husk

Directions:

1. Supply your smoker with wood pellets and follow the start-up procedure. Preheat the grill, with the lid closed, to 325° F.

2. Place green onions directly on the grill grate and cook 15 minutes until lightly charred. Remove from grill and set aside.

3. Sesame-Chile Butter: Take butter out of fridge and let soften. Chop up charred green onions and add to butter along with chile powder and sesame seeds. Mash all ingredients together.

4. Grill corn, rotating occasionally, until husks are blackened (some will flake and fall off) and kernels are tender with some browned and charred spots, about 25 to 35 minutes. Grill: 325 °F

5. Let corn cool slightly, then shuck. Serve with the Sesame-Chile Butter. Enjoy

Smoked Jalapeño Poppers

Servings: 4
Cooking Time: 60 Minutes

Ingredients:

- 12 Medium jalapeño
- 6 Slices bacon, cut in half
- 8 Ounce cream cheese
- 2 Tablespoon Pork & Poultry Rub
- 1 Cup grated cheese

Directions:

1. Supply your smoker with wood pellets and follow the start-up procedure. Preheat the grill, with the lid closed, to 180° F. For optimal flavor, use Super Smoke if available.

2. Slice the jalapeños in half lengthwise. Scrape out any seeds and ribs with a small spoon or paring knife. Mix softened cream cheese with Traeger Pork & Poultry rub and grated cheese. Spoon mixture onto each jalapeño half. Wrap with bacon and secure with a toothpick.

3. Place the jalapeños on a rimmed baking sheet. Place on grill and smoke for 30 minutes. Grill: 180 °F

4. Increase the grill temperature to 375°F and cook an additional 30 minutes or until bacon is cooked to desired doneness. Serve warm, enjoy! Grill: 375 °F

Smoked Macaroni Salad

Servings: 4
Cooking Time: 20 Minutes

Ingredients:

- 1 Pound macaroni, uncooked
- 1/2 Small red onion, diced
- 1 green bell pepper, diced
- 1/2 Cup shredded carrot
- 1 Cup mayonnaise
- 3 Tablespoon white wine vinegar
- 2 Tablespoon sugar
- salt
- black pepper

Directions:

1. Bring a large stock pot of salted water to a boil over medium heat and cook pasta according to package directions. Make sure to cook to al dente, strain, and rinse under cold water.

2. Supply your smoker with wood pellets and follow the start-up procedure. Preheat the grill, with the lid closed, to 225° F.

3. Spread cooked pasta out on a sheet tray and place sheet tray directly on the grill grate. Smoke for 20 minutes, remove from heat, and transfer directly to the refrigerator to cool. Grill: 225 °F

4. While the pasta is cooling mix the dressing. Place all ingredients in a medium bowl and whisk to combine.

5. When pasta is cool combine chopped veggies, smoked pasta and dressing in a large bowl.

6. Cover with plastic wrap and place in the fridge for 20 minutes before serving. Enjoy!

Mashed Red Potatoes

Servings: 4
Cooking Time: 40 Minutes

Ingredients:

- 8 Large red potatoes
- salt
- black pepper
- 1/2 Cup heavy cream
- 1/4 Cup butter

Directions:

1. Supply your smoker with wood pellets and follow the start-up procedure. Preheat the grill, with the lid closed, to 180° F.

2. Slice red potatoes in half, lengthwise then cut in half again to make quarters. Season potatoes with salt and pepper.

3. Increase the heat to High and preheat. Once the grill is hot, set potatoes directly on the grill grate. Grill: 450 °F

4. Every 15 minutes flip potatoes to ensure all sides get color. Continue to do this until potatoes are fork tender.

5. When tender, mash potatoes with cream, butter, salt, and pepper to taste. Serve warm, enjoy!

Roasted Pickled Beets

Servings: 8

Cooking Time: 60 Minutes

Ingredients:

* 6 Medium Red Beets, scrubbed and trimmed
* 1 Cup red wine vinegar
* 1/2 Cup sugar
* 10 Whole peppercorns
* 1 Cup water
* 1 1/2 Teaspoon coarse salt
* 8 whole cloves
* 2 Pieces Star Anise, Broken
* 1 cinnamon stick, broken in half

Directions:

1. Make a foil pouch large enough to enclose the beets. Poke a few holes in the top to allow steam to escape.

2. Supply your smoker with wood pellets and follow the start-up procedure. Preheat the grill, with the lid closed, to 350° F.

3. Roast the beets until they are tender, 50 to 60 minutes. Carefully remove the foil and allow the beets to cool until they can be comfortably handled. Grill: 350 °F

4. Slip the skins off with your fingers. (You may wish to wear latex gloves to avoid staining your hands.) Cut the beets into quarters or slices. (Candy cane beets are especially pretty when sliced.)

5. In the meantime, make the brine: Bring the vinegar, sugar, salt, and water to a boil in a small saucepan over high heat.

6. Put the cloves, peppercorns, star anise, and cinnamon in a clean lidded jar, such as a canning jar

7. Add the beets to the jar. Pour the hot brine over the beets. Put the lid on the jar. Cool the beets to room temperature, then refrigerate for 3 to 5 days before serving. Enjoy!

Baked Kale Chips

Servings: 4

Cooking Time: 20 Minutes

Ingredients:

* 2 Bunch kale, leaves washed and stems removed
* 1 As Needed extra-virgin olive oil
* 1 To Taste sea salt

Directions:

1. Dry the kale leaves well and lay them out on a sheet tray. Drizzle lightly with olive oil and sprinkle with sea salt.

2. Supply your smoker with wood pellets and follow the start-up procedure. Preheat the grill, with the lid closed, to 250° F.

3. Place the sheet tray directly on the grill grate and cook until kale is lightly browned and crispy, about 20 minutes. Enjoy! Grill: 250 °F

Carolina Baked Beans

Servings: 12-15

Cooking Time: 180 Minutes

Ingredients:

* 3 (28-ounce) cans baked beans (I like Bush's brand)
* 1 large onion, finely chopped
* 1 cup The Ultimate BBQ Sauce
* ½ cup light brown sugar
* ¼ cup Worcestershire sauce
* 3 tablespoons yellow mustard
* Nonstick cooking spray or butter, for greasing
* 1 large bell pepper, cut into thin rings
* ½ pound thick-cut bacon, partially cooked and cut into quarters

Directions:

1. Supply your smoker with wood pellets and follow the start-up procedure. Preheat, with the lid closed, to 300°F.

2. In a large mixing bowl, stir together the beans, onion, barbecue sauce, brown sugar, Worcestershire sauce, and mustard until well combined

3. Coat a 9-by-13-inch aluminum pan with cooking spray or butter.

4. Pour the beans into the pan and top with the bell pepper rings and bacon pieces, pressing them down slightly into the sauce.

5. Place a layer of heavy-duty foil on the grill grate to catch drips, and place the pan on top of the foil. Close the lid and cook for 2 hours 30 minutes to 3 hours, or until the beans are hot, thick, and bubbly.

6. Let the beans rest for 5 minutes before serving.

Baked Sweet Potatoes

Servings: 8
Cooking Time: 60 Minutes

Ingredients:

- 1 Cup butter, softened
- 1/4 Cup pure maple syrup
- 1/2 Teaspoon ground cinnamon
- 8 Medium sweet potatoes

Directions:

1. Make the Maple-Cinnamon Butter: In a mixing bowl, combine the butter, maple syrup, and cinnamon and whip with a wooden spoon. (Alternatively, blend the ingredients using a hand-held mixer or a stand mixer.) Transfer to a small bowl, cover, and chill until serving time.

2. Supply your smoker with wood pellets and follow the start-up procedure. Preheat the grill, with the lid closed, to 375° F. Arrange the sweet potatoes on the grill grate and bake until soft, 1 to 1-1/2 hours, depending on the size of the potatoes. Make a slit in the side of each, and squeeze the ends gently to fluff.

3. Serve hot with the Maple-Cinnamon Butter. Enjoy!

Grilled Cabbage Steaks With Warm Bacon Vinaigrette

Servings: 4
Cooking Time: 10 Minutes

Ingredients:

- 3 Strips thick-cut lean bacon, cut into 1/4 inch strips
- 1 Large shallot, minced
- 2 Tablespoon sherry vinegar
- 1 Tablespoon whole grain mustard
- 1 Teaspoon chopped thyme
- 2 Tablespoon olive oil, plus more as needed
- 1 Head green cabbage, cut into 3/4 inch thick slices (about 6 steaks)
- salt and pepper

Directions:

1. Supply your smoker with wood pellets and follow the start-up procedure. Preheat the grill, with the lid closed, to 450° F.

2. For the Vinaigrette: In a large skillet, cook the bacon in 2 tablespoons olive oil over medium-high heat until browned and crisp. Remove bacon from heat and stir in the shallot, vinegar, mustard and thyme then set aside.

3. Brush cabbage steaks with olive oil and season with salt and pepper. Place cabbage steaks directly

on grill grate and grill for 5 minutes per side. Grill: 450 °F

4. Remove cabbage steaks from grill and drizzle with bacon vinaigrette. Enjoy!

Steak Fries With Horseradish Creme

Servings: 6
Cooking Time: 25 Minutes

Ingredients:
- 5 Potatoes, Baking
- 2 Tablespoon extra-virgin olive oil
- 1 Teaspoon butter
- 3 Clove garlic, crushed
- 1 Teaspoon onion powder
- 2 Teaspoon Jacobsen Salt Co. Pure Kosher Sea Salt
- 1 Teaspoon black pepper

Directions:
1. Wash the potatoes thoroughly, and cut them in eighths, then toss them in the olive oil, butter, crushed garlic, onion powder, salt, and pepper.
2. Supply your smoker with wood pellets and follow the start-up procedure. Preheat the grill, with the lid closed, to 450° F.
3. In order to get great grill marks, line up the wedges on the front of the grill and the back of the grill, turning to get grill marks on all sides.
4. Once they have been seared, move them to the center of the grill and finish cooking about ten more minutes, serve hot with the horseradish mayo. Enjoy!

Roasted Garlic Herb Fries

Servings: 4
Cooking Time: 45 Minutes

Ingredients:
- 4 Whole russet potatoes
- 1 Teaspoon salt
- 2 Tablespoon avocado oil
- 1 Teaspoon fresh chopped rosemary
- 1 Teaspoon fresh chopped thyme
- 2 Clove garlic, minced
- 2 Teaspoon flake salt
- 1 Teaspoon chopped parsley, for garnish

Directions:
1. Supply your smoker with wood pellets and follow the start-up procedure. Preheat the grill, with the lid closed, to 425° F.
2. Chop potatoes into fries, (a mandolin works great for this) and place directly into an ice water bath with 1 teaspoon salt for 15 to 30 minutes.
3. Combine oil, rosemary, thyme and garlic in a big bowl. Remove potatoes from ice water and dry thoroughly with paper towels.
4. Toss potatoes in the oil mixture and place them on 2 to 3 parchment-lined baking sheets in a single layer. Sprinkle the flake salt over the fries.
5. Place baking sheets on the grill and roast for 30 minutes, flip the fries, then cook for an additional 15 minutes until golden and crispy. Dust with parsley. Grill: 425 °F
6. Serve with your favorite dipping sauce, side dish or as a nacho base.

Roasted Beet & Bacon Salad

Servings: 4
Cooking Time: 45 Minutes

Ingredients:
- 2 Medium raw beets, peeled and thinly sliced
- 8 Slices bacon
- 1/4 Cup raw pecans or walnuts
- 2 Medium ripe pears, sliced

- 2 Large avocados, diced
- 1 Head red leaf lettuce or baby spinach, torn into bite-size pieces
- 1/4 Cup champagne vinaigrette

Directions:

1. Supply your smoker with wood pellets and follow the start-up procedure. Preheat the grill, with the lid closed, to 400° F.

2. Place beets on a foil-lined baking sheet and top with bacon. Place baking sheet directly on the grill grate (while preheating) and cook for 25 minutes. Grill: 400 °F

3. Toss to coat beets in rendered bacon fat.

4. Spread everything out in a single layer and continue to cook for another 15 minutes, or until beets are tender and bacon is crispy. Grill: 400 °F

5. Add pecans or walnuts and roast for 5 more minutes. Spoon out nuts and place on paper towels to drain and cool.

6. Once bacon is cool to the touch, roughly chop into medium pieces.

7. Place bacon, beets, nuts, pears, avocado and lettuce in a large salad bowl. Drizzle with champagne vinaigrette, toss to coat, and serve. Enjoy!

Sweet Potato Marshmallow Casserole

Servings: 6
Cooking Time: 60 Minutes

Ingredients:

- 5 Yams
- 1 1/2 Stick butter
- 1/2 Cup brown sugar
- 1 Teaspoon vanilla
- 1 Teaspoon kosher salt
- 1 Teaspoon cracked black pepper
- 1 Marshmallows, miniature
- 1/4 Unsalted Butter, Softened

Directions:

1. Supply your smoker with wood pellets and follow the start-up procedure. Preheat the grill, with the lid closed, to 375° F.

2. Pierce the skin of the yams with a fork a few times. Place on a baking sheet or foil tin inside the grill and let roast for 50 minutes or until extremely softened. Grill: 375 °F

3. Remove yams from the grill and set aside until cool enough to handle. While the potatoes cool, with a stiff whisk, whip together 1/2 cup softened butter, the brown sugar, vanilla, salt and pepper.

4. Remove and discard skins from sweet potatoes and mash until smooth. Fold in the butter mixture and transfer to a cast iron pan.

5. Place cast iron on the grill and bake for 15-20 minutes. Remove from the grill, top with marshmallows and dot with remaining 1/4 cup butter.

6. Place back in the grill for 15 minutes until warm and the marshmallows are golden. Enjoy! Grill: 375 °F

Tater Tot Bake

Servings: 4
Cooking Time: 15 Minutes

Ingredients:

- 1 Whole frozen tater tots
- salt and pepper
- 1 Cup sour cream
- 1 Cup shredded cheddar cheese, divided
- 1/2 Cup bacon, chopped
- 1/4 Cup green onion, diced

Directions:

1. Supply your smoker with wood pellets and follow the start-up procedure. Preheat the grill, with the lid closed, to 375° F.

2. Line a baking sheet with aluminum foil for easy clean up and spread frozen tater tots onto sheet.

3. Sprinkle with Veggie Shake or salt and pepper to taste.

4. Place the baking sheet on the preheated grill grate and cook the tater tots for 10 minutes.

5. Drizzle sour cream over cooked tater tots.

6. Sprinkle the cheese, bacon bits and green onions on top of the tater tots.

7. Turn heat up to High heat and cook for 5 more minutes until the cheese melts and serve immediately. Enjoy!

Roasted Artichokes With Garlic Butter

Servings: 2

Cooking Time: 60 Minutes

Ingredients:
- 2 Large artichokes
- 3 Tablespoon olive oil
- sea salt
- 1 Stick unsalted butter
- 2 Clove garlic, chopped
- 2 Tablespoon chives, parsley, tarragon or cilantro
- 1 lemon

Directions:

1. Supply your smoker with wood pellets and follow the start-up procedure. Preheat the grill, with the lid closed, to 375° F.

2. Meanwhile, break off and discard any small outer leaves on the artichokes. Use a knife to slice off the tops of the artichokes, then using scissors, cut off any thorns on the remaining artichoke leaves. Trim the very bottom of the stem, then peel the tough and fibrous outer layer of the stem. Finally, cut artichokes in half and rinse off.

3. Transfer artichokes to a large mixing bowl, drizzle with olive oil and generously sprinkle with sea salt. Toss to coat the artichokes thoroughly. Grill: 375 °F

4. Add the artichokes to the grill, cut side down, and roast at 375°F until the artichoke bottoms are tender when poked with a fork or knife, about 50 to 60 minutes. Grill: 375 °F

5. When artichokes are almost done, add butter, chopped garlic and a pinch of sea salt to a small sauce pan and melt slowly over medium-low heat. Once the butter melts all the way and starts to bubble slightly, add the herbs.

6. When the artichokes are done, transfer to a butcher paper lined tray with the cut sides up. Drizzle half the garlic butter and squeeze half of the lemon over the artichokes. Add a small sprinkle of sea salt over the artichokes.

7. Serve with a ramekin of the remaining butter for dipping and extra wedges of lemon. Enjoy! Chef Tip: You can also serve with a ramekin of good mayonnaise mixed with a bit of hot sauce.

Smoked Parmesan Herb Popcorn

Servings: 2

Cooking Time: 15 Minutes

Ingredients:
- 4 Tablespoon butter
- 2 Teaspoon Italian Seasoning
- 1 Teaspoon garlic powder
- 1 Teaspoon salt
- 1/4 Cup popcorn kernels
- 1/2 Cup Parmesan cheese, grated

Directions:

1. Supply your smoker with wood pellets and follow the start-up procedure. Preheat the grill, with the lid closed, to 250° F.

2. In a small saucepan, melt the butter over medium heat. Add Italian seasoning, garlic powder, and salt and stir to combine. Remove from heat and set aside.

3. Add 1/4 cup of popcorn to a brown paper lunch bag. Fold the top of the bag over twice to close. Place the bag in the microwave and microwave on high for 1 to 2 minutes, or until there are about 5 seconds between pops. Open the bag with care and dump into a large mixing bowl.

4. Pour butter mixture of popcorn in a bowl and toss to combine. Dump popcorn onto a baking sheet and place in grill.

5. Smoke for 10 minutes; remove from grill. Toss with parmesan cheese to serve. Enjoy! Grill: 250 ˚F

Baked Loaded Tater Tots

Servings: 6
Cooking Time: 35 Minutes

Ingredients:
- 2 Pound frozen tater tots
- 1 Can Black Beans
- 1 1/2 Cup leftover chili
- 1 Cup leftover queso
- 1 red onion, finely diced
- 1/2 Cup chopped cilantro
- 1/2 Cup sour cream
- 1 jalapeños, sliced

Directions:
1. Supply your smoker with wood pellets and follow the start-up procedure. Preheat the grill, with the lid closed, to 375° F.

2. Spread frozen tots out on a sheet tray and place directly on the grill grate.

3. Cook for 20 to 25 minutes or until tots are crispy. Grill: 375 ˚F

4. Top with warmed chili, queso and beans. Place back on the grill for 15 minutes. Grill: 375 ˚F

5. Remove from grill and top with red onion, cilantro, sour cream and jalapeño. Enjoy!

Parmesan Roasted Cauliflower

Servings: 4
Cooking Time: 40 Minutes

Ingredients:
- 1 Head cauliflower, cut into florets
- 1 Medium onion, sliced
- 4 Clove garlic, unpeeled
- 4 Tablespoon olive oil
- salt
- black pepper
- 1 Teaspoon fresh thyme
- 1/2 Cup Parmesan cheese, grated

Directions:
1. Supply your smoker with wood pellets and follow the start-up procedure. Preheat the grill, with the lid closed, to 400° F.

2. On a baking tray, mix together cauliflower, onion, thyme, garlic, olive oil, salt and pepper.

3. Place tray on preheated grill and cook until cauliflower is firm and almost tender (about 25 minutes). Grill: 400 ˚F

4. Sprinkle cauliflower with Parmesan cheese and continue to cook on the Traeger for another 10 to 15 minutes. Cauliflower should be tender and the Parmesan crisp. Serve immediately, enjoy!

BAKING RECIPES

Caramel Bourbon Bacon Brownies

Servings: 16
Cooking Time: 60 Minutes

Ingredients:

- 2 Cup All-Purpose Flour
- 1/4 Cup Bourbon
- 1 Cup Brown Sugar
- 1 Cup Canola Oil
- Caramel Sauce
- 1.5 Cup Cocoa Powder
- 1 Tablespoon Hickory Honey Sea Salt
- 2 Tablespoon Instant Coffee
- 6 Large Eggs
- 1/2 Teaspoon Smoked Infused Hickory Honey Sea Salt
- 1 Cup Powdered Sugar
- 6 Slices Bacon, Raw
- 4 Tablespoons Water
- 3 Cups White Sugar

Directions:

1. Supply your smoker with wood pellets and follow the start-up procedure. Preheat the grill, with the lid closed, to 400° F.

2. In a large mixing bowl, whisk together the cocoa, powdered sugar, white sugar, instant coffee and flour.

3. To the flour mixture, add the eggs, oil and water until just combined.

4. Spray the 9 x 13 pan well with cooking spray.

5. Pour half the batter in the pan, drizzle with caramel.

6. Pour other half of batter on top and drizzle with caramel again and add candied bacon to the top.

7. Bake the brownies in the smoker for 1 hour, or until a toothpick inserted in the center of the pan comes out clean.

8. Remove from the smoker and allow to cool before slicing.

Sopapilla Cheesecake By Doug Scheiding

Servings: 8
Cooking Time: 45 Minutes

Ingredients:

- 2 Tablespoon softened butter
- 24 Ounce cream cheese
- 2 Cup granulated sugar, divided
- 2 Teaspoon vanilla
- 2 Can Pillsbury Butter Flake Crescent Rolls
- 1/2 Cup butter, melted
- cinnamon

Directions:

1. Coat a 9x13 inch baking dish with 2 tablespoons softened butter and set aside.

2. Supply your smoker with wood pellets and follow the start-up procedure. Preheat the grill, with the lid closed, to 350° F.

3. In a mixer, combine cream cheese, 1 to 1-1/2 cups of sugar and vanilla. Mix for 60 to 90 seconds on high with paddle attachment.

4. Take crescents out of the refrigerator. Open one can and place into the buttered 9x13 inch rectangular metal pan or glass dish. Make sure to fill in the gaps in this bottom layer of crescents.

5. Put the cream cheese mixture on the top of the crescent layer using a spatula to make it level.

6. Open the second can of crescents and put on top of the cream cheese layer, again filling in the gaps in the crescents to cover middle.

7. Pour 1/2 cup of melted butter on the top of the last layer of crescent. Start on sides first then middle.

8. Then sprinkle 1/4 cup to 1/2 cup of sugar over the entire pan followed by a light, even dusting of cinnamon.

9. Place pan directly on the grill grate and bake for 40 to 50 minutes until top is brown and starting to get crusty. Grill: 350 ˚F

10. Remove from grill and let cool 5 to 10 minutes. This allows the cheesecake to set which makes portioning easier. This dessert can be served warm or cold. Enjoy!

Baked Cast Iron Berry Cobbler

Servings: 6
Cooking Time: 35 Minutes

Ingredients:
- 4 Cup Berries
- 12 Tablespoon sugar
- Cup orange juice
- 2/3 Cup Flour
- 3/4 Teaspoon baking powder
- 1 Pinch salt
- 1/2 Cup butter
- 1 Tablespoon Sugar, raw

Directions:
1. Supply your smoker with wood pellets and follow the start-up procedure. Preheat the grill, with the lid closed, to 350° F.

2. In a 10-inch (25-cm) cast iron or other baking pan, mix together the berries, 4 Tbsp sugar and the orange juice.

3. In a small bowl, mix together the flour, baking powder and salt. Set aside.

4. In a separate bowl, cream together the butter and granulated sugar. Add the egg and vanilla extract and mix to combine. Gradually fold in the flour mixture.

5. Spoon the batter on top of the berries and sprinkle raw sugar on top.

6. Bake the cobbler for approximately 35-45 minutes. Cool slightly and serve with whipped cream. Enjoy! Grill: 350 ˚F

Pound Cake

Servings: 8
Cooking Time: 60 Minutes

Ingredients:
- 1 1/2 Cup butter
- 8 Ounce cream cheese
- 3 Cup sugar
- 6 eggs
- 3 Teaspoon Bourbon Vanilla
- 1 Tablespoon lemon zest
- fresh strawberries
- whipped cream

Directions:
1. In a large bowl, cream the butter, cream cheese, and sugar. Add eggs one at a time, whipping in between. Add vanilla and lemon zest, whip.

2. Pour batter into greased loaf pans, about halfway full to allow cake to rise.

3. Supply your smoker with wood pellets and follow the start-up procedure. Preheat the grill, with the lid closed, to 325° F.

4. Place loaf pans on grill and cook for 1 hour - 1 hour and 15 minutes. Check the cake at 45 minutes, if golden brown, cover loosely with foil and continue to cook until a toothpick inserted comes out clean. Grill: 325 °F

5. Cool loaf in pan for 10 minutes before removing to a wire rack.

6. Cut into 1 inch slices and serve with fresh sliced strawberries, top with smoked whip cream.

Smoked, Salted Caramel Apple Pie

Servings: 4
Cooking Time: 60 Minutes

Ingredients:
- 1 Cup cream
- 1 Cup brown sugar
- 3/4 Cup Light Corn Syrup
- 6 Tablespoon butter
- 1 Teaspoon sea salt
- 1 Pastry for Double-Crust Pie
- 6 Granny Smith Apples, Cut Into Wedges

Directions:
1. Supply your smoker with wood pellets and follow the start-up procedure. Preheat the grill, with the lid closed, to 180° F.

2. Fill a large pan with ice and water. Pour the cream into a smaller, shallow pan. Place the pan with the cream in the ice bath and place them both on the Traeger to smoke for 15-20 minutes. Grill: 180 °F

3. To make the caramel, combine the sugar and corn syrup in a saucepan and cook over medium heat, stirring constantly until it coats the back of your spoon and starts to turn a copper color, then stir in butter, salt, and smoked cream.

4. To assemble the pie, gather the pie crust, salted caramel, and apples. Place one of the pie crusts into the pie plate and fill with apple slices. Pour caramel over the apples. Lay the top crust over the filling, then crimp the top and bottom crusts together.

5. Make slits in the top crust to release the steam and finish by brushing with egg or cream. Sprinkle with raw sugar and sea salt.

6. When ready to bake, set the Traeger to 375°F and preheat, lid closed for 15 minutes.

7. Place the pie on the grill and bake for 20 minutes. Grill: 375 °F

8. Reduce heat to 325°F and cook for 25 more minutes. When ready, the crust should be golden brown and the filling, bubbly. Grill: 325 °F

9. Remove the pie from the grill and let cool. Serve with vanilla ice cream. Enjoy!

Chicken Pizza On The Grill

Servings: 4
Cooking Time: 10 Minutes

Ingredients:
- 3 Boneless, Skinless Chicken Breast
- 5 Cups Flour, Strong
- 3 Cups Georgia Style Bbq Sauce
- 3 Cups Mozzarella Cheese, Shredded
- 1 Tsp Olive Oil
- 3 Cups Georgia Style BBQ Sauce
- 1 1/2 Cups Red Bell Peppers, Diced
- 1 1/2 Cups Red Onion, Diced
- 1 Tsp Sugar
- 1/2 Cup Water, Hot
- 1 1/4 Cup Water, Warm
- 2 Tsb Active Yeast, Instant

Directions:

1. Roll your pizza dough so it forms a base about a 1/2 inch thick. To impress your friends and family, you'll want to aim for a nice, pizza like shape. HINT: use a sprinkle of cornmeal on the countertop to aid in moving the dough.

2. Now for the toppings! Start by spreading 1 cup of Georgia Style BBQ sauce onto each base. Make sure to leave a small portion for the crust! Next, load up with sliced, cooked chicken breasts, diced red onions and red bell peppers before finishing off with a two cups of shredded mozzarella cheese.

3. Supply your smoker with wood pellets and follow the start-up procedure. Preheat the grill, with the lid closed, to 500° F. Place the pizza stone in your grill. Pick up your pizza using a flat surface like a chopping board and slide the pizza carefully onto the hot stone. Close the lid and let your homemade wood-fired pizza bake for 10 - 12 minutes. Remove once your pizza has a golden crust and the cheese is bubbling. Cut and serve for pizza you'll hardly want to share.

Baked Potatoes & Celery Root Au Gratin

Servings: 2

Cooking Time: 60 Minutes

Ingredients:

- 5 Tablespoon butter, softened
- 2 Large leeks, white parts only, cleaned and sliced into half moons
- kosher salt
- freshly ground black pepper
- 5 Small Yukon Gold potatoes, sliced 1/4 inch thick
- 2 Whole celery root, peeled and sliced 1/4 inch thick
- 2 Cup cream
- 1 Tablespoon minced sage
- 1 Cup shredded Gruyere or other hearty Swiss cheese, divided

Directions:

1. Supply your smoker with wood pellets and follow the start-up procedure. Preheat the grill, with the lid closed, to 400° F.

2. Butter a 9x13 baking dish with 1 tablespoon of the softened butter. In a medium frying pan over medium heat, melt the remaining butter. Add the leeks and a generous pinch of salt and pepper and cook, stirring often until softened, about 5 minutes.

3. Remove from the heat and allow to cool. Place the potato and celery root slices into a large mixing bowl. Add the cream, leek mixture, minced sage, 1 teaspoon salt, 1/2 teaspoon pepper and 1 cup cheese. Stir gently to coat.

4. Arrange a layer of potato and celery root slices so they're slightly overlapping in the prepared baking dish. Repeat two more times so there are three layers of potatoes. Pour remaining cream from the bowl over the gratin, then sprinkle the top with the remaining cup of cheese.

5. Cover the dish loosely with foil and bake on the grill for 45 minutes. Remove the foil and continue baking until the top is golden and bubbly and the potatoes are tender when pierced, about 30 to 45 minutes longer. Let stand for 10 minutes before serving. Enjoy!

Baked Bourbon Maple Pumpkin Pie

Servings: 6-8

Cooking Time: 60 Minutes

Ingredients:

- 1/4 Cup Cocoa Powder, Unsweetened
- 1 Tablespoon Cocoa Powder, Unsweetened
- 3 1/2 Tablespoon sugar
- 1 Teaspoon salt
- 1 1/4 Cup all-purpose flour
- 1 Tablespoon all-purpose flour
- 6 Tablespoon butter
- 2 Tablespoon vegetable oil
- 1 Large Egg Yolk
- 1/2 Teaspoon apple cider vinegar
- 1/4 Cup ice water
- 1 Large egg, beaten
- 15 Ounce Pumpkin, canned
- 1/4 Cup sour cream
- 2 Tablespoon bourbon
- 1 Teaspoon ground cinnamon
- 1/2 Teaspoon salt
- 1/4 Teaspoon ground ginger
- 1/4 Teaspoon ground nutmeg
- 1/8 Teaspoon Allspice, ground
- 1/8 Teaspoon Mace, ground
- 3 Large eggs
- 3/4 Cup maple syrup
- 2 Tablespoon sugar
- 1/2 Vanilla Bean, halved
- 1 Cup heavy cream

Directions:

1. For the Chocolate Pie Dough: Pulse cocoa powder, granulated sugar, salt, and 1-1/4 cups plus 1 Tbsp flour in a food processor to combine. Add butter and shortening and pulse until mixture resembles coarse meal with a few pea-sized pieces of butter remaining. Transfer to a large bowl.

2. Whisk together the egg yolk, vinegar, and 1/4 cup ice water in a small bowl. Drizzle half of the egg mixture over flour mixture and, using a fork, mix gently just until combined. Add remaining egg mixture and mix until the dough just comes together (you will have some unincorporated pieces).

3. Turn out dough onto a lightly floured surface, flatten slightly, and cut into quarters. Stack pieces on top of one another. Placing unincorporated dry pieces of dough between layers, and press down to combine. Repeat process twice more (all pieces of dough should be incorporated at this point). Form dough into a 1" thick disk. Wrap in plastic; chill at least 1 hour.

4. Roll out a disk of dough on a lightly floured surface into a 14" round. Transfer to a 9" pie dish. Lift up the edge and allow the dough to slump down into the dish. Trim. Leaving about 1" overhang. Fold overhang under and crimp edge. Chill in freezer 15 minutes.

5. When ready to cook, set the smoker to 350°F and preheat, lid closed for 15 minutes.

6. Line pie with parchment paper or heavy-duty foil, leaving a 1-1/2" overhang. Fill with pie weights or dried beans. Bake until crust is dry around the edge, about 20 minutes.

7. Remove paper and weights and bake until surface of the crust looks dry, 5-10 minutes.

8. Brush bottom and sides of crust with 1 beaten egg. Return to grill and bake until dry and set, about 3 minutes longer.

9. For the Pumpkin Maple Filling: Whisk together pumpkin puree, sour cream, bourbon,

cinnamon, salt, ginger, nutmeg, allspice, mace (optional) and remaining 3 eggs in a large bowl; set aside.

10. Pour maple syrup and 2 tbsp sugar in a small saucepan. Scrape in the seeds from vanilla bean (reserve pod for another use) or add vanilla extract and bring syrup to a boil. Reduce heat to medium-high and simmer, stirring occasionally, until mixture is thickened and small puffs of steam start to release about 3 minutes.

11. Remove from heat and add cream in 3 additions, stirring with a wooden spoon after each addition until smooth. Gradually whisk hot maple cream into pumpkin mixture.

12. Place pie dish on a rimmed baking sheet and pour in pumpkin filling. Bake pie, rotating halfway through, until set around edge but center barely jiggles 50-60 minutes.

13. Transfer pie dish to a wire rack and let the pie cool. Slice and serve. Enjoy!

Baked Peach Cobbler Cupcakes

Servings: 8
Cooking Time: 30 Minutes

Ingredients:
- 2 Large Peaches, fresh
- 3/4 Cup sugar
- 2 Teaspoon lemon juice
- 1/2 Teaspoon ground cinnamon
- Yellow Cake Mix, Boxed
- 1 Can vanilla icing

Directions:
1. Bring a pot of water to a boil. Turn peaches upside down and cut a small shallow X across the bottom. Put peaches in boiling water and boil for 1 minute to help loosen the skin.

2. Drain the peaches into a colander and rinse off with cold water. Peel skin off peaches.

3. Filling: Dice peaches and place into a large pan. Cook peaches over medium heat. As it starts to sizzle, add sugar, lemon and cinnamon. Cook mixture on medium heat for 10-15 minutes until a majority of the juice from the peaches evaporates leaving a thick syrup.

4. Transfer to a bowl to cool.

5. Supply your smoker with wood pellets and follow the start-up procedure. Preheat the grill, with the lid closed, to 350° F.

6. Cupcakes: Follow the directions on box cake mix and put the mixture into cupcake pan with liners.

7. When grill has preheated, bake cupcakes for 13-16 minutes, until a light golden brown. Grill: 350 °F

8. When cupcakes have cooled, use a piping bag to pipe the peach cobbler mixture into the middle of the cupcake.

9. Ice with your favorite vanilla icing. Enjoy!

Traeger Baked Focaccia

Servings: 4
Cooking Time: 40 Minutes

Ingredients:
- 2 1/2 Cup all-purpose flour
- 1 Cup warm water (110°F to 115°F)
- 1 Tablespoon instant yeast
- 1 Teaspoon sugar
- 1 Teaspoon salt
- 3 Tablespoon olive oil, plus more as needed
- 1 Tablespoon fresh herbs such as thyme, rosemary and sage
- 2 Tablespoon freshly grated Parmesan, optional

- flaky sea salt

Directions:

1. Place the flour, water, yeast, sugar, salt and oil in the bowl of a stand mixer and mix for 60 seconds. You may also use a food processor by adding the flour, sugar, salt and yeast to the bowl and process while streaming in the warm water followed by the olive oil. Process until combined and a ball forms.

2. Gently form the sticky dough into a ball, if needed, and place in a well-oiled 12 inch cast iron skillet. Drizzle the top of the dough with more olive oil. Cover with plastic wrap and a kitchen towel and let rise in a warm spot for 45 to 60 minutes.

3. After the dough has risen, press the dough to the edges of the pan and cover it again. Let rise for 15 minutes.

4. Supply your smoker with wood pellets and follow the start-up procedure. Preheat the grill, with the lid closed, to 375° F.

5. Uncover the dough and press it again to the edges of the pan using your fingertips to create divots.

6. Drizzle with olive oil, then sprinkle with herbs, Parmesan and flaky salt.

7. Bake it on the Traeger for 30 to 40 minutes, or until golden brown and cooked through. Allow it to cool slightly before removing from cast iron and slicing. Enjoy! Grill: 375 °F

Lemon Strawberry Rhubarb Pie

Servings: 8
Cooking Time: 30 Minutes

Ingredients:
- 1/3 Cup Flour
- 1 Tbsp Lemon, Zest
- 1 Prepard Pie Shell, Deep
- 3 Stalks Rhubarb
- 2 1/2 Cups Strawberry
- 1 Cup Sugar

Directions:

1. Summer baking never has to stop when you can use your Wood Pellet Grill to bake anything from cookies to pie! In this recipe, we will show you how to bake a delicious barbecued strawberry rhubarb pie without turning your kitchen into an oven.

2. Supply your smoker with wood pellets and follow the start-up procedure. Preheat the grill, with the lid closed, to 400° F.

3. Slice rhubarb and strawberries into bite sized pieces. Combine sugar, flour and lemon zest with rhubarb and strawberries. Pour into prepared pie crust. Cover with top crust.

4. Bake in Grill for 1 hour or until crust is crispy.

5. Serve hot.

Sourdough Pizza

Servings: 4
Cooking Time: 12 Minutes

Ingredients:
- 1 1/2 Cup Fresh Sourdough Starter
- 1 Tablespoon olive oil
- 1 Teaspoon Jacobsen Salt Co. Pure Kosher Sea Salt
- 1 1/4 Cup all-purpose flour

Directions:

1. Supply your smoker with wood pellets and follow the start-up procedure. Preheat the grill, with the lid closed, to 450° F.

2. Mix together the fresh sourdough starter, one tablespoon of oil, Jacobsen salt and 1-1/4 cups of

flour. Add more flour, a little at a time, as needed to form a pizza dough consistency.

3. Allow the dough to rest for 30 minutes, to allow for easier rolling. Roll the dough out into a circle, using a small amount of flour to prevent sticking.

4. Place on a pizza stone. Bake the crust for approximately 7 minutes Grill: 450 °F

5. Remove the crust from the grill; brush on remaining oil to prevent toppings from soaking into the crust. Add the desired toppings and return pizza to grill; bake until the crust browns and the cheese melts.

Sweet Cheese Muffins

Servings: 3
Cooking Time: 15 Minutes

Ingredients:
- 1 package butter cake mix
- 1 package Jiffy Corn Muffin Mix
- 1 cup self-rising or cake flour
- 12 tablespoons (1½ sticks) unsalted butter, softened, plus 8 tablespoons (1 stick) melted
- 3½ cups shredded Cheddar cheese
- 2 eggs, beaten, at room temperature
- 2¼ cups buttermilk
- Nonstick cooking spray or butter, for greasing
- ¼ cup packed brown sugar

Directions:
1. Supply your smoker with wood pellets and follow the start-up procedure. Preheat, with the lid closed, to 375°F.

2. In a large mixing bowl, combine the cake mix, corn muffin mix, and flour.

3. Slice the 1½ sticks of softened butter into pieces and cut into the dry ingredients. Add the cheese and mix thoroughly.

4. In a medium bowl, combine the eggs and buttermilk, then add to the dry ingredients, stirring until well blended.

5. Coat three 12-cup mini muffin pans with cooking spray and spoon ¼ cup of batter into each cup.

6. Transfer the pans to the grill, close the lid, and smoke, monitoring closely, for 12 to 15 minutes, or until the muffins are lightly browned.

7. While the muffins are cooking, make the topping: In a small bowl, stir together the remaining 1 stick of melted butter and the brown sugar until well combined.

8. Remove the muffins from the grill. Brush the tops with the sweet butter and serve warm.

Crescent Rolls

Servings: 8
Cooking Time: 12 Minutes

Ingredients:
- 1 Crescent Dough, Can

Directions:
1. Supply your smoker with wood pellets and follow the start-up procedure. Preheat the grill, with the lid closed, to 375° F.

2. Unroll the dough and separate into triangles. Roll up the triangles and place on an ungreased nonstick cookie sheet. Bake for 10 -12 minutes on your Grill. You will know that they are finished when the rolls are golden brown.

Baked Irish Creme Cake

Servings: 4
Cooking Time: 60 Minutes

Ingredients:
- 1 Cup Pecans, pieces
- 1 Yellow Cake Mix, Boxed

- 1 Vanilla Pudding Mix, Instant Package (3.4oz)
- 4 Large eggs
- 1/2 Cup water
- 1/2 Cup vegetable oil
- 1 Cup Irish Cream Liquor
- 1/2 Cup butter
- 1 Cup sugar

Directions:

1. Grease and flour a 10" (25 cm) Bundt pan. Sprinkle pecans along the bottom.

2. In a large bowl, with a mixer, combine yellow cake mix, pudding mix, eggs, water, oil, and Irish Cream liquor. Pour batter over nuts in the pan.

3. Supply your smoker with wood pellets and follow the start-up procedure. Preheat the grill, with the lid closed, to 325° F.

4. Place Bundt pan on the Traeger and bake for 1 hour, or until a toothpick comes out clean. Remove from heat, cool for 10 minutes. Grill: 325 °F

5. While the cake is cooling, combine the butter, water and sugar and bring to a boil. Boil for 5 minutes, stirring constantly. Remove from heat and add Irish cream liquor.

6. Use a bamboo skewer to poke holes in the cooled cake. Spoon glaze over the cake. Allow cake to absorb the glaze. Enjoy!

Strawberry Basil Daiquiri

Servings: 2

Cooking Time: 20 Minutes

Ingredients:

- 4 strawberries, stemmed
- 6 Tablespoon granulated sugar, divided
- 6 basil leaves
- 3 Ounce white rum
- 2 Ounce lime juice
- 1 Ounce Smoked Simple Syrup
- 2 fresh basil leaves, for garnish
- 2 lime slice, for garnish

Directions:

1. Supply your smoker with wood pellets and follow the start-up procedure. Preheat the grill, with the lid closed, to 375° F.

2. Cut strawberries in half and coat in 2 tablespoons granulated sugar. Place directly on grill grate and cook for 15 to 20 minutes. Remove from heat and cool. Grill: 375 °F

3. Add 1 tablespoon granulated sugar and basil leaves to shaking tin and lightly muddle. Add strawberries and muddle again.

4. Pour in white rum, lime juice and Smoked Simple Syrup. Shake with ice.

5. Strain contents into a chilled glass and garnish with large fresh basil leaf and sliced lime. Enjoy!

Mint Butter Chocolate Chip Cookies

Servings: 24

Cooking Time: 12 Minutes

Ingredients:

- 1/2 Cup Butter, Melted
- 1 Package Chocolate Chip Cookie Mix
- 8-10 Drop Food Coloring
- 1/2 Tsp Mint, Extract

Directions:

1. Supply your smoker with wood pellets and follow the start-up procedure. Preheat the grill, with the lid closed, to 350° F.

2. Follow the directions on the back of the Chocolate Chip Cookie mix and also add the

mint extract and green food coloring. Mix until combined.

3. On a baking sheet lined with parchment paper, drop balls of dough about 2 tbsp in size onto the pan.

4. Place in your Grill and bake for 10-12 minutes. Let cool for a couple minutes before removing from the pan. Enjoy!

Baked Pumpkin Pie

Servings: 6
Cooking Time: 50 Minutes

Ingredients:

- 4 Ounce cream cheese
- 15 Ounce pumpkin puree
- 1/3 Cup Cream, whipping
- 1/2 Cup brown sugar
- 1 Teaspoon pumpkin pie spice
- 3 Large eggs
- 1 frozen pie crust, thawed

Directions:

1. Supply your smoker with wood pellets and follow the start-up procedure. Preheat the grill, with the lid closed, to 325° F.

2. Mix cream cheese, puree, milk, sugar, and spice. One at a time, incorporate an egg to the mixture. Pour mixture into pie shell.

3. Bake for 50 minutes, edges should be golden and pie should be firm around edges with slight movement in middle. Let cool before whip cream is applied. Serve and enjoy! Grill: 325 °F

Sweet And Spicy Baked Pork Beans

Servings: 20
Cooking Time: 120 Minutes

Ingredients:

- 1 - 21 Oz Apple Pie Filling, Can
- 1 Gallon Baked Beans
- 1 Tbs Chilli, Powder
- 1 Green Bell Pepper, Diced
- 1 10 Oz Drained Jalapeno, Can Diced
- 1 Cup Maple Syrup
- 1 Onion, Diced
- 1 Lb Pork, Pulled

Directions:

1. Supply your smoker with wood pellets and follow the start-up procedure. Preheat the grill, with the lid closed, to 350° F.

2. Place all ingredients in mixing bowl and mix well.

3. Pour bean mixture into foil pans.

4. Bake in grill till bubbling throughout – about 2 hours.

5. Rest at least 15 minutes before serving.

Chicken Pot Pie

Servings: 6
Cooking Time: 60 Minutes

Ingredients:

- 2 Chicken, Boneless/Skinless
- 1 Cream Of Chicken Soup, Can
- 1 Tsp Curry Powder
- 1/2 Cup Mayo
- 1 1/2 Cups Mixed Frozen Vegetables
- 1 Onion, Sliced
- 2 Frozen Pie Shell, Deep
- 1/2 Cup Sour Cream

Directions:

1. Supply your smoker with wood pellets and follow the start-up procedure. Preheat the grill, with the lid closed, to 425° F.

2. Cut the onion in half and place on the grates of the grill. If you"re using fresh chicken breasts, barbecue the chicken at the same time as the onions. The chicken is fully cooked when the internal temperature reached 170F. While the onion and chicken are cooking, prepare the pie crust by putting one crust in a pie plate. When the chicken and onions are done, shred chicken and chop onion into small pieces and place in the prepared pie plate along with the mixed vegetables.

3. Combine cream of chicken soup, mayo, sour cream, and curry powder in a bowl. Pour into the pie crust with the chicken and mix to combine. Wet the sides of the bottom crust with a small amount of water and top with the second pie crust. Push gently along the sides of the crust to seal the two pie crusts together.

4. Place in the and bake for 40 minutes, or until the crust is golden brown. Serve hot.

Vanilla Cheesecake Skillet Brownie

Servings: 2
Cooking Time: 30 Minutes

Ingredients:
- 1 Box Brownie Mix
- 1 Package Cream Cheese
- 2 Egg
- 1/2 Cup Oil
- 1 Can Pie Filling, Blueberry
- 1/2 Cup Sugar
- 1 Tsp Vanilla
- 1/4 Cup Water, Warm

Directions:
1. Combine all brownie ingredients and mix. In a separate bowl, combine cream cheese, sugar, egg and vanilla and mix until smooth. Grease skillets

and pour in brownie batter. Top with cheesecake and cherry pie filling, using a knife to blend to give it that marbled look.

2. Supply your smoker with wood pellets and follow the start-up procedure. Preheat the grill, with the lid closed, to 350°F and bake for about 30 minutes.

3. Let cool for about 10 minutes and enjoy!

Baked Bourbon Monkey Bread

Servings: 6
Cooking Time: 40 Minutes

Ingredients:
- 3 Can Pillsbury Grands Buttermilk Biscuits
- 1 Cup sugar
- 3 Teaspoon ground cinnamon
- 1 Cup Butter, unsalted
- 1 Cup dark brown sugar
- Tablespoon bourbon

Directions:
1. Supply your smoker with wood pellets and follow the start-up procedure. Preheat the grill, with the lid closed, to 350° F.

2. Cut each biscuit into quarters. In a Ziploc bag, combine sugar and cinnamon and add quartered biscuits. Toss to coat in cinnamon sugar.

3. Dump coated biscuit dough into a bundt pan coated with non-stick spray.

4. In a small saucepan, combine the brown sugar, butter, and bourbon. Cook over medium heat until the sugar has dissolved.

5. Pour the butter mixture over the biscuits in the bundt pan.

6. Place in the center of the grill and cook for 40 minutes or until dark golden brown.

7. Let cool on the counter for 5-10 minutes, then flip out onto a serving plate. Enjoy!

Savory Cheesecake With Bourbon Pecan Topping

Servings: 6

Cooking Time: 75 Minutes

Ingredients:

- Crust
- 12 ounce Oreos
- 6 ounce melted butter
- Filling
- 24 ounces cream cheese - room temperature
- 1 cup granulated sugar
- 3 tbs cornstarch
- 2 large eggs
- 2/3 cup heavy cream
- 1 tbs vanilla
- 1 1/2 tbs bourbon
- Topping
- 3 large eggs beaten
- 1/3 cup granulated sugar
- 1/3 cup brown sugar
- 8 tbsp corn syrup dark corn syrup recommended
- 2 tbsp bourbon
- 1/2 tbsp vanilla
- 1/8 tbsp salt
- 3/4 cup rough chopped pecans (smoked pecans recommended)

Directions:

1. Supply your smoker with wood pellets and follow the start-up procedure. Preheat the grill, with the lid closed, to 350 °F.
2. Wrap foil on the bottom and up the sides of a 9" spring-form pan (outside of pan).
3. Butter the bottom & insides of the pan.
4. Crust
5. Throw ingredients in a food processor until they are finely ground.
6. Spread in 9" cheesecake pan on bottom & about ½ way upsides.
7. Filling
8. Place 8 oz of cream cheese in mixer bowl with 1/3 of sugar & cornstarch.Mix until smooth andcreamy.
9. Add another 8 oz cream cheese andbeat until smooth, then add remaining cream cheese,beating until smooth.
10. Then mix in the rest of the sugar, bourbon & vanilla.
11. Add eggs one at a time beating well after each one.
12. Add the heavy cream and mix just until smooth. Reminder: Do not over mix.
13. Pour batter into the prepared crust.
14. Topping
15. Mix all together except pecans.
16. Sprinkle pecans on top of cheesecake batter.
17. Pour topping over cheesecake batter.
18. Place in a pan big enough to hold a spring-form pan. Pour boiling water in the roasting pan to come up about ½ way up the spring-form pan.
19. Bake at 350 °F for 75 minutes until the top just barely jiggles. Carefully take the pan out of water-bath and put on cooling rack.
20. Let cool for 2 hours in pan. After 2 hours put in fridge until totally chilled then serve.

Chili Cheese Fries

Servings: 6

Cooking Time: 10 Minutes

Ingredients:

- 1 Cup Cheddar Cheese, Shredded
- 1 Cup Chili Con Carne, Prepared

- 1 Bag French Fries
- 1 Tablespoon Olive Oil
- 1 Tablespoon Sweet Heat Rub

Directions:

1. Supply your smoker with wood pellets and follow the start-up procedure. Preheat the grill, with the lid closed, to 350° F. If you're using charcoal or gas, set it up for medium high heat.

2. Bake the fries according to manufacturer's instructions. Once the fries are done, place them in a large bowl and add the olive oil and Sweet Heat Rub. Toss the fries to coat. Once everything is well coated with the oil and seasoning, spread the fries on a baking sheet.

3. Top the fries with the chili and the shredded cheddar cheese. Place the baking sheet on the grill and grill for 7-10 minutes, or until the cheese is melted and bubbly, and the chili is warm all the way through.

4. Remove the baking sheet from the grill and serve the fries immediately.

Double Chocolate Chip Brownie Pie

Servings: 8-12

Cooking Time: 45 Minutes

Ingredients:

- 1/2 Cup Semisweet Chocolate Chips
- 1 Cup butter
- 1 Cup brown sugar
- 1 Cup sugar
- 4 Whole eggs
- 2 Teaspoon vanilla extract
- 2 Cup all-purpose flour
- 333/500 Cup Cocoa Powder, Unsweetened
- 1 Teaspoon baking soda
- 1 Teaspoon salt
- 1 Cup Semisweet Chocolate Chips
- 3/4 Cup White Chocolate Chips
- 3/4 Cup Nuts (optional)
- 1 Whole Hot Fudge Sauce, 8oz
- 2 Tablespoon Guinness Beer

Directions:

1. Coat the inside of a 10-inch (25 cm) pie plate with non-stick cooking spray.

2. When ready to cook, set the grill temperature to 350°F (180 C)and preheat, lid closed for 15 minutes.

3. Melt 1/2 cup (100 g) of the semi sweet chocolate chips in the microwave. Cream together butter, brown sugar and granulated sugar. Beat in the eggs, adding one at a time and mixing after each egg, and the vanilla. Add in the melted chocolate chips.

4. On a large piece of wax paper, sift together the cocoa powder, flour, baking soda and salt. Lift up the corners of the paper and pour slowly into the butter mixture.

5. Beat until the dry ingredients are just incorporated. Stir in the remaining semi sweet chocolate chips, white chocolate chips, and the nuts. Press the dough into the prepared pie pan.

6. Place the brownie pie on the grill and bake for 45-50 minutes or until the pie is set in the middle. Rotate the pan halfway through cooking. If the top or edges begin to brown, cover the top with a piece of aluminum foil.

7. In a microwave-safe measuring cup, heat the fudge sauce in the microwave. Stir in the Guinness.

8. Once the brownie pie is done, allow to sit for 20 minutes. Slice into wedges and top with the fudge sauce. Enjoy.

Pretzel Rolls

Servings: 6
Cooking Time: 20 Minutes

Ingredients:

- 2 3/4 Cup Bread Flour
- 1 Quick-Rising Yeast, envelope
- 1 Teaspoon salt
- 1 Teaspoon sugar
- 1/2 Teaspoon celery seed
- 1/2 Teaspoon Caraway Seeds
- 1 Cup hot water
- As Needed Cornmeal
- 8 Cup water
- 1/4 Cup baking soda
- 2 Tablespoon sugar
- 1 Whole Egg White
- Coarse salt

Directions:

1. Combine bread flour, 1 envelope yeast, salt, 1 teaspoon sugar, caraway seeds and celery seeds in food processor or standing mixer with dough hook and blend.

2. With machine running, gradually pour hot water, adding enough water to form smooth elastic dough. Process 1 minute to knead. (You could also knead it by hand for a few minutes.)

3. Grease medium bowl. Add dough to bowl, turning to coat. Cover bowl with plastic wrap, then towel; let dough rise in warm draft-free area until doubled in volume, about 35 minutes.

4. Flour a large baking sheet. Punch dough down and knead on lightly floured surface until smooth. Divide into 8 pieces. Form each dough piece into a ball.

5. Place dough balls on prepared sheet, flattening each slightly. Using serrated knife, cut X in top center of each dough ball. Cover with towel and let dough balls rise until almost doubled in volume, about 20 minutes.

6. When ready to cook, start the smoker on Smoke with the lid open until a fire is established (4-5 minutes). Turn temperature to 375 F (190 C) and preheat, lid closed, for 10 to 15 minutes.

7. Grease another baking sheet and sprinkle with cornmeal. Bring water to boil in large saucepan. Add baking soda and sugar (water will foam up). Add 3 rolls (or however many will fit comfortably in the pot) and cook 30 seconds per side.

8. Using slotted spoon, transfer rolls to prepared sheet, arranging X side up. Repeat with remaining rolls. Brush rolls with egg white glaze. Sprinkle rolls generously with coarse salt.

9. Bake rolls until brown, about 20 to 25 minutes. Transfer to racks and cool 10 minutes. Serve rolls warm or at room temperature. Enjoy!

S'mores Dip Skillet

Servings: 4-6
Cooking Time: 8 Minutes

Ingredients:

- 2 tablespoons salted butter, melted
- ¼ cup milk
- 12 ounces semisweet chocolate chips
- 16 ounces Jet-Puffed marshmallows
- Graham crackers and apple wedges, for serving

Directions:

1. Supply your smoker with wood pellets and follow the start-up procedure. Preheat, with the lid closed, to 450°F.

2. Place a cast iron skillet on the preheated grill grate and pour in the melted butter and milk, stirring for about 1 minute.

3. Once the mixture starts to heat, top with the chocolate chips in an even layer and arrange the marshmallows standing up to cover all of the chocolate.

4. Close the lid and smoke for 5 to 7 minutes, or until the marshmallows are lightly toasted.

5. Remove from the heat and serve immediately with graham crackers and apple wedges for dipping.

Vanilla Chocolate Chip Cookies

Servings: 12

Cooking Time: 20 Minutes

Ingredients:

- 3/4 cup brown sugar
- 3/4 cup white sugar
- 1 stick butter, room temp
- 2 eggs
- 1 tsp vanilla
- 2 1/2 cups flour
- 1/2 tsp salt
- 1 tsp baking soda
- 1 cup Chocolate Chips

Directions:

1. Cream your butter and sugar together in a mixing bowl using a hand mixer or stand mixer on medium speed for about 4-5 minutes.

2. Once the butter is creamed, add the eggs and vanilla. Continue mixing for an additional minute.

3. Put flour, salt, and baking soda in a sifter. Sift it into your creamed butter mixture.

4. Scrape the sides of your mixing bowl with a rubber spatula, and then turn your mixer on to low speed.

5. Let it mix a little, and then scrape the sides again. Stop mixing when there are one or two streaks of flour left in the cookie dough.

6. Scrape the sides of your bowl and pour in a cup of chocolate chips, and turn the mixer to low again to mix the chocolate. It should take just a few turns for the chocolate pieces to be well incorporated.

7. Line a large baking sheet with parchment paper. Using a medium cookie scoop (about 1.5 tbsp), drop evenly spaced dollops of cookie dough onto the cookie sheet.

8. Supply your smoker with wood pellets and follow the start-up procedure. Preheat the grill, with the lid closed, to 350° F. Place the cookie sheet in your smoker, and let them cook for about 12 minutes.

9. Let them sit on a cooling rack while you continue to cook the additional cookies.

10. Cool for a few minutes to let cookies set.

11. Enjoy!

Delicious Pellet Grill Cornbread

Servings: 6

Cooking Time: 35 Minutes

Ingredients:

- 1 cup flour
- 1 cup cornmeal
- 2 teaspoons baking powder
- 2 teaspoons salt
- 3/4 cup sugar
- 2 tablespoons honey
- 1/2 cup butter
- 1 cup sour cream
- 3 eggs
- 1 cup milk

Directions:

1. Supply your smoker with wood pellets and follow the start-up procedure. Preheat the grill, with the lid closed, to 350° F.

2. Grease a 12-inch cast iron skillet or an equivalent baking pan.

3. Add flour, cornmeal, baking powder, salt, sugar, honey, butter, sour cream, eggs, and milk into a mixing bowl.

4. Mix well then pour into pan and bake on the grill for 30-35 minutes or until the cornbread is baked through in the center.

Green Bean Casserole Circa 1955

Servings: 6
Cooking Time: 30 Minutes

Ingredients:
- 1 1/2 Pound Green Beans, fresh
- 1 Can cream of mushroom soup
- 1/2 Cup milk
- 2 Teaspoon soy sauce
- 1/2 Teaspoon Worcestershire sauce
- 1/2 Teaspoon black pepper
- 1.334 Cup French's Original Crispy Fried Onions
- 1/4 Cup red bell pepper, diced

Directions:
1. In a mixing bowl, combine the beans (trimmed and cooked until tender, or may use 2 16 oz. cans), soup, milk, soy sauce, Worcestershire sauce, black pepper, 2/3 cup of the onion rings, and red pepper, if using. Transfer to a 1-1/2 quart casserole dish.

2. Supply your smoker with wood pellets and follow the start-up procedure. Preheat the grill, with the lid closed, to 375° F.

3. Cook the casserole until the filling is hot and bubbling, 25 to 30 minutes. Top with the remaining onions and cook for 5 to 10 minutes more, or until the onions are crisp and beginning to brown. Grill: 375 °F

Smoked Lemon Cheesecake

Servings: 16
Cooking Time: 130 Minutes

Ingredients:
- For the crust
- Vegetable oil, for oiling the pan
- 12 ounces gingersnaps (about 36) or chocolate icebox cookies (about 36)
- 3 tablespoons light brown sugar
- 8 tablespoons (1 stick) unsalted butter, melted
- For the filling
- 4 packages (8 ounces each) cream cheese, at room temperature
- 1 cup firmly packed light brown sugar
- 2 teaspoons pure vanilla extract
- 2 teaspoons finely grated lemon zest
- 1 tablespoon fresh lemon juice
- 2 tablespoons (1/4 stick) unsalted butter, melted
- 5 large eggs
- Burnt Sugar Sauce (recipes follows, optional)

Directions:
1. Supply your smoker with wood pellets and follow the start-up procedure. Preheat the grill, with the lid closed, to 400° F. Lightly oil the springform pan with vegetable oil and wrap a sheet of aluminum foil around the outside.

2. Make the crust: Break the cookies into pieces and grind with the brown sugar to a fine powder in a food processor. You'll want about 1 3/4 cups of crumbs. Add the melted butter and run the processor in short bursts to obtain a crumbly dough. Press the mixture evenly across the bottom and halfway up the sides of the springform pan. Indirect-grill or bake the crust until lightly browned, 5 to 8 minutes. Transfer the pan to a wire rack and let cool.

3. Make the filling: Wipe out the food processor bowl. Add the cream cheese, brown sugar, vanilla, lemon zest, lemon juice, and butter, and process until smooth. Work in the eggs one by one, processing until smooth after each addition. (You can also use a stand mixer, beating the cream cheese mixture until smooth and beating in the eggs one at a time.) Pour the filling into the crust. Gently tap the pan on the countertop a few times to knock out any air bubbles.

4. Supply your smoker with wood pellets and follow the start-up procedure. Preheat the grill, with the lid closed, to 225 °F-250 °F.

5. Place the cheesecake in the smoker. Smoke until the top is bronzed with smoke and the filling is set, 1 1/2 to 2 hours. To test for doneness, gently poke the side of the pan—the filling will jiggle, not ripple. Alternatively, insert a slender metal skewer in the center of the cake; it should come out clean.

6. Transfer the cheesecake in its pan to a wire rack to cool to room temperature. Refrigerate until serving; the cheesecake can be made up to 8 hours ahead. Run a slender knife around the inside of the springform pan. Unclasp and remove the ring. (You'll serve the cheesecake off the bottom of the pan.) Let the cheesecake warm slightly at room temperature before serving.

7. If serving with the sauce, pour some of it over the cheesecake and the rest into a pitcher. Cut into wedges and pass the remaining sauce.

Pull-apart Dinner Rolls

Servings: 8
Cooking Time: 10 Minutes

Ingredients:
- 1/4 Cup warm water (110°F to 115°F)
- 1/3 Cup vegetable oil
- 2 Tablespoon active dry yeast
- 1/4 Cup sugar
- 1/2 Teaspoon salt
- 1 egg
- 3 1/2 Cup all-purpose flour
- cooking spray

Directions:
1. Supply your smoker with wood pellets and follow the start-up procedure. Preheat the grill, with the lid closed, to 400° F.
2. In the bowl of a stand mixer, combine warm water, oil, yeast and sugar. Let mixture rest for 5 to 10 minutes, or until frothy and bubbly.
3. With a dough hook, mix in salt, egg and 2 cups of flour until combined. Add remaining flour 1/2 cup at a time (dough will be sticky).
4. Prepare a cast iron pan with cooking spray and set aside.
5. Spray your hands with cooking spray and shape the dough into 12 balls.
6. After shaped, place in the prepared cast iron pan and let rest for 10 minutes. Bake in Traeger for about 10 to 12 minutes, or until tops are lightly golden. Enjoy! Grill: 400 °F

Pizza Bites

Servings: 6
Cooking Time: 20 Minutes

Ingredients:
- 4 1/2 Cup Bread Flour
- 1 1/2 Tablespoon sugar
- 2 Teaspoon Instant Yeast
- 2 Teaspoon kosher salt
- 3 Tablespoon extra-virgin olive oil
- 15 Fluid Ounce Water, Lukewarm
- 8 Ounce Pepperoni, sliced

- 1 Cup pizza sauce
- 1 Cup mozzarella cheese
- 1 Whole egg, for egg wash
- 1 As Needed salt

Directions:

1. For the Pizza Dough: Combine flour, sugar, salt, and yeast in food processor. Pulse 3 to 4 times until incorporated evenly. Add olive oil and water. Run food processor until mixture forms ball that rides around the bowl above the blade, about 15 seconds. Continue processing 15 seconds longer.

2. Transfer dough ball to lightly floured surface and knead once or twice by hand until smooth ball is formed. Divide dough into three even parts and place each into a 1 gallon zip top bag. Place in refrigerator and allow to rise at least one day.

3. At least two hours before baking, remove dough from refrigerator and shape into balls by gathering dough towards bottom and pinching shut. Flour well and place each one in a separate medium mixing bowl. Cover tightly with plastic wrap and allow to rise at warm room temperature until roughly doubled in volume.

4. When ready to cook, set the grill temperature to 350°F and preheat, lid closed for 15 minutes.

5. After the first rise remove the dough from the fridge and let come to room temperature. Roll dough on a flat surface. Cut dough into long strips 3" wide by 18" long.

6. Slice pepperoni into strips.

7. In a medium bowl combine the pizza sauce, mozzarella and pepperoni.

8. Spoon 1 TBSP of the pizza filling onto the pizza dough every two inches, about halfway down the length of the dough. Dip a pastry brush into the egg wash and brush around pizza filling.

Fold the half side of the dough (without the pizza filling) over the other the half that contains the pizza filling.

9. Press down between each pizza bite slightly with your fingers. With a ravioli or pizza cutter, cut around each filling- creating a rectangle shape and sealing the crust in.

10. Transfer each pizza bite onto a parchment lined cookie sheet. Cover with a kitchen towel and let them rise for 30 minutes.

11. When ready to cook, preheat the grill to 350 ⊠ F with the lid closed for 10-15 minutes.

12. Brush the bites with remaining egg wash, sprinkle with salt and place directly on the sheet tray. Bake 10-15 minutes until the exterior is golden brown.

13. Remove from grill and transfer to a serving dish. Serve with extra pizza sauce for dipping and enjoy!

Anzac Coconut Biscuits

Servings: 4
Cooking Time: 30 Minutes

Ingredients:
- This recipe makes a dozen biscuits.
- 1 cup rolled oats
- 3/4 cup raw sugar
- 3/4 cup desiccated coconut
- 1 cup plain flour, sifted
- 125 g butter, melted
- 2 tablespoons Golden Syrup
- 1/2 tsp bicarb soda
- 3 tablespoons boiling water

Directions:

1. Combine and mix thoroughly sifted flour, oats, sugar and coconut in a large bowl.

2. Melt the butter and Golden Syrup over low heat.

3. Add boiling water to the bicarb soda, once dissolved add into the butter/syrup mix, it will bubble/fizz up a bit.

4. Add the liquid into the dry ingredients and mix throughly.

5. Rolls the mix into golf ball size balls and layout on grease proof paper on baking tray and flatten the tops just slightly.

6. Space the balls with about 3 fingers between each ball as they will flatten to about triple the diameter as they cook.

7. Supply your smoker with wood pellets and follow the start-up procedure. Preheat the grill, with the lid closed, to 350° F. Cook for 25-30 minutes until golden brown.

8. Rest on cooling rack until at room temperature then store in air-tight container.

Bacon Chocolate Chip Cookies

Servings: 2
Cooking Time: 10-12 Minutes

Ingredients:
- 2¾ cups all-purpose flour
- 1½ teaspoons baking soda
- ½ teaspoon salt
- 12 tablespoons (1½ sticks) unsalted butter, softened
- 1 cup light brown sugar
- 1 cup granulated sugar
- 2 eggs, at room temperature
- 2½ teaspoons apple cider vinegar
- 1 teaspoon vanilla extract
- 2 cups semisweet chocolate chips
- 8 slices bacon, cooked and crumbled

Directions:

1. In a large bowl, combine the flour, baking soda, and salt, and mix well.

2. In a separate large bowl, using an electric mixer on medium speed, cream the butter and sugars. Reduce the speed to low and mix in the eggs, vinegar, and vanilla.

3. With the mixer speed still on low, slowly incorporate the dry ingredients, chocolate chips, and bacon pieces.

4. Supply your smoker with wood pellets and follow the start-up procedure. Preheat, with the lid closed, to 375°F.

5. Line a large baking sheet with parchment paper.

6. Drop rounded teaspoonfuls of cookie batter onto the prepared baking sheet and place on the grill grate. Close the lid and smoke for 10 to 12 minutes, or until the cookies are browned around the edges.

Donut Bread Pudding

Servings: 8
Cooking Time: 40 Minutes

Ingredients:
- 16 Cake Donuts
- 1/2 Cup Raisins, seedless
- 5 eggs
- 3/4 Cup sugar
- 2 Cup heavy cream
- 2 Teaspoon vanilla extract
- 1 Teaspoon ground cinnamon
- 3/4 Cup Butter, melted, cooled slightly
- Ice Cream

Directions:

1. Lightly butter a 9- by 13-inch baking pan. Layer the donuts in an even thickness in the pan.

Distribute the raisins over the top, if using. Drizzle evenly with the butter.

2. Make the custard: In a medium bowl, whisk together the sugar, eggs, cream, vanilla, and cinnamon. Whisk in the butter. Pour over the donuts. Let sit for 10 to 15 minutes, periodically pushing the donuts down into the custard. Cover with foil.

3. Supply your smoker with wood pellets and follow the start-up procedure. Preheat the grill, with the lid closed, to 350° F.

4. Bake the bread pudding for 30 to 40 minutes, or until the custard is set. Remove the foil and continue to bake for 10 additional minutes to lightly brown the top. Grill: 350 °F

5. Let cool slightly before cutting into squares. Drizzle with melted ice cream, if desired. Enjoy!

Smokin' Lemon Bars

Servings: 8-12

Cooking Time: 60 Minutes

Ingredients:

- 3/4 Cup lemon juice
- 1 1/2 Cup sugar
- 2 eggs
- 3 Egg Yolk
- 1 1/2 Teaspoon cornstarch
- Pinch sea salt
- 4 Tablespoon unsalted butter
- 1/4 Cup olive oil
- 1/2 Tablespoon lemon zest
- 1 1/4 Cup flour
- 1/4 Cup granulated sugar
- 3 Tablespoon Confectioner's Sugar
- 1 Teaspoon lemon zest
- 1/4 Teaspoon Sea Salt, Fine
- 10 Tablespoon Unsalted Butter, Cut Into Cubes

Directions:

1. When ready to cook, set grill temperature to 180°F and preheat, lid closed for 15 minutes.

2. In a small mixing bowl, whisk together lemon juice, sugar, eggs and yolks, cornstarch and fine sea salt. Pour into a sheet tray or cake pan and place on grill. Smoke for 30 minutes whisking mixture halfway through smoking. Remove from grill and set aside.

3. Pour mixture into a small saucepan. Place on stove top set to medium heat until boiling. Once boiling, boil for 60 seconds. Remove from heat and strain through a mesh strainer into a bowl. Whisk in cold butter, olive oil, and lemon zest.

4. To make a crust, pulse together the flour, granulated sugar, confectioners' sugar, lemon zest and salt in a food processor. Add butter and pulse until just mixed into a crumbly dough. Press dough into a prepared 9" by 9" baking dish lined with parchment paper that is long enough to hang over 2 of the sides.

5. When ready to cook, set the smoker to 350°F and preheat, lid closed for 15 minutes.

6. Bake until crust is very lightly golden brown, about 30 to 35 minutes.

7. Remove from grill and pour the lemon filling over the crust. Return to grill and continue to bake until filling is just set about 15 to 20 minutes.

8. Allow to cool at room temperature, then refrigerate until chilled before slicing into bars. Sprinkle with confectioners' sugar and flaky sea salt right before serving. Enjoy!

Easy Smoked Cornbread

Servings: 4

Cooking Time: 75 Minutes

Ingredients:

- 2 cups self rising flour
- 1 1/2 cups white corn meal
- 2 cups sharp cheddar cheese
- 1/2 cup sour cream
- 1/2 cup sugar
- 1 Tbsp baking powder
- 1 teaspoon sea salt
- 1 12 oz can of evaporated milk
- 1/2 cup vegetable oil
- 2 large eggs beaten

Directions:

1. Mix all ingredients together well and fold into a greased baking pan (such as a round cake Pan).

2. Supply your smoker with wood pellets and follow the start-up procedure. Preheat the grill, with the lid closed, to 375° F. Smoke on 375 °F for 1 hour and 15 minutes or until toothpick comes clean and edges look brown.

3. Rub some butter on top and sprinkle a little Fred's Butt Rub on top before serving.

4. Enjoy!

Chocolate Peanut Cookies

Servings: 4

Cooking Time: 12 Minutes

Ingredients:

- 1/2 Tsp Baking Soda
- 1/2 Cup Brown Sugar
- 1/2 Cup + 1 Tbsp Butter, Unsalted
- 1/3 Cup Cocoa Powder, Dark And Unsweetened
- 2 Eggs, Beaten
- 1 1/2 Cups Flour, All-Purpose
- 1/3 Cup Miniature Chocolate Chips
- 2 Cups Peanut Butter Chips, Divided
- 1/4 Tsp Sea Salt
- 1/2 Cup Sugar, Granulated
- 1 Tsp Vanilla Extract

Directions:

1. Supply your smoker with wood pellets and follow the start-up procedure. Preheat the grill, with the lid closed, to medium-low heat. If using a gas or charcoal grill, preheat a cast iron skillet.

2. In a mixing bowl, whisk together the flour, cocoa powder, baking soda, and salt. Set aside.

3. Set a metal saucepan on the griddle, then add ½ cup of butter to melt. Whisk in the sugars and vanilla extract and cook for 2 minutes. Remove the pan from the griddle, and transfer contents to a large mixing bowl.

4. Slowly pour the beaten eggs into the sugar mixture, whisking constantly to temper the eggs.

5. Add the dry mixture to the wet ingredients until just combined. Fold in 1 cup of peanut butter chips and chocolate chips. Refrigerate mixture for 15 to 30 minutes.

6. Remove the dough from the refrigerator, then add an additional cup of peanut butter chips.

7. Portion dough into 16 to 18 cookie balls.

8. Melt 1 tablespoon of butter on the griddle, then transfer the cookie balls to the griddle. Press down gently on the cookies, then cook for 10 to 12 minutes, flipping halfway.

9. Transfer cookies to a cooling rack for 5 minutes before enjoying.

PORK RECIPES

Smoked Rendezvous Ribs

Servings: 4
Cooking Time: 120 Minutes

Ingredients:

- 1/2 Cup apple cider vinegar
- 1/2 Cup water
- 1/2 Cup BBQ Sauce
- 2 Tablespoon Pork & Poultry Rub
- 3 Rack baby back pork ribs, membrane removed
- 1 As Needed Pork & Poultry Rub

Directions:

1. In a mixing bowl, combine vinegar, water, barbecue sauce, and Traeger Pork and Poultry rub. Set the sauce and a barbecue mop or basting brush grill-side.

2. Supply your smoker with wood pellets and follow the start-up procedure. Preheat the grill, with the lid closed, to 325° F.

3. Arrange the ribs on the grill grate, meat-side up.

4. Grill for 30 minutes, then start mopping. Mop every 15 minutes. After 2 hours, check the ribs for doneness. Grill: 325 ˚F

5. Insert a toothpick between the bones in the center of a rack. If there is little or no resistance, the ribs are done (or close to it). If the ribs are not to your liking, continue to grill them in 30-minute increments, mopping every 15 minutes. Grill: 325 ˚F

6. When the ribs are done, transfer them to a cutting board and give them a final dose of the mop sauce. Sprinkle lightly with Traeger Pork and Poultry Rub.

7. Let the ribs rest for a few minutes before cutting into half slabs or individual ribs. Enjoy!

Grilled Pork Tacos Al Pastor

Servings: 8
Cooking Time: 15 Minutes

Ingredients:

- 2 Tsp Annatto Powder
- Cilantro, Chopped
- Corn Tortillas
- 2 Tsp Cumin
- 1 Tsp Granulated Garlic
- 2 Tbsp Guajillo Chili Powder
- Jalapeno Pepper, Minced
- Lime, Wedges
- 1 Tsp Oregano, Dried
- 1/2 Tsp Pepper
- 1/2 Cup Pineapple, Juice
- 1/2 Pineapple, Skinned & Cored
- 2 Lbs Pork Shoulder, Boneless, Sliced Thin
- 1 1/2 Tsp Salt
- 2 Tbsp Tomato Paste
- 2 Tbsp Vegetable Oil
- 1/4 Cup White Vinegar
- Yellow Onion, Chopped

Directions:

1. Prepare marinade: In a mixing bowl, whisk together pineapple juice, vinegar, oil, tomato paste, chili powder, annatto, cumin, granulated garlic, oregano, salt, and pepper. Set aside.

2. Slice pork shoulder into thin slices (around ¼" thick), then place in a resealable plastic bag. Pour marinade over pork, seal bag, and turn to coat. Refrigerate overnight.

3. Supply your smoker with wood pellets and follow the start-up procedure. Preheat the grill, with the lid open, to 450° F. If using a gas or charcoal grill, set it up for high heat.

4. Remove the pork from the marinade and set on the grill. Grill over high heat for 3 to 5 minutes, turning frequently. Transfer to a cutting board to rest for 10 minutes, then slice thin.

5. Grill pineapple for 3 minutes, turning once. Set aside on a cutting board, and chop once cooled.

6. Assemble tacos: tortillas, pork, pineapple, jalapeño, onion, and cilantro. Serve warm with fresh lime wedges.

Baby Back Ribs With Mustard Slather

Servings: 4

Cooking Time: 120 Minutes

Ingredients:

- 2 racks of baby back ribs, each about 2lb (1kg)
- all-purpose barbecue rub
- low-carb barbecue sauce (optional)
- for the mustard
- ½ cup yellow or brown mustard
- 2 tbsp dill pickle juice or apple cider vinegar

Directions:

1. Supply your smoker with wood pellets and follow the start-up procedure. Preheat the grill, with the lid closed, to 325° F.

2. Remove the thick membrane on the bone side of the ribs. Don't remove the thin membrane on top of the bones because it holds them together. Trim off any odd bits of meat or excess fat. Place the ribs on a rimmed sheet pan.

3. In a small bowl, make the mustard slather by combining the mustard and pickle juice. Brush the ribs on both sides with the mixture and then season with the barbecue rub.

4. Place the ribs on the grate and smoke until the ribs are tender, about 1½ to 2 hours. (A toothpick inserted between bones should go in with little resistance. The meat will also have pulled back from the bone about ½ inch [1.25cm].) Brush the ribs with barbecue sauce (if using) during the last 10 minutes of smoking. Place the ribs meat side down on the grate for 5 minutes. Turn and grill for 5 minutes more. This sets the sauce.

5. Transfer the ribs to a cutting board. Use a sharp knife to cut the slabs in half or into individual ribs. Serve immediately with more barbecue sauce.

Bbq Pulled Pork With Sweet & Heat Bbq Sauce

Servings: 4

Cooking Time: 540 Minutes

Ingredients:

- 10 Pound Bone-In Pork Butt
- 2 Tablespoon Pork & Poultry Rub
- 1 1/2 Cup apple juice
- 4 Tablespoon brown sugar
- 1 Tablespoon salt
- 1 To Taste salt
- 1 To Taste Pork & Poultry Rub
- 1 As Needed Sweet & Heat BBQ Sauce

Directions:

1. Trim pork butt of all excess fat leaving 1/4" of the fat cap attached. Combine 2 Tbsp Pork and Poultry rub, apple juice, brown sugar, and salt in a small bowl stirring until most of the sugar and salt are dissolved. Inject the pork butt every square inch or so with the apple juice mixture.

Season the exterior of the pork butt with remaining rub.

2. Supply your smoker with wood pellets and follow the start-up procedure. Preheat the grill, with the lid closed, to 225° F.

3. Place pork butt directly on the grill grate and cook for about 6 hours or until the internal temperature reaches 160°F. Grill: 225 °F Probe: 160 °F

4. Wrap the pork butt in two layers of foil and pour in 1/2 cup of apple juice. Secure tin foil tightly to contain the apple juice. Increase temperature to 275°F and return to grill in a pan large enough to hold the pork butt in case of leaks. Cook an additional 3 hours or until internal temperature reaches 205°F. Grill: 275 °F Probe: 205 °F

5. Remove from the grill and discard the bone. Shred the pork removing any excess fat or tendons. Season with additional Pork and Poultry Rub and salt if needed.

6. Add Sweet & Heat BBQ sauce and serve. Enjoy!

Scalloped Potatoes With Ham, Corn And Bacon

Servings: 4-6
Cooking Time: 60 Minutes

Ingredients:
- 1 1/2 Cups Cooked Bacon, Chopped
- 1 Tablespoon Butter
- 1 1/2 Cup Cooked Ham, Cubed
- 5-6 Large Potatoes, Red
- Salt And Pepper
- 1 Cup Whole Kernel Corn
- Milk

Directions:

1. Supply your smoker with wood pellets and follow the start-up procedure. Preheat the grill, with the lid open, to 350° F.

2. Smear softened butter all over the bottom of a baking dish. Slice potatoes as uniformly as possible.

3. Place enough potatoes in the pan to cover the bottom. Add some of the bacon, ham and corn on top of the potatoes. Repeat this until you've created a few layers and have used all the potatoes, ham, corn and bacon.

4. Add 1 tbsp of butter and cover with milk, till it's almost covering the mixture. Add salt and pepper to taste.

5. Place on the grill for 1 hour and enjoy!

Spicy Ribs

Servings: 4
Cooking Time: 300 Minutes

Ingredients:
- 2 Finely Minced Chipotle In Adobo
- 1 Cup (Any Kind) Barbecue Sauce
- 1/2 Cup Brown Sugar
- 1/4 Cup Honey
- 1/4 Cup Olive Oil
- 1 Rack St. Louis-Style Rib(S)
- 3 Tablespoons Sweet Heat Rub

Directions:

1. Remove the ribs from their packaging, drain, and pat dry. Using a paper towel, grip the membrane on the back of the ribs and pull off. Discard the membrane and paper towel.

2. In a small mixing bowl, combine the brown sugar, olive oil, honey, BBQ sauce, and chiles in adobo. Using a basting brush, brush the front and back of the ribs generously with the BBQ mixture.

Save the basting brush for later along with half of the sauce.

3. Generously season the ribs with Sweet Heat rub, making sure to focus especially on the front of the ribs.

4. Supply your smoker with wood pellets and follow the start-up procedure. Preheat the grill, with the lid open, to 225° F. If you're using a gas or charcoal grill, set it up for low heat. Place the ribs on the grill and smoke at 225°F for 4-6 hours making sure to baste in the sauce every 2 hours.

5. Remove from the grill and serve with additional barbecue sauce.

Pork Loin Porchetta

Servings: 8
Cooking Time: 120 Minutes

Ingredients:

- 1 center-cut pork loin roast, about 2½ to 3lb (1.2 to 1.4kg)
- Mustard Caviar
- for the paste
- 4 garlic cloves, peeled and coarsely chopped
- zest and juice of 1 lemon
- ½ cup coarsely chopped fresh curly or flat-leaf parsley
- 2 tbsp coarsely chopped fresh rosemary
- 2 tbsp coarsely chopped fresh sage
- 2 tsp fennel seeds
- 1 tsp coarse salt, plus more
- 1 tsp freshly ground black pepper, plus more
- 1 tsp crushed red pepper flakes
- ¼ cup extra virgin olive oil, plus more

Directions:

1. Supply your smoker with wood pellets and follow the start-up procedure. Preheat the grill, with the lid closed, to 450° F.

2. Use a sharp, slender knife to slice the pork almost in half lengthwise, leaving a 1-inch (5cm) hinge. (This is called "butterflying.") Open like a book and make a similar lengthwise cut on either side of the first cut—stopping when you reach the last 1 inch (2.5cm) of meat.

3. In a food processor, make the seasoning paste by combining the garlic, lemon zest and juice, parsley, rosemary, sage, fennel seeds, salt and pepper, and red pepper flakes. With the machine running, add the olive oil in a thin stream. Thinly spread the paste on the interior surfaces of the pork loin, leaving a 1-inch (2.5cm) border. Starting on a long side, reform the pork loin and tie at 2-inch (5cm) intervals with butcher's twine. Brush the outside surface with olive oil and then season with salt and pepper.

4. Place the pork on the grate and roast for 30 minutes. Lower the temperature to 325°F (163°C) and continue to roast the pork until the internal temperature reaches 145°F (63°C), about 60 to 90 minutes more.

5. Transfer the porchetta to a cutting board and let rest for 10 minutes. Remove the butcher's twine and carve the meat into finger-thick slices. Serve with the mustard caviar or a good-quality aged balsamic vinegar.

3-2-1 Spare Ribs

Servings: 4
Cooking Time: 180 Minutes

Ingredients:

- 2 racks of St. Louis–cut pork spare ribs, each about 3lb (1.4kg)
- all-purpose barbecue rub
- 3 tbsp unsalted butter, cut into cubes
- 1 cup apple juice or apple cider

- low-carb barbecue sauce

Directions:

1. Supply your smoker with wood pellets and follow the start-up procedure. Preheat the grill, with the lid closed, to 225° F.

2. Place the ribs on a rimmed sheet pan and dust with the rub. Place the ribs bone side down on the grate and smoke for 3 hours.

3. Tear off 2 large sheets of heavy-duty aluminum foil. Place one rack of ribs bone side down on the foil and top with half the butter cubes. Place the second rack of ribs bone side down on the butter cubes and top with the remaining butter cubes.

4. Bring up all 4 sides of the foil and pour in the apple juice. Crimp the edges of the foil so the ribs are tightly enclosed. Place the foil package on the grate and smoke for 2 hours more.

5. Transfer the ribs to a workspace and carefully open the foil package. (Be careful of escaping steam.) Discard the foil and any accumulated juices. Brush the ribs on both sides with barbecue sauce. Place the ribs on the grate and smoke for 1 hour more to set the sauce and firm up the bark.

6. Transfer the ribs to a cutting board. Use a sharp knife to cut the slabs in half or into individual ribs. Serve immediately.

Smoked Pork Tenderloin

Servings: 4
Cooking Time: 180 Minutes

Ingredients:
- 1/2 Cup apple juice
- 3 Tablespoon honey
- 3 Tablespoon Pork & Poultry Rub
- 1/4 Cup brown sugar
- 2 Tablespoon thyme leaves
- 1/2 Tablespoon black pepper
- 2 (1-1/2 lb) pork tenderloins, silverskin removed

Directions:

1. For the Marinade: In a large bowl, add the apple juice, honey (warmed), Traeger Pork & Poultry rub, brown sugar, thyme leaves and black pepper. Whisk to combine.

2. Add pork loins to the bowl with the marinade. Turn pork to coat and cover bowl with plastic wrap.

3. Transfer to the refrigerator and marinate for 2 to 3 hours.

4. Supply your smoker with wood pellets and follow the start-up procedure. Preheat the grill, with the lid closed, to 225° F.

5. Place the tenderloins directly on the grill grate and smoke until the internal temperature registers 145°F, about 2-1/2 to 3 hours. Grill: 225 °F Probe: 145 °F

6. Remove from grill and let rest 5 minutes before slicing. Enjoy!

3-2-1 Bbq Baby Back Ribs

Servings: 6
Cooking Time: 360 Minutes

Ingredients:
- 2 Rack baby back pork ribs
- 1/3 Cup yellow mustard
- 1/2 Cup apple juice, divided
- 1 Tablespoon Worcestershire sauce
- Pork & Poultry Rub
- 1/2 Cup dark brown sugar
- 1/3 Cup honey, warmed
- 1 Cup 'Que BBQ Sauce

Directions:

1. If your butcher has not already done so, remove the thin silverskin membrane from the bone-side of the ribs by working the tip of a butter knife or a screwdriver underneath the membrane over a middle bone. Use paper towels to get a firm grip, then tear the membrane off.

2. In a small bowl, combine the mustard, 1/4 cup of apple juice (reserve the rest) and the Worcestershire sauce. Spread the mixture thinly on both sides of the ribs and season with Traeger Pork & Poultry Rub.

3. Supply your smoker with wood pellets and follow the start-up procedure. Preheat the grill, with the lid closed, to 180° F.Smoke the ribs, meat-side up for 3 hours.

4. After the ribs have smoked for 3 hours, transfer them to a rimmed baking sheet and increase the grill temperature to 225°F.

5. Tear off four long sheets of heavy-duty aluminum foil. Top with a rack of ribs and pull up the sides to keep the liquid enclosed. Sprinkle half the brown sugar on the rack, then top with half the honey and half the remaining apple juice. Use a bit more apple juice if you want more tender ribs. Lay another piece of foil on top and tightly crimp the edges so there is no leakage. Repeat with the remaining rack of ribs.

6. Return the foiled ribs to the grill and cook for an additional 2 hours.

7. Carefully remove the foil from the ribs and brush the ribs on both sides with Traeger 'Que Sauce. Discard the foil. Arrange the ribs directly on the grill grate and continue to grill until the sauce tightens, 30 to 60 minutes more.

8. Let the ribs rest for a few minutes before serving. Enjoy!

Apricot Glazed Breakfast Sausage

Servings: 6
Cooking Time: 20 Minutes

Ingredients:

- 1/2 Cup Apricot BBQ Sauce or Apricot Jam
- 1 Tablespoon Dijon mustard
- 1 Pound Breakfast Sausage Links

Directions:

1. In a small saucepan, combine the Traeger Barbecue sauce and mustard and warm over low heat. Keep warm.

2. Supply your smoker with wood pellets and follow the start-up procedure. Preheat the grill, with the lid closed, to 350° F.

3. Arrange the sausage links on the grill grate, turning once or twice with tongs, until cooked through, 10 to 15 minutes. Using tongs, roll several sausages at a time in the barbecue sauce and mustard mixture, and return to the grill for 2 to 3 minutes to set the glaze. Grill: 350 °F

4. Serve with the remaining glaze. Enjoy!

Pineapple-pepper Pork Kebabs

Servings: 12-15
Cooking Time: 240 Minutes

Ingredients:

- 1 (20-ounce) bottle hoisin sauce
- ½ cup Sriracha
- ¼ cup honey
- ¼ cup apple cider vinegar
- 2 tablespoons canola oil
- 2 teaspoons minced garlic
- 2 teaspoons onion powder
- 1 teaspoon ground ginger
- 1 teaspoon salt
- 1 teaspoon freshly ground black pepper

- 2 pounds thick-cut pork chops or pork loin, cut into 2-inch cubes
- 10 ounces fresh pineapple, cut into chunks
- 1 red onion, cut into wedges
- 1 bag mini sweet peppers, tops removed and seeded
- 12 metal or wooden skewers (soaked in water for 30 minutes if wooden)

Directions:

1. In a small bowl, stir together the hoisin, Sriracha, honey, vinegar, oil, minced garlic, onion powder, ginger, salt, and black pepper to create the marinade. Reserve ¼ cup for basting.

2. Toss the pork cubes, pineapple chunks, onion wedges, and mini peppers in the remaining marinade. Cover and refrigerate for at least 1 hour or up to 4 hours.

3. Supply your smoker with wood pellets and follow the start-up procedure. Preheat, with the lid closed, to 450°F.

4. Remove the pork, pineapple, and veggies from the marinade; do not rinse. Discard the marinade.

5. Use the double-skewer technique to assemble the kebabs (see Tip below). Thread each of 6 skewers with a piece of pork, a piece of pineapple, a piece of onion, and a sweet mini pepper, making sure that the skewer goes through the left side of the ingredients. Repeat the threading on each skewer two more times. Double-skewer the kebabs by sticking another 6 skewers through the right side of the ingredients.

6. Place the kebabs directly on the grill, close the lid, and smoke for 10 to 12 minutes, turning once. They are done when a meat thermometer inserted in the pork reads 160°F.

Grilled Raspberry Chipotle Pork Ribs

Servings: 4
Cooking Time: 180 Minutes

Ingredients:
- Baby Back Rib
- Original Bbq Sauce
- Raspberry Chipotle Spice Rub

Directions:

1. Begin by gently rinsing off your ribs in cool water. Pat dry and remove the flavor blocker (thin membrane on the underside of the ribs) to allow the seasoning to permeate right into the meat.

2. Generously season your ribs with Raspberry Chipotle seasoning and place in the refrigerator for an hour for flavor to set in.

3. Supply your smoker with wood pellets and follow the start-up procedure. Preheat the grill, with the lid open, to 250° F. Place your seasoned rack of ribs on the grill and let cook for 2 hours. Next, lather on a thick coating of Original BBQ Sauce, turn up the grill to 300°F and let your ribs roast for another hour. Remove, cut and serve for a meal that will surely make its way into the weekly rotation.

Baked Candied Bacon Cinnamon Rolls

Servings: 6
Cooking Time: 35 Minutes

Ingredients:
- 12 Slices Bacon, sliced
- 1/3 Cup brown sugar
- pre-made cinnamon rolls
- 2 Ounce cream cheese

Directions:

1. Supply your smoker with wood pellets and follow the start-up procedure. Preheat the grill, with the lid closed, to 350° F.

2. Dredge 8 of the slices of bacon in brown sugar, making sure to cover both sides of the bacon.

3. Place the brown sugared bacon slices along with the other slices of bacon on a cooling rack placed on top of a large baking sheet.

4. Cook the bacon on the Traeger for 15-20 minutes or until the fat renders but bacon is still pliable. Turn the Traeger down to 325°F.

5. Open and unroll the cinnamon rolls. While bacon is still warm, place 1 slice of the brown sugared bacon on top of 1 of the unrolled rolls and roll back up. Repeat for all the rolls.

6. Place cinnamon rolls in an 8" x 8" baking dish or cake pan that has been sprayed with nonstick cooking spray. Cook the cinnamon rolls at 325°F for 10 to 15 minutes or until golden. Rotate the pan a half turn halfway through cooking time. Grill: 325 °F

7. Meanwhile, take the provided cream cheese frosting and mix in the softened cream cheese. Crumble the cooked bacon and add into the cream cheese frosting.

8. Spread frosting over warm cinnamon rolls. Serve warm, enjoy!

Bbq Baby Back Ribs With Bacon Pineapple Glaze By Scott Thomas

Servings: 4

Cooking Time: 180 Minutes

Ingredients:

- 2 Rack baby back ribs
- 1 As Needed salt and pepper
- 1 As Needed Your Favorite Spicy Rub
- 6 Slices bacon
- 6 Fluid Ounce pineapple juice
- 1 Teaspoon garlic, minced
- 2 Tablespoon honey

Directions:

1. Remove the membrane from the bone side of the ribs and apply the salt, pepper and rub to that side. Flip the ribs over and season the meat side.

2. Supply your smoker with wood pellets and follow the start-up procedure. Preheat the grill, with the lid closed, to 350° F.

3. While the grill heats up, cook the bacon in a frying pan. As the bacon is cooking, pour the pineapple juice, garlic and honey into an oven safe pot.

4. Remove the bacon from the grease and let the pan and bacon fat cool down. After the pan has cooled for a while, pour the bacon grease in with the pineapple juice, garlic and honey and stir to combine.

5. Place the ribs and the pot on the grill and close the lid. After an hour, the slurry will have reduced down a bit and can be applied to the ribs. Slather the ribs with the reduction every 15 minutes. When the bones peek out about a quarter to a third of an inch, the ribs are done which is about 2 hours and 15 minutes. Grill: 350 °F

6. For fall off the bone ribs, go another 30-45 minutes, continuing to glaze every 15 minutes. Grill: 350 °F

7. The sweet and savory of the reduction will temper the heat of the spicy rub forming an outstanding and complex blend of flavors. Enjoy!

Barbecued Tenderloin

Servings: 4-6
Cooking Time: 30 Minutes

Ingredients:

- 2 (1-pound) pork tenderloins
- 1 batch Sweet and Spicy Cinnamon Rub

Directions:

1. Supply your smoker with wood pellets and follow the start-up procedure. Preheat the grill, with the lid closed, to 350°F.
2. Generously season the tenderloins with the rub. Using your hands, work the rub into the meat.
3. Place the tenderloins directly on the grill grate and smoke until their internal temperature reaches 145°F.
4. Remove the tenderloins from the grill and let them rest for 5 to 10 minutes, before thinly slicing and serving.

Crown Roast Of Pork

Servings: 4
Cooking Time: 60 Minutes

Ingredients:

- 1 Whole Crown Roast of Pork, 12-14 ribs
- 1/4 Cup Pork & Poultry Rub
- 1 Cup apple juice
- 1 Cup Apricot BBQ Sauce

Directions:

1. Supply your smoker with wood pellets and follow the start-up procedure. Preheat the grill, with the lid closed, to 375° F.
2. Season the pork roast liberally with Traeger Pork and Poultry Rub. Let sit at room temperature for 30 minutes. Wrap each tip of the crown roast in a small piece of aluminum foil. This will protect the bones during the cook and prevent them from turning black.
3. Place the roast directly on the grill grate and cook for about 90 minutes spraying with apple juice every 30 minutes or so.
4. When the roast reaches an internal temperature of 125 degrees F, remove the aluminum foil from the bones and return to the grill.
5. Spray again with apple juice and continue to cook until the internal temperature reaches 135 degrees F in the thickest part of the roast. In the last ten minutes, baste the roast with the Apricot BBQ Sauce to let the glaze set.
6. Remove from the grill, tent with foil, and let it rest 15-20 minutes before slicing. Enjoy!

Jalapeño-bacon Pork Tenderloin

Servings: 4-6
Cooking Time: 150 Minutes

Ingredients:

- ¼ cup yellow mustard
- 2 (1-pound) pork tenderloins
- ¼ cup Pork Rub
- 8 ounces cream cheese, softened
- 1 cup grated Cheddar cheese
- 1 tablespoon unsalted butter, melted
- 1 tablespoon minced garlic
- 2 jalapeño peppers, seeded and diced
- 1½ pounds bacon

Directions:

1. Slather the mustard all over the pork tenderloins, then sprinkle generously with the dry rub to coat the meat.
2. Supply your smoker with wood pellets and follow the start-up procedure. Preheat, with the lid closed, to 225°F.

3. Place the tenderloins directly on the grill, close the lid, and smoke for 2 hours.

4. Remove the pork from the grill and increase the temperature to 375°F.

5. In a small bowl, combine the cream cheese, Cheddar cheese, melted butter, garlic, and jalapeños.

6. Starting from the top, slice deeply along the center of each tenderloin end to end, creating a cavity.

7. Spread half of the cream cheese mixture in the cavity of one tenderloin. Repeat with the remaining mixture and the other piece of meat.

8. Securely wrap one tenderloin with half of the bacon. Repeat with the remaining bacon and the other piece of meat.

9. Transfer the bacon-wrapped tenderloins to the grill, close the lid, and smoke for about 30 minutes, or until a meat thermometer inserted in the thickest part of the meat reads 160°F and the bacon is browned and cooked through.

10. Let the tenderloins rest for 5 to 10 minutes before slicing and serving.

Baked Honey Glazed Ham

Servings: 8
Cooking Time: 120 Minutes

Ingredients:
- 1 (6-8 lb) Snake River Farms Kurobuta Half Bone-In Ham
- 20 whole cloves
- 1 Stick butter, softened
- 1/4 Cup dark corn syrup
- 1 Cup honey, room temperature

Directions:

1. Supply your smoker with wood pellets and follow the start-up procedure. Preheat the grill, with the lid closed, to 325° F.

2. Score ham. Smear the entire ham with softened butter and stud with the whole cloves and place ham in foil-lined pan.

3. Combine the dark corn syrup and honey. Warm to combine if needed. Pour 3/4 of the glaze over ham, and bake for 1-1/2 to 2 hours on the grill or until the ham reaches 140°F. Grill: 325 °F Probe: 140 °F

4. Baste ham every 20 minutes with remaining honey glaze. Grill: 325 °F Probe: 140 °F

5. Remove from grill and let rest a few minutes.

6. Slice and serve. Enjoy!

Spiced Pulled Pork Shoulder

Servings: 16
Cooking Time: 600 Minutes

Ingredients:
- 5-8 lb Bone-in Pork Shoulder
- Maple Chili Rub
- Maple Sugar
- Kosher Salt
- Fresh Ground Black Pepper
- Roasted Garlic Powder
- Onion Powder
- Cumin
- Chipotle Powder
- Chili Powder
- Cinnamon Powder

Directions:

1. Supply your smoker with wood pellets and follow the start-up procedure. Preheat the grill, with the lid closed, to 225° F. Using apple pellets for this dish will impart a slightly sweeter smoke that goes great with the rub.

2. In a bowl combine rub ingredients.

3. Trim excess fat from pork shoulder, score fat with a sharp knife (only slice about 1/8" into pork), then cover with rub. Reserve some rub to be sprinkled on the meat after it has been shredded.

4. Place the pork onto the smoker.

5. Continue to smoke pork until internal temperature reaches 203 °F, about 10 hours. You can wrap pork in butcher paper once it reaches 160 °F if you want to speed up cooking time (your final bark won't be as good though).

6. Once Pork reaches 203 °F, remove from smoker then wrap tightly in aluminum foil. Place wrapped Pork into a cooler for 1 hour.

7. After 1 hour remove pork from the foil, pull out the bones, using 2 forks shred the pork to your desired consistency.

8. Sprinkle left over rub onto the pork and toss to coat.

9. Enjoy!

Everything Pigs In A Blanket

Servings: 4

Cooking Time: 15 Minutes

Ingredients:

- 2 Tablespoon poppy seeds
- 1 Tablespoon dried minced onion
- 2 Teaspoon garlic, minced
- 2 Tablespoon sesame seeds
- 1 Teaspoon salt
- 8 Ounce (8 oz) Can Pillsbury Original Crescent Rolls
- 1/4 Cup Dijon mustard
- 1 Large egg, beaten

Directions:

1. Supply your smoker with wood pellets and follow the start-up procedure. Preheat the grill, with the lid closed, to 350° F.

2. Mix together poppy seeds, dried minced onion, dried minced garlic, salt and sesame seeds. Set aside.

3. Cut each triangle of crescent roll dough into thirds lengthwise, making 3 small strips from each roll.

4. Brush the dough strips lightly with Dijon mustard. Put the mini hot dogs on 1 end of the dough and roll up.

5. Arrange them, seam side down, on a greased baking pan. Brush with egg wash and sprinkle with seasoning mixture.

6. Bake in Traeger until golden brown, about 12 to 15 minutes.

7. Serve with mustard or dipping sauce of your choice. Enjoy!

Hawaiian Pineapple Pork Butt

Servings: 8 - 10

Cooking Time: 720 Minutes

Ingredients:

- 6 - 8 Pineapple Rings
- 2 Cups Pineapple, Juice
- 1 8-10Lb Pork Butt Roast, Bone-In
- ¼ Cup Sweet Heat Rub

Directions:

1. Supply your smoker with wood pellets and follow the start-up procedure. Preheat the grill, with the lid open, to 225° F. If not using a pellet smoker, set up the smoker for indirect smoking.

2. Remove the pork butt from its packaging and drain any excess liquid from the pork butt. Pat the pork butt dry with paper towels and discard the paper towels.

3. Generously season the pork butt with the Sweet Heat seasoning, making sure that the roast is coated on all sides.

4. Place the pineapple rings evenly over the pork shoulder, fat side up, and pin with toothpicks. Place the pork butt into the 9x13 pan and pour the pineapple juice over the top.

5. Set the pan into the smoker. Make sure that the pork butt is placed as close to the center of the rack as possible for even cooking.

6. Place a temperature probe into the thickest part of the pork butt, and smoke the pork until it reaches an internal temperature of 201°F. The pork should be deeply browned and smell very porky.

7. Once the pork butt reaches its internal temperature, remove the pork butt from the grill and wrap it tightly in foil. Allow the roast to rest for at least 1 hour before shredding.

8. After the roast has rested for an hour, shred the pork with your meat claws, discarding any large chunks of fat. Serve immediately.

Bacon Onion Ring

Servings: 6
Cooking Time: 60 Minutes

Ingredients:

- 16 Slices bacon
- 2 Whole Vidalia onion, sliced
- 1 Tablespoon Chili Garlic Sauce
- 1 Tablespoon yellow mustard
- 1 Teaspoon honey

Directions:

1. Wrap a piece of bacon around an individual onion ring; continue until bacon is gone. Some onion slices may be larger and require 2 pieces of bacon to complete a ring.

2. Place a skewer through the bacon-wrapped onion slice, to keep bacon from unraveling while cooking.

3. Supply your smoker with wood pellets and follow the start-up procedure. Preheat the grill, with the lid closed, to 400° F.

4. Meanwhile, mix chili garlic sauce and yellow mustard in a small bowl until incorporated; add honey.

5. Place skewers on the grill grate and cook for approximately 90 minutes, flipping after 45 minutes. Enjoy! Grill: 400 °F

Competition Style Bbq Pulled Pork

Servings: 8
Cooking Time: 600 Minutes

Ingredients:

- 1 (8-10 lb) bone-in pork butt
- 1 Cup Pork & Poultry Rub, divided
- 2 3/4 Cup apple juice, divided
- 1/4 Cup Butcher BBQ Pork Injection
- meat injector

Directions:

1. Supply your smoker with wood pellets and follow the start-up procedure. Preheat the grill, with the lid closed, to 225° F.

2. While the grill heats up, trim excess fat from pork.

3. In a small bowl, mix together half the Traeger Pork & Poultry Rub, 2 cups apple juice and butchers pork injection. Thoroughly inject pork butt throughout using an injector.

4. Season the pork with a layer of Traeger Pork & Poultry Rub. Let pork rest for 20 minutes.

5. Place pork on the grill and cook for 4-1/2 to 5-1/2 hours. After 4-1/2 hours, check the internal

temperature of the pork. It should be between 155-165°F. If not, check again in 30 minutes. Grill: 225 °F Probe: 155 °F

6. When the temperature reaches 155-165°F, wrap the pork in a double layer of heavy duty aluminum foil. Pour 3/4 cup reserved apple juice in a foil packet with the pork and place back on the grill.

7. Turn the grill temperature up to 250°F and cook for another 3 to 4 hours. Check the internal temperature after 3 hours. The desired temperature is between 204°F and 206°F in the thickest part of the pork. If the pork is not to temperature, check back every 30 minutes until it reaches 204-206°F. The entire cook time should be between 8-10 hours depending on the size of the pork. Grill: 250 °F Probe: 204 °F

8. Remove pork from grill and open the foil packet to vent for 10 minutes. Seal back up and let rest for 45 minutes to one hour.

9. After resting, pour the liquid out of the foil and separate the fat from the broth using a fat separator. Remove the bone and pull the meat. Add 2 cups of the broth to the pulled meat. Add extra broth, if necessary, to achieve desired moisture level. Enjoy!

Hawaiian Pulled Pig

Servings: 4
Cooking Time: 300 Minutes

Ingredients:

- 7 Pound bone-in pork shoulder
- 3 Tablespoon Jacobsen Salt Co. Pure Kosher Sea Salt
- ground black pepper
- 2 Whole Banana Leaves

Directions:

1. Season the pork shoulder with Jacobsen Salt and pepper.

2. Place a banana leaf on your work surface. Lay the pork shoulder in the center of it, and draw up the ends as if you were wrapping a gift. Lay the second banana leaf at right angles to the first and draw up the ends to enclose the meat. Wrap the entire package tightly in aluminum foil. Refrigerate overnight.

3. Supply your smoker with wood pellets and follow the start-up procedure. Preheat the grill, with the lid closed, to 300° F.

4. Place the wrapped pork directly on the grill grate and cook until the pork is falling-apart-tender, 5 to 6 hours, or until it has reached an internal temperature of 190 degrees F. Grill: 300 °F Probe: 190 °F

5. Transfer the pork to a cutting board and let rest, still wrapped, for 20 minutes. Carefully unwrap the pork and save any juices that accumulated in the foil.

6. Tear the pork into chunks and shreds, discarding any lumps of fat or bone. Enjoy!

Bbq Brown Sugar Pork Belly

Servings: 8
Cooking Time: 180 Minutes

Ingredients:

- 1 (3-4 lb) pork belly
- 4 Tablespoon brown sugar
- 4 Tablespoon salt

Directions:

1. The night before you plan to cook, take your pork belly out of the fridge and pat dry with paper towels. Score fat with a very sharp knife in a diamond pattern making sure not to cut into the meat.

2. Combine salt and brown sugar and rub pork belly on all sides. Place on a drying rack on a pan and refrigerate uncovered overnight.

3. Thirty minutes before cooking, remove pork belly from fridge. Rinse under cold water and pat very dry with paper towels.

4. Supply your smoker with wood pellets and follow the start-up procedure. Preheat the grill, with the lid closed, to 450° F.

5. Place the pork belly directly on grill grate, fat side up, for 30 minutes. Grill: 500 °F

6. After 30 minutes, reduce the grill temperature to 325°F and cook for 3 hours or until pork is tender and fat is crisp. Grill: 325 °F

7. Remove from grill and allow to rest for 30 minutes before slicing.

8. Serve with baked beans, potato salad, coleslaw, white bread, BBQ sauce, or your favorite BBQ sides. Enjoy!

Cuban Onion Pork Sandwich

Servings: 4

Cooking Time: 270 Minutes

Ingredients:

- 1 Tbsp Butter
- 3 Cups Chicken Stock
- 4 Ciabatta Bread Or Torta Rolls, Halved
- 1/4 Cup Dijon Mustard
- 4 Dill Pickle, Slice
- 1 Lb Ham Or Prosciutto
- 1/4 Cup Mayonnaise
- Pulled Pork Rub
- 3 1/2 Lbs Pork Shoulder
- 8 Oz Swiss Cheese, Sliced
- 1 Tbsp Vegetable Oil
- 1 White Onion, Sliced

Directions:

1. Supply your smoker with wood pellets and follow the start-up procedure. Preheat the grill, with the lid open, to 250° F. If using a gas or charcoal grill, set it up for low, indirect heat.

2. Generously season pork shoulder with Pulled Pork Rub, then transfer to the grill grate. Smoke for 1 hour, then flip pork and smoke for an additional hour.

3. Place onion and chicken stock in a deep cast iron skillet, or metal grill pan. Transfer the pork to the skillet, then cover with a shallow cast iron skillet, or aluminum foil. Braise for 2 hours, then increase grill temperature to 300° F, and braise for 1 more hour.

4. Remove the cover then pull pork with tongs while still on the grill. The stock will have reduced, so be sure and toss the pork in the reduced, seasoned stock and onions. Remove from the grill and set aside.

5. Preheat the griddle to medium-low flame. If using a different grill, preheat a clean cast iron skillet on medium low heat.

6. Heat butter and oil on the griddle, then toast rolls, pressing down by hand or with a metal spatula. Combine mustard and mayonnaise, then spread onto both sides of rolls. Set aside.

7. Divide pork into 4 portions, and place on the griddle, along with the sliced ham. Cook for 2 to 3 minutes, rotating ham and pork. Layer pork, ham, cheese, and pickles. Cover for 1 minute to allow cheese to melt. Return rolls to the griddle, cut each portion of filling in half, then stack 2 per prepared rolls. Press each sandwich down with the bottom of a metal spatula. Carefully flip, and press down again.

8. Remove sandwiches from the griddle and serve warm.

Delicious Smoked Bone-in Pork Chops

Servings: 4

Cooking Time: 90 Minutes

Ingredients:

- 1/2 Cup Apple Cider Vinegar
- 4 Pork Butt Roast, Bone-In
- 2 Tbsp Salt
- 1 Tbsp Sugar
- 4 Tablespoons Tennessee Apple Butter Seasoning
- 1/4 Cup Vinegar, Red Wine
- 1/4 Cup Water

Directions:

1. Supply your smoker with wood pellets and follow the start-up procedure. Preheat the grill, with the lid closed, to 250° F.

2. In a large mixing bowl, combine the sugar, red wine vinegar, salt, 2 tablespoons of Tennessee Apple Butter and water to create a brine for the pork chops. Whisk the brine well until the sugar, salt and Tennessee Apple Butter have dissolved.

3. Generously rub the pork chops on all sides with olive oil and season on all sides with the Tennessee Apple Butter. Make sure the meat is coated on all sides.

4. Place the pork chops in the smoker, insert a temperature probe into the thickest part of one of the pork chops, and smoke until the internal temperature reaches 145°F, or about 1 hour 30 minutes. The pork chops should have developed a good color and be juicy, but no longer be pink in the center.

5. Remove the pork chops from the smoker and allow them to rest for 5-10 minutes under tented aluminum foil, then slice along the grain and serve.

Baked Maple And Brown Sugar Bacon

Servings: 4

Cooking Time: 60 Minutes

Ingredients:

- 1 Pound cold bacon
- 1/2 Cup pure maple syrup, warmed
- 1/2 Cup brown sugar, plus more as needed

Directions:

1. Supply your smoker with wood pellets and follow the start-up procedure. Preheat the grill, with the lid closed, to 300° F.

2. Line a rimmed baking sheet with foil and place a wire rack on top. Lay bacon strips in a single layer on the wire rack.

3. Using a pastry brush, brush each strip of bacon on both sides with the warmed maple syrup, then sprinkle brown sugar evenly on both sides.

4. Put the baking sheet in the grill and cook bacon for 60-75 minutes, or until bacon browns and appears to be crisping. Grill: 300 °F

5. Allow the bacon to cool slightly before eating. Enjoy!

Traeger Pork Chops

Servings: 2

Cooking Time: 30 Minutes

Ingredients:

- 2 (1-1/2 inch thick) pork chops
- Blackened Saskatchewan Rub
- kosher or sea salt

Directions:

1. Rub salt and Traeger Blackened Saskatchewan Rub into pork chops.

2. Supply your smoker with wood pellets and follow the start-up procedure. Preheat the grill, with the lid closed, to 450° F.

3. Place pork chops directly on grill grate and cook for 30 minutes flipping once halfway through. Grill: 450 ℉

4. Remove from grill and let rest 5 minutes. Enjoy!

Maple Baby Backs

Servings: 4-6

Cooking Time: 240 Minutes

Ingredients:

- 2 (2- or 3-pound) racks baby back ribs
- 2 tablespoons yellow mustard
- 1 batch Sweet Brown Sugar Rub
- ½ cup plus 2 tablespoons maple syrup, divided
- 2 tablespoons light brown sugar
- 1 cup Pepsi or other non-diet cola
- ¼ cup The Ultimate BBQ Sauce

Directions:

1. Supply your smoker with wood pellets and follow the start-up procedure. Preheat the grill, with the lid closed, to 180°F.

2. Remove the membrane from the backside of the ribs. This can be done by cutting just through the membrane in an X pattern and working a paper towel between the membrane and the ribs to pull it off.

3. Coat the ribs on both sides with mustard and season them with the rub. Using your hands, work the rub into the meat.

4. Place the ribs directly on the grill grate and smoke for 3 hours.

5. Remove the ribs from the grill and place them, bone-side up, on enough aluminum foil to wrap the ribs completely. Drizzle 2 tablespoons of maple syrup over the ribs and sprinkle them with 1 tablespoon of brown sugar. Flip the ribs and repeat the maple syrup and brown sugar application on the meat side.

6. Increase the grill's temperature to 300°F.

7. Fold in three sides of the foil around the ribs and add the cola. Fold in the last side, completely enclosing the ribs and liquid. Return the ribs to the grill and cook for 30 to 45 minutes.

8. Remove the ribs from the grill and unwrap them from the foil.

9. In a small bowl, stir together the barbecue sauce and remaining 6 tablespoons of maple syrup. Use this to baste the ribs. Return the ribs to the grill, without the foil, and cook for 15 minutes to caramelize the sauce.

10. Cut into individual ribs and serve immediately.

Lip-smackin' Pork Loin

Servings: 8

Cooking Time: 180 Minutes

Ingredients:

- ¼ cup finely ground coffee
- ¼ cup paprika
- ¼ cup garlic powder
- 2 tablespoons chili powder
- 1 tablespoon packed light brown sugar
- 1 tablespoon ground allspice
- 1 tablespoon ground coriander
- 1 tablespoon freshly ground black pepper
- 2 teaspoons ground mustard
- 1½ teaspoons celery seeds
- 1 (1½- to 2-pound) pork loin roast

Directions:

1. Supply your smoker with wood pellets and follow the start-up procedure. Preheat, with the lid closed, to 250°F.

2. In a small bowl, combine the ground coffee, paprika, garlic powder, chili powder, brown sugar, allspice, coriander, pepper, mustard, and celery seeds to create a rub, and generously apply it to the pork loin roast.

3. Place the pork loin on the grill, fat-side up, close the lid, and roast for 3 hours, or until a meat thermometer inserted in the thickest part of the meat reads 160°F.

4. Let the pork rest for 5 minutes before slicing and serving.

Pork Belly Burnt Ends

Servings: 8-10
Cooking Time: 360 Minutes

Ingredients:
- 1 (3-pound) skinless pork belly (if not already skinned, use a sharp boning knife to remove the skin from the belly), cut into 1½- to 2-inch cubes
- 1 batch Sweet Brown Sugar Rub
- ½ cup honey
- 1 cup The Ultimate BBQ Sauce
- 2 tablespoons light brown sugar

Directions:
1. Supply your smoker with wood pellets and follow the start-up procedure. Preheat the grill, with the lid closed, to 250°F.

2. Generously season the pork belly cubes with the rub. Using your hands, work the rub into the meat.

3. Place the pork cubes directly on the grill grate and smoke until their internal temperature reaches 195°F.

4. Transfer the cubes from the grill to an aluminum pan. Add the honey, barbecue sauce, and brown sugar. Stir to combine and coat the pork.

5. Place the pan in the grill and smoke the pork for 1 hour, uncovered. Remove the pork from the grill and serve immediately.

Baked Sage & Sausage Stuffing

Servings: 4
Cooking Time: 45 Minutes

Ingredients:
- 1 Pound Sage-Flavored Sausage, Such as Bob Evans Or Jimmy Dean
- 1/2 Cup onion, diced
- 1/2 Cup celery, diced
- 14 Ounce (14 oz) package herb seasoned stuffing
- 1/2 Cup dried sweetened cranberries
- 2 Cup low sodium chicken broth
- 6 Tablespoon butter
- butter

Directions:
1. Brown the sausage in a large frying pan, breaking up the sausage with a wooden spoon.

2. Add the onion and celery and cook until softened. Drain any excess fat. Transfer to a large mixing bowl. Add the stuffing mix and cranberries, if using.

3. Warm the chicken broth over medium-low heat; add butter and cook until melted. Toss with the bread/sausage mixture and mix lightly.

4. Butter a 3-qt casserole or baking dish. Do not compress the mixture or it will be dense.

5. Supply your smoker with wood pellets and follow the start-up procedure. Preheat the grill, with the lid closed, to 350° F.

6. Bake the stuffing, covered, for 35 to 45 minutes; uncover during the last 20 minutes of cooking if you prefer a crunchier texture. Grill: 350 °F

7. Remove from grill and serve. Enjoy!

Honey Pork Belly Burnt Ends

Servings: 4

Cooking Time: 270 Minutes

Ingredients:

- 2/3 Cup Bbq Sauce
- 2 Tbsp Butter, Melted
- 2 Tbsp Honey
- 2 Tbsp Olive Oil
- Blackened Sriracha Rub
- 3 Lbs Pork Belly, Skin Removed

Directions:

1. Supply your smoker with wood pellets and follow the start-up procedure. Preheat the grill, with the lid open, to 225° F. If using a gas or charcoal grill, set it up for low, indirect heat.

2. Cut pork belly into 2-inch cubes and place into a large mixing bowl.

3. Drizzle olive oil over pork belly, then generously season with Blackened Sriracha.

4. Transfer seasoned pork belly to a wire rack and place on the grill grate. Cook for 3 hours.

5. Remove the pork belly from the wire rack and transfer into a foil-lined aluminum pan or disposable foil pan.

6. Whisk together BBQ sauce, melted butter, and honey, then pour mixture over pork.

7. Toss to coat, then cover the pan with aluminum foil and return to the grill rack.

8. Cook for another 1 to 1 ½ hours, until the internal temperature reaches 200° F.

9. Remove the foil, transfer pork belly to a cast iron skillet and place in the center of the grill.

10. Open the sear slide and continue cooking for another 5 to 7 minutes, turning halfway, to crisp up the pork.

11. Remove pork belly from the grill, and serve warm.

Double-decker Pulled Pork Nachos With Smoked Cheese

Servings: 4

Cooking Time: 55 Minutes

Ingredients:

- 8 Ounce pepper jack cheese
- 8 Ounce Cheese, sharp cheddar
- tortilla chips
- 2 Cup leftover pulled pork
- black olives
- jalapeño, diced
- cilantro

Directions:

1. Supply your smoker with wood pellets and follow the start-up procedure. Preheat the grill, with the lid closed, to 165° F.

2. Place the cheese (frozen) on a rack on top of a tray filled with ice. You may want to cut the cheese into smaller portions, maybe 2 or 3 chunks per block, to help it smoke more quickly.

3. Smoke the cheeses for 45 to 60 minutes; allow to cool. Shred the cheeses (about 1 cup of each), and set aside. Grill: 165 °F

4. Turn the heat on the Traeger up to 350 degrees and preheat, lid closed, for 10 to 15 minutes. Grill: 350 °F

5. Lay out your tortilla chips on large baking sheet and top evenly with the shredded, smoked cheeses. Place the baking sheet on the Traeger

grill grate and cook for about 10 minutes, or until the cheese is melted and bubbly. Grill: 350 ˚F

6. Remove the pan from the Traeger and start to assemble the double-decker nachos. Assemble the nachos with a layer of cheesy chips on the bottom, some pulled pork, and more cheesy chips on top. Finish it off with your favorite nacho toppings. Serve warm.

Spiced Orange Ribs

Servings: 4
Cooking Time: 180 Minutes

Ingredients:
- 1 Tablespoon Adobo Sauce
- 2 (2 1/2-Pound) Racks Baby Back Rib
- 1/3 Cup Firmly Packed Light Brown Sugar
- 1 Tablespoon Chili Powder
- 5 In Adobo Sauce Chipotle Peppers
- 1/3 Cup Leaves Cilantro, Fresh
- 1 Teaspoon Ground Cumin
- 1/4 Cup Honey
- 1/4 Cup Ketchup
- 2 Tablespoons Lime Juice
- 1 Cup Orange Juice, Fresh
- 5 Tablespoons Sweet Heat Rub

Directions:
1. First, make the barbecue sauce. Into the bowl of a blender, add ¾ cup of orange juice, cilantro, honey, ketchup, lime juice, 2 chipotles in adobo, adobo sauce, and 1 tablespoon of the Sweet Heat Rub. Place the lid on the blender and blend until completely smooth. Pour into a bowl, reserve ½ cup and set aside.

2. Prepare the ribs. Using the paper towels, pull the membrane off of the back of the ribs and discard. In the bowl of a blender, add the orange juice, brown sugar, chipotle peppers, chili powder,

ground cumin, and Sweet Heat. Place the lid on the blender and blend until smooth. Pour this mixture over the ribs and massage into the meat. Place the ribs in the refrigerator and marinade for 8 hours.

3. Supply your smoker with wood pellets and follow the start-up procedure. Preheat the grill, with the lid open, to 275˚ F. Place the ribs, meat side up, and grill for 1 ½ hours. Baste the ribs with the reserved barbecue sauce, then BBQ for another 1 ½ hours, or until the ribs are extremely tender. Remove the ribs from the grill and serve with barbecue sauce.

Smoked Curry Ketchup Pork Ribs

Servings: 4
Cooking Time: 205 Minutes

Ingredients:
- 1 Tsp Chili Powder
- 1 Tbsp Curry Powder
- 1/2 Tsp Ground Mustard
- 2 Tsp Honey
- To Taste, Kansas City Barbecue Rub Seasoning
- 1 Cup Ketchup
- 2 Pork Back Rib Racks, Membrane Removed
- 2 Tsp Smoked Paprika
- 2 Tsp Worcestershire Sauce

Directions:
1. Supply your smoker with wood pellets and follow the start-up procedure. Preheat the grill, with the lid open, to 225˚ F. If using a gas or charcoal grill, set it up for low, indirect heat.

2. Place rib racks on a sheet tray, then season both sides with Kansas City Barbeque Rub. Transfer ribs to the grill and smoke for 1 hour.

3. Meanwhile, prepare the curry ketchup: In a mixing bowl, add ketchup, curry powder, smoked paprika, chili powder, ground mustard, Worcestershire, and honey and whisk to incorporate. Set aside.

4. Rotate the rib racks and increase temperature to 250 F. Cook for another hour, then remove the ribs from the grill and place on butcher paper. Brush ribs with sauce then wrap with paper.

5. Return ribs to the grill. Cook for one more hour, until tender.

6. Remove ribs from the grill, cut open the butcher paper, and baste with remaining curry ketchup. Place racks back on the grill, increase the temperature to 275 F, then cook for an additional 15 minutes. Remove ribs from the grill, cut open the butcher paper, and baste with remaining curry ketchup. Place racks back on the grill, increase the temperature to 275 F, then cook for an additional 15 minutes.

7. Remove ribs from the grill, rest for 10 minutes, then slice and serve warm.

Game Day Cheese Dip

Servings: 6

Cooking Time: 18 Minutes

Ingredients:

- 8 Slices bacon
- 8 cream cheese, softened
- 1/2 Cup mayonnaise
- 2 Teaspoon Dijon mustard
- 1 3/4 Cup Swiss cheese
- 3 scallions, chopped
- 2 Teaspoon Horseradish, fresh

Directions:

1. Supply your smoker with wood pellets and follow the start-up procedure. Preheat the grill, with the lid closed, to 400° F.

2. In a mixing bowl, combine cream cheese, mayonnaise, dijon mustard, swiss cheese (except cheese for topping), scallions, horseradish and crumbled bacon.

3. Transfer to a shallow small casserole or baking dish. Top the dip with the additional 1/4 cup of extra swiss cheese.

4. Place the casserole dish on the Traeger grill grate and cook until golden and bubbly at edges, 15 to 18 minutes. Grill: 400 °F

5. Top with chopped scallions. Enjoy!

SEAFOOD RECIPES

Cajun-blackened Shrimp

Servings: 4
Cooking Time: 20 Minutes

Ingredients:

- 1 pound peeled and deveined shrimp, with tails on
- 1 batch Cajun Rub
- 8 tablespoons (1 stick) butter
- ¼ cup Worcestershire sauce

Directions:

1. Supply your smoker with wood pellets and follow the start-up procedure. Preheat the grill, with the lid closed, to 450°F and place a cast-iron skillet on the grill grate. Wait about 10 minutes after your grill has reached temperature, allowing the skillet to get hot.
2. Meanwhile, season the shrimp all over with the rub.
3. When the skillet is hot, place the butter in it to melt. Once the butter melts, stir in the Worcestershire sauce.
4. Add the shrimp and gently stir to coat. Smoke-braise the shrimp for about 10 minutes per side, until opaque and cooked through. Remove the shrimp from the grill and serve immediately.

Grilled Whole Steelhead Fillet

Servings: 6
Cooking Time: 30 Minutes

Ingredients:

- (2-1/2 to 3 lb) steelhead or salmon fillet, skin-on

- 2 Tablespoon Montana Mex Sweet Seasoning
- 1 Teaspoon Montana Mex Jalapeño Seasoning Blend
- 1 Teaspoon Montana Mex Mild Chile Seasoning Blend
- 2 Tablespoon Montana Mex Avocado Oil
- 2 Tablespoon freshly grated ginger
- 1 lemon, thinly sliced

Directions:

1. Coat fillet evenly with all three dry seasonings, avocado oil, grated ginger and thinly sliced lemon.
2. Supply your smoker with wood pellets and follow the start-up procedure. Preheat the grill, with the lid closed, to 380° F.
3. Place the fish skin-side down on the grill grate and cook for 20 minutes. Grill: 380 °F
4. Remove fillet from grill and let rest for 5 minutes. Enjoy!

Grilled Trout With Citrus & Basil

Servings: 4
Cooking Time: 10 Minutes

Ingredients:

- 6 Whole Trout
- 2 Teaspoon Blackened Saskatchewan Rub
- 10 Sprig fresh basil
- 2 Lemons, cut in half
- extra-virgin olive oil

Directions:

1. Supply your smoker with wood pellets and follow the start-up procedure. Preheat the grill, with the lid closed, to 450° F.

2. Season the center cavity of the trout with the Traeger Blackened Saskatchewan. Place two sprigs of Basil in each cavity, then add 4 lemon halves.

3. Next tie the fish closed using the Butchers twine, and then rub with olive oil.

4. Place the trout on the hot grill and cook 5 minutes on each side. Enjoy! Grill: 450 °F

Charleston Crab Cakes With Remoulade

Servings: 4
Cooking Time: 45 Minutes

Ingredients:

- 1¼ cups mayonnaise
- ¼ cup yellow mustard
- 2 tablespoons sweet pickle relish, with its juices
- 1 tablespoon smoked paprika
- 2 teaspoons Cajun seasoning
- 2 teaspoons prepared horseradish
- 1 teaspoon hot sauce
- 1 garlic clove, finely minced
- 2 pounds fresh lump crabmeat, picked clean
- 20 butter crackers (such as Ritz brand), crushed
- 2 tablespoons Dijon mustard
- 1 cup mayonnaise
- 2 tablespoons freshly squeezed lemon juice
- 1 tablespoon salted butter, melted
- 1 tablespoon Worcestershire sauce
- 1 tablespoon Old Bay seasoning
- 2 teaspoons chopped fresh parsley
- 1 teaspoon ground mustard
- 2 eggs, beaten
- ¼ cup extra-virgin olive oil, divided

Directions:

1. For the remoulade:

2. In a small bowl, combine the mayonnaise, mustard, pickle relish, paprika, Cajun seasoning, horseradish, hot sauce, and garlic.

3. Refrigerate until ready to serve.

4. For the crab cakes:

5. Supply your smoker with wood pellets and follow the start-up procedure. Preheat, with the lid closed, to 375°F.

6. Spread the crabmeat on a foil-lined baking sheet and place over indirect heat on the grill, with the lid closed, for 30 minutes.

7. Remove from the heat and let cool for 15 minutes.

8. While the crab cools, combine the crushed crackers, Dijon mustard, mayonnaise, lemon juice, melted butter, Worcestershire sauce, Old Bay, parsley, ground mustard, and eggs until well incorporated.

9. Fold in the smoked crabmeat, then shape the mixture into 8 (1-inch-thick) crab cakes.

10. In a large skillet or cast-iron pan on the grill, heat 2 tablespoons of olive oil. Add half of the crab cakes, close the lid, and smoke for 4 to 5 minutes on each side, or until crispy and golden brown.

11. Remove the crab cakes from the pan and transfer to a wire rack to drain. Pat them to remove any excess oil.

12. Repeat steps 6 and 7 with the remaining oil and crab cakes.

13. Serve the crab cakes with the remoulade.

Lemon Scallops Wrapped In Bacon

Servings: 4

Cooking Time: 20 Minutes

Ingredients:

- 3 Tbsp Lemon, Juice
- Pepper
- 12 Scallop

Directions:

1. Start your grill on smoke with the lid open until a fire is established in the burn pot (3-7 minutes).

2. Supply your smoker with wood pellets and follow the start-up procedure. Preheat the grill, with the lid closed, to 400° F.Cut the bacon rashers in half, wrap each half around a scallop and use a toothpick to keep it in place.

3. Next drizzle the lemon juice over the scallops, and then place them on a baking tray.

4. Place in the grill, and grill for about 15-20 minutes, or until the bacon is crisp, remove from the grill, then serve.

Florentine Shrimp Al Cartoccio

Servings: 4

Cooking Time: 13 Minutes

Ingredients:

- 6 tbsp unsalted butter, melted
- ½ cup heavy whipping cream
- ½ cup grated Parmesan cheese
- 2 garlic cloves, peeled and minced
- 1 cup thinly sliced button mushrooms, cleaned and destemmed
- 1 cup baby spinach leaves
- 2 tbsp chopped sun-dried, oil-packed tomatoes
- ½ tsp dried oregano
- ½ tsp dried basil
- ½ tsp crushed red pepper flakes, plus more
- ½ tsp coarse salt
- ½ tsp freshly ground black pepper
- 20 to 24 jumbo shrimp, about 1lb (450g) total, peeled and deveined
- sprigs of fresh rosemary, basil, thyme, or oregano

Directions:

1. Supply your smoker with wood pellets and follow the start-up procedure. Preheat the grill, with the lid closed, to 400° F.

2. In a large bowl, combine the butter and whipping cream. Stir in the Parmesan, garlic, mushrooms, spinach, tomatoes, oregano, basil, red pepper flakes, and salt and pepper. Add the shrimp and stir gently to coat.

3. Place four 12-inch (30.5cm) sheets of wide heavy-duty aluminum foil on a workspace and pull up the sides. Divide the shrimp mixture evenly between the sheets of foil. Roll and crimp the top and sides of the foil to create sealed packages.

4. Place the packets seam side up on the grate and grill until the shrimp are cooked through, about 10 to 13 minutes. (You can carefully open one package to check on the shrimp.)

5. Transfer the packets to plates. Carefully open the packets to avoid any steam. Scatter fresh herbs over the shrimp before serving.

Oysters Margarita

Servings: 4

Cooking Time: 10minutes

Ingredients:

- 24 fresh oysters in the shell

- 4oz (120ml) freshly squeezed lime juice
- 2oz (60ml) tequila
- 2oz (60ml) orange liqueur, such as triple sec
- 6 tbsp cold butter, cut into 24 cubes
- crunchy salt, such as margarita rimming salt
- lime wedges
- hot sauce (optional)

Directions:

1. Supply your smoker with wood pellets and follow the start-up procedure. Preheat the grill, with the lid closed, to 450° F.

2. Carefully shuck each oyster to remove the top shell. Run your shucking knife under the oyster to release it from the bottom shell, but don't spill the juices. Discard the top shells, but keep the oysters in the bottom shells. Balance each oyster on a wire rack placed on a rimmed sheet pan.

3. Place 1 teaspoon of lime juice, ½ teaspoon of tequila, ½ teaspoon of orange liqueur, and 1 cube of butter on each oyster.

4. Place the pan on the grate and smoke until the butter has melted and the juices are bubbling, about 8 to 10 minutes. (The oysters should be just barely cooked.)

5. Remove the pan from the grill. Sprinkle a pinch of salt on each oyster. Serve immediately with lime wedges and hot sauce (if using).

Swordfish With Sicilian Olive Oil Sauce

Servings: 4
Cooking Time: 10 Minutes

Ingredients:
- 1/2 Cup extra-virgin olive oil, plus 2 tablespoons for oiling the fish
- 1 Whole lemon, juiced
- 2 Clove garlic, minced

- 3 Tablespoon finely chopped fresh parsley
- 1 Tablespoon finely chopped fresh oregano or 1 teaspoon dried oregano
- 1 Tablespoon brined capers, drained (optional)
- 4 (6 to 8 oz) swordfish, halibut, tuna or salmon steaks, 1 inch thick
- salt and pepper

Directions:

1. Put 1/2 cup of olive oil in a small saucepan and warm over low heat.

2. Whisk in lemon juice and 2 tablespoons hot water. Stir in garlic, parsley, oregano, capers (if using), and salt and pepper to taste (go easy on the salt if you're using capers). Keep warm.

3. Supply your smoker with wood pellets and follow the start-up procedure. Preheat the grill, with the lid closed, to 400° F.

4. Brush the fish steaks with 2 tablespoons of olive oil and season with salt and pepper. Grill: 400 ℉

5. Arrange on the grill grate and grill until the fish is opaque and flakes easily when pressed with a fork, about 18 minutes. (If you prefer your tuna or salmon on the rare side, cook them for less time.) Grill: 400 ℉

6. Transfer the fish steaks to a platter or plates and drizzle with the warm olive oil sauce.

7. Serve the remaining sauce on the side. Enjoy!

Grilled Crab Legs With Herb Butter

Servings: 2
Cooking Time: 15 Minutes

Ingredients:
- 12 Tablespoon butter
- 3 Tablespoon Fresh Herbs (Parsley, Chives, Tarragon), finely chopped

- 4 Pound King Crab Legs or Dungeness Crab Leg Clusters
- 3 Whole Lemons, cut into wedges

Directions:

1. Supply your smoker with wood pellets and follow the start-up procedure. Preheat the grill, with the lid closed, to 375° F.

2. Place the butter, garlic, herbs, and a pinch of salt into a small cast iron sauce pan. Place on grill for 5 minutes to melt. Remove from grill and stir. Grill: 375 °F

3. If using king crab legs, split down the center and pour herb butter over meat reserving a quarter for serving. If using crab clusters, toss clusters with herb butter in a large mixing bowl reserving a quarter for serving.

4. Place crab legs directly on the grill grate, meat side up. Grill for 5 to 10 minutes or until hot and beginning to develop a little char on the shell. Grill: 375 °F

5. Serve crab legs with lemon wedges and reserved herb butter. Enjoy!

Honey-soy Garlic Salmon

Servings: 4
Cooking Time: 6 Minutes

Ingredients:

- 1 Tsp Chili Paste
- Chives, Chopped
- 2 Grate Garlic, Cloves
- 2 Tbsp Minced Ginger, Fresh
- 1 Tsp Honey
- 2 Tbsp Lemon, Juice
- 4 Salmon, Fillets (Skin Removed)
- 1 Tsp Sesame Oil
- 2 Tbsp Soy Sauce, Low Sodium

Directions:

1. Supply your smoker with wood pellets and follow the start-up procedure. Preheat the grill, with the lid closed, to 400° F.

2. Take the salmon and place it in a large resealable plastic bag, and then top with all remaining ingredients, except the chives. Seal the plastic bag and toss evenly to coat the salmon. Marinade in the refrigerator for 20 minutes.

3. After the salmon has been marinading for 20 minutes, place salmon on a flat pan or right on the grates and grill for about 3 minutes, and then flip and grill on the second side for about 3 minutes. Turn off the Grill, remove the pan from grill, plate, garnish with chives, and enjoy!

Delicious Smoked Trout

Servings: 8
Cooking Time: 120 Minutes

Ingredients:

- 6 rainbow trout fillets
- Brine:
- 2 Tablespoons kosher salt
- 2 Tablespoons brown sugar
- 4 cups cool water

Directions:

1. For the brine, dissolve the kosher salt and brown sugar in water.

2. Place the trout fillets in the brine, skin side up, and brine the fillets for 15 minutes.

3. Supply your smoker with wood pellets and follow the start-up procedure. Preheat the grill, with the lid closed, to 180° F.

4. Remove the trout from the brine and transfer it to the grill grates.

5. Smoke the trout for 1.5 to 2 hours with the lid closed, depending on the thickness of your fillets.

6. Smoke until the trout reaches an internal temperature of 145 °F, or until the trout flakes easily.

7. Remove the trout from the smoker and serve warm, or let it cool completely and serve chilled with your favorite accouterments.

Shrimp Cabbage Tacos With Lime Cream

Servings: 4
Cooking Time: 10 Minutes

Ingredients:
- 1/4 Cabbage, Shredded
- 2 Tsp Cilantro, Chopped
- Corn Tortillas
- 1/2 Lime, Wedges
- 1/4 Cup Mayonnaise
- Blackened Sriracha Rub
- 1/4 Red Bell Pepper, Chopped
- 1 Lb Shrimp, Peeled & Deveined
- 1/4 Cup Sour Cream
- 2 Tsp Vegetable Oil
- 1/2 White Onion, Chopped

Directions:
1. Place shrimp In a medium bowl. Season with Blackened Sriracha Rub, then drizzle with vegetable oil. Toss by hand to coat well then set aside.

2. In a small mixing bowl, stir together mayonnaise, sour cream, and fresh lime juice. Season to taste with Blackened Sriracha. Set aside.

3. In a small mixing bowl, combine jalapeño, onion, red bell pepper, and cilantro. Set aside.

4. Supply your smoker with wood pellets and follow the start-up procedure. Preheat the grill, with the lid closed, till over medium heat. If using a grill, preheat a cast iron skillet over medium-heat.

5. Place tortillas on the griddle to warm each side, then turn off the burner below.

6. Transfer shrimp to the hot griddle, and cook for 4 to 6 minutes, tossing occasionally, until opaque. For spicier shrimp, season with additional Blackened Sriracha.

7. Assemble tacos: shredded cabbage, shrimp, pepper mixture, then drizzle with sauce. Serve warm with fresh lime wedges.

Grilled Albacore Tuna With Potato-tomato Casserole

Servings: 8
Cooking Time: 20 Minutes

Ingredients:
- 6 Tuna Steaks, 6oz
- 1 Whole lemon zest
- 1 chile de árbol, thinly sliced
- 1 Tablespoon thyme
- 1 Tablespoon fresh parsley

Directions:
1. To make the fish: Season the fish with the lemon zest, chile, thyme, and parsley. Cover and refrigerate at least 4 hours.

2. Remove fish from the refrigerator 30 minutes before cooking to come to room temperature.

3. Season the fish with salt and pepper on both sides. Grill 2-3 minutes per side (next to the cast iron with the casserole) rotating it once or twice. The tuna should be well seared but still rare.

Mexican Mahi Mahi With Baja Cabbage Slaw

Servings: 4
Cooking Time: 10 Minutes

Ingredients:

- 1½lb (680g) skinless mahi mahi, cod, or other firm white fish fillets
- coarse salt
- freshly ground black pepper
- chili powder
- lime wedges
- for the slaw
- 2 cups finely shredded green cabbage
- 2 cups finely shredded purple cabbage
- 4 tbsp reduced-fat mayo
- 2 tsp hot sauce, plus more
- 2 tsp freshly squeezed lime juice
- ½ tsp coarse salt
- for the marinade
- ¼ cup freshly squeezed orange juice
- ¼ cup freshly squeezed lime juice
- 2 tbsp extra virgin olive oil

Directions:

1. In a medium bowl, make the slaw by combining the ingredients. Stir well. Transfer to a serving bowl. Cover and refrigerate until ready to serve.

2. Place the fish fillets in a baking dish and pour the orange and lime juices and olive oil over them. Turn the fillets to coat thoroughly. Cover and refrigerate for 15 to 20 minutes.

3. Supply your smoker with wood pellets and follow the start-up procedure. Preheat the grill, with the lid closed, to 450° F.

4. Drain the fish and pat dry with paper towels. (Discard the marinade.) Season the fillets on both sides with salt and pepper and chili powder. Place the fillets on the grate and grill until golden brown, about 4 to 5 minutes per side, turning with a thin-bladed spatula.

5. Transfer the fish to a platter. Serve with the slaw and lime wedges.

Traeger Crab Legs

Servings: 4
Cooking Time: 30 Minutes

Ingredients:

- 3 Pound crab legs, thawed and halved
- 1 Cup butter, melted
- 2 Tablespoon fresh lemon juice
- 2 Clove garlic, minced
- 1 Tablespoon Fin & Feather Rub or Old Bay Seasoning, plus more to taste
- lemon wedges
- Italian Parsley, chopped

Directions:

1. If the crab legs are too long to fit in the roasting pan, break them down at the joints by twisting, or use a heavy knife or cleaver. Split the shells open lengthwise. Transfer to the roasting pan.

2. Combine the butter, lemon juice and garlic; whisk to mix. Pour mixture over the crab legs, turning the legs to coat. Sprinkle the Traeger Fin & Feather Rub or Old Bay Seasoning over the legs.

3. Supply your smoker with wood pellets and follow the start-up procedure. Preheat the grill, with the lid closed, to 350° F.

4. Cook the crab legs, basting once or twice with the butter sauce from the bottom of the pan, for 20 to 30 minutes (depending on the size of the crab legs) or until warmed through. Grill: 350 °F

5. Transfer the crab legs to a large platter and divide the sauce and accumulated juices between 4 dipping bowls. Enjoy!

Smoked Mango Shrimp

Servings: 4

Cooking Time: 5 Minutes

Ingredients:

- 2 Tablespoon Olive Oil
- 1 Pound Raw Tail-On, Thawed And Deveined Shrimp, Uncooked

Directions:

1. Supply your smoker with wood pellets and follow the start-up procedure. Preheat the grill, with the lid closed, to 425° F. Rinse shrimp off in sink with cold water. Place in bowl and season generously with Mango Magic seasoning and olive oil. Toss well in bowl.

2. Thread several shrimp onto a skewer, so that they are all just touching each other. Repeat with other skewers and remaining shrimp.

3. Grill shrimp for 2 - 3 minutes on each side, or until pink and opaque all the way through. Remove from grill and serve immediately.

Grilled Fresh Fish

Servings: 2

Cooking Time: 15 Minutes

Ingredients:

- 1 Whole fillet of firm white fish: sea bass, halibut or cod
- Fin & Feather Rub
- 2 Whole lemons

Directions:

1. Supply your smoker with wood pellets and follow the start-up procedure. Preheat the grill, with the lid closed, to 325° F.

2. Season fish with Traeger Fin & Feather Rub and let sit for 30 minutes. Slice lemons in half.

3. Place the fish and the lemons (cut side down) directly on the grill grates. Cook for 10 to 15 minutes until the fish is flaky and is at least 145°F in the thickest part of fish. Be careful not to over cook.

4. Serve with the grilled lemons. Enjoy!

Garlic Pepper Shrimp Pesto Bruschetta

Servings: 12

Cooking Time: 15 Minutes

Ingredients:

- 12 Slices Bread, Baguette
- 1/2 Tsp Chili Pepper Flakes
- 1/2 Tsp Garlic Powder
- 4 Cloves Garlic, Minced
- 2 Tbsp Olive Oil
- 1/2 Tsp Paprika, Smoked
- 1/4 Tsp Parsley, Leaves
- Pepper
- Pesto
- Salt
- 12 Shrimp, Jumbo

Directions:

1. Supply your smoker with wood pellets and follow the start-up procedure. Preheat the grill, with the lid closed, to 350° F. Place the baguette slices on a baking sheet lined with foil. Stir together the olive oil, and minced garlic, then brush both sides of the baguette slices with the mix. Place the pan inside the grill, and bake for about 10-15 minutes.

2. In a skillet, add a splash of olive oil, shrimp, chili powder, garlic powder, smoked paprika, salt pepper, and grill on medium-high heat for about 5 minutes (until the shrimp is pink). Be sure to stir often. Once pink, remove pan from heat. Once the baguettes are toasted, let them cool for 5 minutes, then spread a layer of pesto onto each one, then top with a shrimp, and serve.

Honey Balsamic Salmon

Servings: 2

Cooking Time: 25 Minutes

Ingredients:

- 1 Medium salmon fillet
- Fin & Feather Rub
- 1/2 Cup balsamic vinegar
- 1 Tablespoon minced garlic
- 2 Tablespoon honey

Directions:

1. Season the fillet with the Traeger Fin & Feather Rub.

2. Make the glaze: Combine the vinegar, garlic and honey in a small saucepan. Simmer over medium heat until reduced by half. Usually 10 to 15 minutes. The glaze will be properly reduced when it coats the back of a spoon. Using a basting brush, coat the fillet with the glaze.

3. Supply your smoker with wood pellets and follow the start-up procedure. Preheat the grill, with the lid closed, to 350° F.

4. Arrange the salmon fillet on the grill grate. Grill for 25 to 30 minutes, or until the salmon is opaque and flakes easily with a fork. Grill: 350 °F

5. Transfer to a platter or plates and serve immediately. If desired, heat any remaining glaze to a boil and drizzle over top of the salmon. Enjoy!

Oysters In The Shell

Servings: 4

Cooking Time: 20 Minutes

Ingredients:

- 8 medium oysters, unopened, in the shell, rinsed and scrubbed
- 1 batch Lemon Butter Mop for Seafood

Directions:

1. Supply your smoker with wood pellets and follow the start-up procedure. Preheat the grill, with the lid closed, to 375°F.

2. Place the unopened oysters directly on the grill grate and grill for about 20 minutes, or until the oysters are done and their shells open.

3. Discard any oysters that do not open. Shuck the remaining oysters, transfer them to a bowl, and add the mop. Serve immediately.

Grilled Artichoke Cheese Salmon

Servings: 12

Cooking Time: 270 Minutes

Ingredients:

- 28 Oz Artichoke Hearts, Whole, Canned
- 1/2 Cup Breadcrumbs
- 1/2 Cup Brown Sugar
- 8 Oz Cream Cheese
- 1 Tbsp Garlic Powder
- 1 Cup Italian Cheese Blend, Shredded
- 1/4 Cup Kosher Salt
- 1 Cup Mayonnaise
- 2 Tsp Olive Oil
- 1 Tbsp Onion Powder
- 1/2 Cup Parmesan Cheese
- 2 Tbsp Parsley, Chopped
- Blackened Sriracha Rub
- 1 1/4 Lbs Salmon, Fillet, Scaled And Deboned
- Sour Cream
- 1/2 Tsp White Pepper, Ground

Directions:

1. In a small mixing bowl, whisk together the brown sugar, salt, garlic powder, onion powder, and white pepper. This will make twice the cure needed, so be sure and place the remaining half in

a resealable plastic bag and save for smoking fish at a later date.

2. Lay a sheet of plastic wrap on a sheet tray and sprinkle a thin layer of the cure on it. Place the salmon skin-side down on top of the cure, then sprinkle a couple tablespoons of cure on top. Gently press the cure on top of the salmon flesh, then wrap in plastic wrap.

3. Refrigerate for 8 hours, or overnight.

4. Remove salmon from the refrigerator and wash off the cure in the sink, under cold water.

5. Blot salmon with a paper towel, then set salmon skin side on a wire rack. Dry at room temperature for two hours, or until a yellowish shimmer appears on the salmon.

6. Supply your smoker with wood pellets and follow the start-up procedure. Preheat the grill, with the lid closed, to 250° F. If using a gas, charcoal or other grill, set it to low, indirect heat.

7. Place the salmon in the upper cabinet. Smoke for 2 hours, then increase the grill temperature to 350° F to maintain a cabinet temperature of 225°F and smoke another 1 to 2 hours, until salmon reaches an internal temperature of 145° F.

8. Remove salmon from the cabinet and set aside to rest for 15 minutes, then flake apart. Reserve ½ cup to top dip after grilling.

9. While the salmon is resting, drain the artichokes, then skewer onto metal skewers (if using wooden skewers, make sure to soak in water for 1 hour prior to grilling, or you can use a grill basket as well).

10. Season with Blackened Sriracha, then set on the grill. Grill for 2 to 3 minutes, until lightly browned.

11. Remove from the grill, cool slightly, then roughly chop. Set aside.

12. In a mixing bowl, combine shredded Italian cheese, grated parmesan, breadcrumbs and parsley. Set aside.

13. Place cream cheese, mayonnaise, and sour cream in a cast iron skillet. Stir frequently, with a wooden spoon, for about 5 minutes, until the mixture is smooth.

14. Carefully fold in flaked salmon and grilled artichoke hearts, then spread breadcrumb mixture over dip.

15. Drizzle with olive oil, then close the grill lid and bake for 25 to 30 minutes, until dip begins to bubble around the edges, and cheese begins to caramelize on top.

16. Remove dip from the grill, top with reserved salmon and a pinch of parsley. Serve warm with bagel chips, crackers, or crusty bread.

Thai-style Swordfish Steaks With Peanut Sauce

Servings: 4

Cooking Time: 8 Minutes

Ingredients:

- 4 center-cut swordfish steaks, each about 6oz (170g) and 1 inch (2.5cm) thick
- Peanut Sauce
- lime wedges
- for the marinade
- ½ cup light Thai-style unsweetened coconut milk
- 2 garlic cloves, peeled and smashed with a chef's knife
- juice and zest of 1 lime
- 1-inch (2.5cm) piece of fresh ginger, peeled and roughly chopped
- ½ Thai bird's eye chili pepper or serrano pepper, deseeded and thinly sliced, plus more

- 2 tbsp fresh cilantro leaves, coarsely chopped
- 1 tbsp Asian fish sauce
- 1 tbsp light soy sauce or liquid aminos
- 1 tbsp light brown sugar or low-carb substitute
- 1 tsp ground coriander
- ½ tsp ground turmeric

Directions:

1. In a medium bowl, make the marinade by whisking together the ingredients. Whisk until the brown sugar dissolves.

2. Place the swordfish steaks in a single layer in a nonreactive baking dish and pour the marinade over them, turning the steaks to coat thoroughly. Refrigerate for 1 hour.

3. Supply your smoker with wood pellets and follow the start-up procedure. Preheat the grill, with the lid closed, to 450° F.

4. Remove the swordfish from the marinade and scrape off any solids. (Discard the marinade.) Place the steaks on the grate and grill until the fish easily flakes when pressed with a fork, about 3 to 4 minutes per side, turning with a thin-bladed spatula.

5. Transfer the swordfish steaks to a platter. Serve with the peanut sauce and lime wedges.

Garlic Bacon Wrapped Shrimp

Servings: 4
Cooking Time: 11 Minutes

Ingredients:

- 8 Bacon, Strip
- 1/4 Cup Butter Style Shortening (Melted)
- 1 Clove Garlic, Minced
- 1 Tsp Lemon, Juice
- Pepper
- Salt

- 16 (Peeled And Veined) Shrimp, Jumbo

Directions:

1. Supply your smoker with wood pellets and follow the start-up procedure. Preheat the grill, with the lid closed, to 450° F.

2. Take one slice of bacon, and wrap it around each piece of shrimp, and lock it in place with a wooden toothpick.

3. Place the shortening into a mixing bowl and whisk in the garlic and lemon juice. Brush each shrimp with the sauce on both sides.

4. Place on the grill, and barbecue for 11 minutes.

5. Turn the grill off, remove the shrimp, serve and enjoy!

Grilled Lemon Shrimp Scampi

Servings: 4
Cooking Time: 6 Minutes

Ingredients:

- 1 ½ pounds medium shrimp, peeled and deveined
- ¼ cup olive oil
- ¼ cup lemon juice
- 3 tablespoons chopped fresh parsley
- 1 tablespoon minced garlic
- ground black pepper to taste
- ¼ teaspoon crushed red pepper flakes to taste

Directions:

1. In a large, non-reactive bowl, stir together the olive oil, lemon juice, parsley, garlic, and black pepper. Season with crushed red pepper, if desired. Add shrimp, and toss to coat. Marinate in the refrigerator for 30 minutes.

2. Supply your smoker with wood pellets and follow the start-up procedure. Preheat the grill, with the lid closed, to high heat.

3. Thread shrimp onto skewers, piercing once near the tail and once near the head. Discard any remaining marinade.

4. Lightly oil grill grate. Place the shrimp skewers on the grill grates.

5. Grill for 2 to 3 minutes per side, or until opaque.

Seared Ahi Tuna Steak With Soy Sauce

Servings: 2
Cooking Time: 60 Minutes

Ingredients:

- 1/2 Cup Gluten Free Soy Sauce
- 1 Large Sushi Grade Ahi Tuna Steak, Patted Dry
- 1/4 Cup Lime Juice
- 2 Tablespoons Rice Wine Vinegar
- 2 Tablespoons Sesame Oil, Divided
- 2 Tablespoons Sriracha Sauce
- 4 Tablespoons Sweet Heat Rub
- 2 Cups Water

Directions:

1. Supply your smoker with wood pellets and follow the start-up procedure. Preheat the grill, with the lid closed, to 400° F. If using gas or charcoal, set it up for high heat over direct heat.

2. In the glass baking dish, pour in the water, soy sauce, lime juice, rice wine vinegar, 1 tablespoon sesame oil, sriracha sauce, and mirin. Whisk the marinade together with the whisk until everything is well combine. Place the ahi steak into the marinade and place the glass baking dish with the ahi steak in the refrigerator for 30 minutes. After 30 minutes, flip the ahi steak over so that the ahi has the chance to fully marinate on all sides, and allow to marinate for 30 more minutes.

3. After the tuna steak has finished marinating, drain off the marinade and pat the steak dry with paper towels on all sides. Pour the Sweet Heat Rub onto the plate and rub the remaining tablespoon of sesame oil generously on all sides of the tuna steak, and then gently place the tuna steak into the seasoning on the plate, turning on all sides to coat evenly.

4. Insert a temperature probe into the thickest part of the ahi steak and place the steak on the hottest part of the grill. Grill the ahi tuna steak for 45 seconds on each side, or just until the outside is opaque and has grill marks. Flip the steak and allow it to grill for another 45 seconds until the outside is just cooked through. The ahi tuna steak's internal temperature should be just at 115°F.

5. Remove the steak from the grill once it reaches 115°F, and immediately slice and serve. The inside of the steak should still be cool and ruby pink.

Lemon Herb Grilled Salmon

Servings: 4
Cooking Time: 25 Minutes

Ingredients:

- 1 1/2 pounds salmon with skin
- 1/2 tablespoon lemon zest
- 1 tablespoon lemon juice
- 1 tablespoon unsalted butter
- 1/2 teaspoon sea salt
- 1/2 teaspoon ground black pepper
- 2 teaspoons freshly chopped dill
- 1 teaspoon freshly chopped parsley
- lemon slices for the garnish

Directions:

1. Supply your smoker with wood pellets and follow the start-up procedure. Preheat the grill, with the lid closed, to 325° F.

2. In a small bowl, combine the lemon zest, lemon juice, softened unsalted butter, dill, parsley, sea salt, and ground black pepper.

3. Generously slather the top of the salmon fillet with the mixture and top with a slice of lemon. You may allow marinating for about 10 minutes or so to absorb the mixture.

4. Place the salmon fillets on the hot grill grate, skin-side facing down.

5. Cook the salmon for 20 to 25 minutes, until it reaches an internal temperature of 145 °F and flakes easily, or until the salmon is cooked to your preferred taste.

6. Serve with lemon slices. Enjoy!

Vodka Brined Smoked Wild Salmon

Servings: 4
Cooking Time: 60 Minutes

Ingredients:

- 1 Cup brown sugar
- 1 Tablespoon black pepper
- 1/2 Cup coarse salt
- 1 Cup vodka
- 1 (1-1/2 to 2 lb) wild caught salmon
- 1 lemon wedges
- capers

Directions:

1. In a small bowl, whisk together brown sugar, pepper, salt and vodka.

2. Place the salmon in a large resealable bag. Pour in marinade and massage into the salmon. Refrigerate for 2 to 4 hours.

3. Remove from bag, rinse and dry with paper towels.

4. Supply your smoker with wood pellets and follow the start-up procedure. Preheat the grill, with the lid closed, to 180° F.

5. Smoke the salmon, skin-side down for 30 minutes.

6. Increase grill temperature to 225°F and continue to cook salmon for an additional 45 to 60 minutes or until the internal temperature in the thickest part of the fish reaches 140°F or the fish flakes easily when pressed with a finger or fork. Grill: 225 °F Probe: 140 °F

7. Serve with lemons and capers. Enjoy!

Cedar Smoked Garlic Salmon

Servings: 6
Cooking Time: 60 Minutes

Ingredients:

- 1 Tsp Black Pepper
- 3 Cedar Plank, Untreated
- 1 Tsp Garlic, Minced
- 1/3 Cup Olive Oil
- 1 Tsp Onion, Salt
- 1 Tsp Parsley, Minced Fresh
- 1 1/2 Tbsp Rice Vinegar
- 2 Salmon, Fillets (Skin Removed)
- 1 Tsp Sesame Oil
- 1/3 Cup Soy Sauce

Directions:

1. Soak the cedar planks in warm water for an hour or more.

2. In a bowl, mix together the olive oil, rice vinegar, sesame oil, soy sauce, and minced garlic.

3. Add in the salmon and let it marinate for about 30 minutes.

4. Start your grill on smoke with the lid open until a fire is established in the burn pot (3-7 minutes).

5. Supply your smoker with wood pellets and follow the start-up procedure. Preheat the grill, with the lid closed, to 225° F.

6. Place the planks on the grate. Once the boards start to smoke and crackle a little, it's ready for the fish.

7. Remove the fish from the marinade, season it with the onion powder, parsley and black pepper, then discard the marinade.

8. Place the salmon on the planks and grill until it reaches 140°F internal temperature (start checking temp after the salmon has been on the grill for 30 minutes).

9. Remove from the grill, let it rest for 10 minutes, then serve.

Whole Vermillion Red Snapper

Servings: 6

Cooking Time: 20 Minutes

Ingredients:
- 1 Whole Vermillion Red Snapper, scaled & gutted
- 4 Clove garlic, chopped
- 1 Whole lemon, thinly sliced
- 2 Sprig rosemary sprigs
- sea salt and freshly ground black pepper

Directions:
1. Supply your smoker with wood pellets and follow the start-up procedure. Preheat the grill, with the lid closed, to High heat.

2. Stuff the cavity of the fish with chopped garlic. Sprinkle the fish with sea salt, pepper, rosemary, and lemon.

3. Grill fish directly on the grill grate. Cook for 20-25 minutes. Serve. Enjoy!

Lobster Tail

Servings: 2

Cooking Time: 25 Minutes

Ingredients:
- 2 lobster tails
- Salt
- Freshly ground black pepper
- 1 batch Lemon Butter Mop for Seafood

Directions:
1. Supply your smoker with wood pellets and follow the start-up procedure. Preheat the grill, with the lid closed, to 375°F.

2. Using kitchen shears, slit the top of the lobster shells, through the center, nearly to the tail. Once cut, expose as much meat as you can through the cut shell.

3. Season the lobster tails all over with salt and pepper.

4. Place the tails directly on the grill grate and grill until their internal temperature reaches 145°F. Remove the lobster from the grill and serve with the mop on the side for dipping.

Traeger Baked Rainbow Trout

Servings: 2

Cooking Time: 20 Minutes

Ingredients:
- 2 Tablespoon olive oil, divided
- 2 Whole rainbow trout, gutted and cleaned, heads and tails still on
- 1/2 Teaspoon fresh dill
- 1/2 Teaspoon fresh thyme
- 1 Teaspoon Jacobsen Salt Co. Pure Kosher Sea Salt

- 1/2 Large onion, sliced
- 1 Large lemon, thinly sliced
- 1 Teaspoon freshly ground black pepper

Directions:

1. Supply your smoker with wood pellets and follow the start-up procedure. Preheat the grill, with the lid closed, to 400° F.

2. Grease a 9x13 inch baking dish with 1 tablespoon olive oil.

3. Place trout in the prepared baking dish and coat fish with remaining olive oil. Season the inside and outside of fish with dill, thyme and salt. Stuff each fish with onion and lemon slices then grind pepper over the top. Place 1 lemon slice on each fish.

4. Bake in the Traeger for 10 minutes. Add 2 tablespoons hot water to the baking dish. Continue baking until fish flakes easily with a fork, about 10 more minutes. Enjoy! Grill: 400 ˚F

Bacon Wrapped Scallops

Servings: 8
Cooking Time: 20 Minutes

Ingredients:

- 24 jumbo deep sea diver scallops, dry-packed
- 1/2 Cup butter
- salt
- freshly ground black pepper
- 1 Clove garlic, minced
- 12 Slices thin-cut bacon, cut in half crosswise
- lemon wedges, for serving

Directions:

1. Remove the small, crescent-shaped muscle from the side of each scallop, if still attached. Dry the scallops thoroughly on paper towels, then transfer to a medium bowl.

2. Melt butter in a small saucepan, add garlic and cook for 1 minute. Let cool slightly then pour over the scallops. Season with salt and pepper and gently toss to coat.

3. Wrap a piece of bacon around each scallop and secure with a toothpick.

4. Supply your smoker with wood pellets and follow the start-up procedure. Preheat the grill, with the lid closed, to 400° F.

5. Arrange the scallops directly on the grill grate. Grill for 15 to 20 minutes, or until the scallop is opaque and the bacon has begun to crisp. If desired, you can turn the scallops on their side, bacon-side down, turning occasionally to crisp the bacon. Do not overcook. Grill: 400 ˚F

6. Transfer the scallops to a platter and serve with lemon wedges.

Spiced Smoked Swordfish

Servings: 4
Cooking Time: 60 Minutes

Ingredients:

- 4 swordfish fillets (about 4 ounces each)
- For the brine:
- 1 gallon water
- ½ cup kosher salt
- ½ cup brown sugar
- For the rub:
- 1 tablespoon olive oil
- 1 tablespoon kosher salt
- 1 tablespoon coarse ground black pepper
- 1 tablespoon garlic powder
- 1 tablespoon onion powder

Directions:

1. Make the brine by mixing the water, salt,and sugar in a large pot and stir. Add swordfish fillets

to the bowl and refrigerate overnight in the mixture.

2. Supply your smoker with wood pellets and follow the start-up procedure. Preheat the grill, with the lid closed, to 225° F.

3. Remove the fillets from the brine, rinse,and blot dry.

4. Brush a coat of olive oil on each fillet and mix salt, pepper, garlic powder,and onion powder in a small bowl for the rub. Apply the rub liberally to each fillet.

5. Put the fillets skin-side down on the smoker and cook for about 1 hour or until the internal temperature in the thickest part of the fillets reaches 145 °F.

6. Enjoy.

Lemon Shrimp Scampi

Servings: 3
Cooking Time: 10 Minutes

Ingredients:

- 2 Tsp Blackened Sriracha Rub Seasoning
- 1/2 Cup Butter, Cubed, Divided
- 1/2 Tsp Chili Pepper Flakes
- 3 Garlic Cloves, Minced
- To Taste, Lemon Wedges, For Serving
- 1 Lemon, Juice & Zest
- Linguine, Cooked
- 3 Tbsp Parsley, Chopped
- 1 1/2 Lbs Shrimp, Peeled & Deveined
- Toasted Baguette, For Serving

Directions:

1. Supply your smoker with wood pellets and follow the start-up procedure. Preheat the grill, with the lid closed, to medium-high heat. If using a gas or charcoal grill, set it up for medium-high heat.

2. Add half of the butter to the griddle, then sauté the garlic, Blackened Sriracha, and chili flakes for 1 minute, until fragrant.

3. Add the shrimp, turning occasionally for 2 minutes, until opaque.

4. Add the remaining butter, parsley, lemon zest and juice. Toss the shrimp to coat in lemon butter, then remove from the griddle, and transfer to a serving bowl.

5. Serve immediately, with fresh lemon wedges, and toasted baguette. Serve over linguine, spaghetti or zucchini noodles, if desired.

Spicy Shrimp Skewers

Servings: 4
Cooking Time: 6 Minutes

Ingredients:

- 2 Pound shrimp, peeled and deveined
- 6 Thai chiles
- 6 Clove garlic
- 2 Tablespoon Winemaker's Napa Valley Rub
- 1 1/2 Teaspoon sugar
- 1 1/2 Tablespoon white vinegar
- 3 Tablespoon olive oil

Directions:

1. If using bamboo skewers, place them in cold water to soak for 1 hour before grilling.

2. Place shrimp in a bowl and set aside. Combine all remaining ingredients in a blender and blend until a coarse-textured paste is reached. Note: if a milder flavor is preferred, feel free to adjust amount of chiles to taste.

3. Add chile-garlic mixture to the shrimp and place in fridge to marinate for at least 30 minutes.

4. Remove from fridge and thread shrimp onto bamboo or metal skewers.

5. Supply your smoker with wood pellets and follow the start-up procedure. Preheat the grill, with the lid closed, to 450° F.

6. Place shrimp on grill and cook for 2 to 3 minutes per side or until shrimp are pink and firm to touch. Enjoy! Grill: 450 °F

Cold-smoked Salmon Gravlax

Servings: 6
Cooking Time: 30 Minutes

Ingredients:
- 1 Cup kosher salt
- 1 Cup sugar
- 1 Tablespoon freshly ground black pepper
- 2 Pound Sushi-Grad Salmon Fillet, Skin-on, Pin Bones Removed
- 2 Bunch Dill Weed, fresh
- capers, drained
- red onion, sliced
- cream cheese
- lemons

Directions:
1. In a bowl stir together the salt, sugar and black pepper until thoroughly combined. On a work surface, turn salmon skin side up and sprinkle about half of salt mixture all over and rub in.
2. Arrange half the dill on the bottom of a baking dish large enough to hold the salmon. Set salmon skin side down on bed of dill.
3. Rub remaining salt mixture all over top and sides of salmon, then top with remaining dill. Cover with plastic, then top with a weight on a smaller baking dish or a plate with cans of beans on top, then place in refrigerator and allow to cure for 2 days.

4. Remove salmon from refrigerator, rinse under cold water and pat dry with paper towels. Allow to sit at room temperature on the counter for 1 hour

5. Supply your smoker with wood pellets and follow the start-up procedure. Preheat the grill, with the lid closed, to 180° F. Place salmon onto a baking pan. Fill another baking pan with ice and place baking pan with salmon over ice. Place onto grill and smoke for 30 minutes.

6. Remove from grill and slice thin. Serve with capers, red onion, dill, cream cheese, and lemon. Enjoy!

Baked Whole Fish In Sea Salt

Servings: 4
Cooking Time: 30 Minutes

Ingredients:
- 3 Pound Whole Branzino, (1.5 each)
- 10 Sprig thyme sprigs
- 1 Medium lemon, thinly sliced
- 5 Cup sea salt
- 10 Whole egg white
- olive oil
- 1 Whole lemon juice

Directions:
1. Supply your smoker with wood pellets and follow the start-up procedure. Preheat the grill, with the lid closed, to High heat.
2. Clip the fins and remove the gills from the fish. Stuff cavity with thyme and lemon slices. Whip the egg whites to soft peaks and fold in the sea salt.
3. Place directly on the grill grate and bake for 30 minutes or until a thermometer poked through the salt crust and into the flesh of the fish registers an internal temperature of 135-140

degrees F. Remove fish from the grill and let stand 10 minutes.

4. Using a wooden spoon, strike the crust to crack it open and brush remaining salt from the surface of the fish.

5. Remove the skin and drizzle fish with good olive oil and a squeeze of lemon. Enjoy!

Cider Hot-smoked Salmon

Servings: 4
Cooking Time: 60 Minutes

Ingredients:
- 1 1/2 Pound Wild Caught Salmon Fillet, skinned, pin bones removed
- 12 Ounce apple juice or cider
- 4 Pieces juniper berries
- 1 Pieces Star Anise, Broken
- 1 Pieces bay leaf, coarsely crumbled
- 1/2 Cup kosher salt
- 1/4 Cup brown sugar
- 2 Teaspoon Blackened Saskatchewan Rub
- 1 Teaspoon coarse ground black pepper, divided

Directions:
1. Rinse the salmon fillet under cold running water and check for pin bones by running a finger over the fleshy part of the fillet. If you feel a bone, remove it with kitchen tweezers or a needle-nose pliers.

2. In a sturdy resealable plastic bag, combine the cider, crushed juniper berries, star anise, and bay leaf. Add the salmon fillet and put the bag in a bowl or pan in the refrigerator. Let sit for at least 8 hours, or overnight.

3. Remove the salmon from the bag and discard the cider mixture. Dry the salmon well on paper towels. Make the cure: In a small mixing bowl, combine the kosher salt, brown sugar, and Traeger rub.

4. Pour half into a shallow plate, or baking dish. Put the salmon fillet, skin-side down, on top of the cure. Generously sprinkle the top with the remaining cure, cover with plastic wrap, and refrigerate for 1 to 1-1/2 hours. Any longer, and the fish will get too salty.

5. Remove the salmon from the cure and pat dry with paper towels. Sprinkle the black pepper on top of the fillet.

6. Supply your smoker with wood pellets and follow the start-up procedure. Preheat the grill, with the lid closed, to 200° F.

7. Lay the salmon skin-side down on the grill grate. Cook for 1 hour, or until the internal temperature in the thickest part of the fish reaches 150 or the fish flakes easily when pressed with a finger or fork. Grill: 200 °F Probe: 150 °F

8. Let cool slightly. Turn the fillet over and remove the skin; it should come off in one piece.

9. If not serving immediately, let the salmon cool completely, then wrap in plastic wrap and refrigerate for up to 2 days. Transfer to a platter and serve with some or all of the suggested accompaniments. Enjoy!

Mezcal Shrimp With Salsa De Molcajete

Servings: 4
Cooking Time: 14 Minutes

Ingredients:
- 18 to 24 jumbo shrimp, about 1½lb (680g) total, peeled and deveined
- ⅓ cup mezcal
- juice of ½ lime
- 2 tbsp extra virgin olive oil

- 2 tsp coarse salt
- 1 tsp ground cumin
- lime wedges
- for the salsa
- 2 Roma tomatoes
- 2 tomatillos, husked and washed
- 2 garlic cloves, peeled and impaled on a toothpick
- 1 jalapeño or serrano pepper
- 1 small white onion, halved
- ½ tsp coarse salt, plus more
- juice of ½ lime
- ¼ cup loosely packed fresh cilantro leaves

Directions:

1. Supply your smoker with wood pellets and follow the start-up procedure. Preheat the grill, with the lid closed, to 450° F.

2. In a large bowl, combine the shrimp, mezcal, lime juice, olive oil, salt, and ground cumin. Toss with your hands to mix thoroughly. Set aside for 15 minutes and then toss once more.

3. Begin to make the salsa by placing the tomatoes, tomatillos, garlic, jalapeño, and onion on the grate. Grill until they begin to char, about 3 minutes for the garlic and about 6 to 8 minutes for the other vegetables, turning as needed. Transfer the vegetables to a rimmed sheet pan. Remove the skewers from the garlic. Let everything cool. Coarsely chop the vegetables and leave them in separate piles.

4. Place the garlic in the molcajete and add the salt. Mash the garlic to a purée using the temolote. Add the onion and grind it into the garlic paste. Stir in the jalapeño (deseeded for a milder salsa), tomatoes, and tomatillos. Stir in the lime juice and cilantro leaves. Taste, adding salt. (If you don't own a molcajete or temolote, prepare the salsa using a small food processor.)

5. Drain the shrimp and discard the marinade. Thread the shrimp on wood or bamboo skewers. Place the shrimp on the grate and grill until they're white and opaque, about 4 to 6 minutes, tossing with tongs.

6. Transfer the shrimp to a platter. Serve with the salsa and lime wedges.

POULTRY RECIPES

Smoked Airline Chicken

Servings: 4

Cooking Time: 120 Minutes

Ingredients:

- 2 boneless chicken breasts with drumettes attached
- ½ cup soy sauce
- ½ cup teriyaki sauce
- ¼ cup canola oil
- ¼ cup white vinegar
- 1 tablespoon minced garlic
- ¼ cup chopped scallions
- 2 teaspoons freshly ground black pepper
- 1 teaspoon ground mustard

Directions:

1. Place the chicken in a baking dish.

2. In a bowl, whisk together the soy sauce, teriyaki sauce, canola oil, vinegar, garlic, scallions, pepper and ground mustard, then pour this marinade over the chicken, coating both sides.

3. Refrigerate the chicken in marinade for 4 hours, turning over every hour.

4. When ready to smoke the chicken, supply your smoker with wood pellets and follow the start-up procedure. Preheat, with the lid closed, to 250°F.

5. Remove the chicken from the marinade but do not rinse. Discard the marinade.

6. Arrange the chicken directly on the grill, close the lid, and smoke for 1 hour 30 minutes to 2 hours, or until a meat thermometer inserted in the thickest part of the meat reads 165°F.

7. Let the meat rest for 3 minutes before serving.

Traeger Mandarin Wings

Servings: 2

Cooking Time: 30 Minutes

Ingredients:

- 1 Bottle (12 oz) mandarin orange sauce
- Beef Rub
- Chicken Rub
- 2 Pound chicken wings, flats and drumettes separated

Directions:

1. Coat chicken wings with mandarin sauce. Sprinkle Traeger Beef Rub and Traeger Chicken Rub onto wings. Marinate for at least 30 minutes.

2. Supply your smoker with wood pellets and follow the start-up procedure. Preheat the grill, with the lid closed, to 350° F.

3. Place wings directly on the grill grate and cook for 30 minutes. Enjoy! Grill: 350 ˚F Probe: 165 ˚F

Texas Style Black Pepper Turkey

Servings: 6

Cooking Time: 240 Minutes

Ingredients:

- 1/2 Cup Coarse Black Pepper
- 1Lb Butter
- 1/2 Cup Salt, Kosher
- 1 Brined Turkey

Directions:

1. Supply your smoker with wood pellets and follow the start-up procedure. Preheat the grill, with the lid closed, to 300° F.

2. Liberally season Turkey with equal parts kosher salt and coarse black pepper.

3. Cook on grill until Internal temp reaches approximately 145°F or the skin has darkened to your liking.

4. Place turkey in a roasting pan topped with a pound of chopped butter and cover.

5. Return to the grill until internal temp of the thigh and breast reaches 165°F

6. Let rest for 30 minutes, carve and serve.

Smoked Avocado Turkey Tamale Pie

Servings: 6
Cooking Time: 240 Minutes

Ingredients:
- 1 Avocado, Diced (For Topping)
- 15 Oz Black Beans, Drained (For Filling)
- To Taste, Blackened Sriracha Rub Seasoning
- 2 Tsp Blackened Sriracha Rub Seasoning (For Filling)
- To Taste, Blackened Sriracha Rub Seasoning (For Polenta)
- 2 Tbsp Butter (For Polenta)
- 2 Tbsp Cilantro, Chopped (For Topping)
- 1 Cup Corn Kernels (For Filling)
- 2 Cups Enchilada Sauce (For Filling)
- 1/2 Jalapeño, Minced (For Topping)
- 2 Cups Milk Or Water (For Polenta)
- 1 Cup Polenta, Or Fine Cornmeal (For Polenta)
- 2 Scallions, Sliced (For Topping)
- 2 Cups Smoked Turkey Breast, Shredded (For Filling)
- 2 1/2 Lbs Split Turkey Breast , Bone-In
- 2 Cups Turkey Stock (For Polenta)
- 4 Oz White Cheddar, Shredded (For Polenta)
- 4 Oz White Cheddar, Shredded (For Topping)

Directions:
1. Supply your smoker with wood pellets and follow the start-up procedure. Preheat the grill, with the lid closed, to 225° F. If using a gas or charcoal grill, set it up for low, indirect heat.

2. Season the turkey breast with Blackened Sriracha, then transfer to the grill, on a rack, over indirect heat.

3. Smoke the turkey breast for 2 ½ to 3 hours, until an internal temperature of 160° F. Remove the turkey from the grill, allow to rest for 20 minutes, then shred with 2 forks.

4. While the turkey is resting, prepare the polenta:

5. Place a deep, cast iron skillet on the grill, then increase the temperature to 375° F. Add chicken broth and milk to a skillet and bring to a boil.

6. Whisk in the polenta, then reduce the heat to a simmer, stirring often for 5 minutes. Season with Blackened Sriracha, then stir in cheese and butter. Remove the skillet from the grill and smooth out the polenta in an even layer.

7. In a large glass measuring cup or mixing bowl, combine the turkey, enchilada sauce, black beans, corn and Blackened Sriracha.

8. Spoon the turkey mixture over the polenta, then top with 4 ounces of shredded cheese. Place on the grill, over indirect heat and bake for 20 to 25 minutes, until the filling is bubbling along the edge and the cheese is melted.

9. Remove the skillet from the grill and allow it to rest for 10 minutes. Serve warm, garnished with avocado, scallions, jalapeño, and fresh cilantro.

Spicy Bbq Whole Chicken

Servings: 4

Cooking Time: 180 Minutes

Ingredients:

- 6 Thai chiles
- 2 Tablespoon sweet paprika
- 1 Scotch bonnet pepper
- 2 Tablespoon sugar
- 3 Tablespoon salt
- 1 white onion
- 5 Clove garlic
- 4 Cup grapeseed oil
- 1 whole chicken

Directions:

1. In a food processor or blender, puree the Thai chiles, paprika, Scotch bonnet pepper, sugar, salt, onion, garlic and grapeseed oil together until smooth.

2. Smother the chicken with mixture and let rest in fridge overnight.

3. Supply your smoker with wood pellets and follow the start-up procedure. Preheat the grill, with the lid closed, to 300° F.

4. Place chicken on grill, breast side up and smoke for 3 hours, or until it reaches an internal temperature of 165°F in the breast. Grill: 300 °F Probe: 165 °F

5. Remove from grill and allow to rest for 10 to 15 minutes before slicing. Serve with sides of choice. Enjoy!

Bbq Breakfast Sausage

Servings: 4 - 6

Cooking Time: 35 Minutes

Ingredients:

- 1/4 Cup Bbq Sauce
- 1 Tbsp Brown Sugar
- 4 Oz Cheddar Cheese, Cut Into Sticks
- To Taste, Cracked Black Pepper
- 6 Eggs, Scrambled
- 4 Oz Ham, Diced
- 1 Package, Approx 1 Lb Shady Brook Farms Ground Turkey Sausage
- 10 Oz Turkey Bacon

Directions:

1. Supply your smoker with wood pellets and follow the start-up procedure. Preheat the grill, with the lid closed, to 375° F. If using a gas or charcoal grill, set it up for medium-high heat.

2. Lay out a piece of plastic wrap then make a bacon weave using your favorite turkey bacon. Top with the Shady Brooks Farms Turkey Sausage and spread out into an even layer with your fingers.

3. Spoon the scrambled eggs into the center of the sausage, then place half of the cheese sticks in the middle, followed by ham, then remaining cheese.

4. Gently lift up one end of the plastic wrap and begin rolling the "not so fatty." Once the roll is completed, remove the plastic wrap and secure the ends of the bacon together with toothpicks, if needed.

5. Set in a cast iron skillet, sprinkle with brown sugar, and season with cracked pepper. Transfer to the grill and cook for 30 minutes, until an internal temperature of 155°F.

6. Baste with BBQ sauce and cook for an additional 5 minutes until the sauce is set and the internal temperature increased to 165°F.

7. Remove from the grill and rest for 5 minutes before slicing and serving warm.

Grilled Honey Garlic Wings

Servings: 4

Cooking Time: 60 Minutes

Ingredients:

- 2 1/2 Pound chicken wings
- Pork & Poultry Rub
- 4 Tablespoon butter
- 3 Clove garlic, minced
- 1/4 Cup honey
- 1/2 Cup hot sauce
- 1 1/2 Cup blue cheese or ranch dressing

Directions:

1. Start by segmenting the wings into three pieces, cutting through the joints. Discard the wing tips or save them to make a stock.

2. Lay out the remaining pieces on a rimmed baking sheet lined with nonstick foil or parchment paper. Season well with Traeger Pork & Poultry Rub.

3. Supply your smoker with wood pellets and follow the start-up procedure. Preheat the grill, with the lid closed, to 350° F.

4. Place the baking sheet with wings directly on the grill grate and cook for 45 to 50 minutes or until they are no longer pink at the bone. Grill: 350 ˚F

5. To make the sauce: Melt butter in a small saucepan. Add the garlic and sauté for 2 to 3 minutes. Add in the honey and hot sauce and cook for a few minutes until completely combined. Keep sauce warm while the wings are cooking.

6. After 45 minutes, pour the spicy honey-garlic sauce over the wings, turning with tongs to coat.

7. Place wings back on the grill and cook for an additional 10 to 15 minutes to set the sauce. Grill: 350 ˚F

8. Serve with ranch or blue cheese dressing. Enjoy!

Smoked Chicken Leg & Thigh Quarters

Servings: 6

Cooking Time: 120 Minutes

Ingredients:

- 8 chicken legs (thigh and drumstick)
- 3 Tablespoon olive oil
- Pork & Poultry Rub

Directions:

1. Place the chicken pieces in a large mixing bowl. Pour oil over the chicken to coat each piece, then season to taste with the Traeger Pork & Poultry Rub. Massage the chicken pieces to encourage the oil and seasonings get under the skin. Cover and refrigerate for at least 1 to 2 hours.

2. Supply your smoker with wood pellets and follow the start-up procedure. Preheat the grill, with the lid closed, to 180° F.

3. Remove the chicken from the refrigerator, letting any excess oil drip back into the bowl. Grill: 180 ˚F

4. Arrange the chicken on the grill grate and smoke for 1 hour. Increase Traeger temperature to 350˚F and continue to roast the chicken until the internal temperature in the thickest part of a thigh is 165˚F or the chicken is golden brown and the juices run clear, about 50 to 60 minutes. Grill: 350 ˚F Probe: 165 ˚F

5. Remove from the grill and allow the chicken to rest for 8 to 10 minutes and serve. Enjoy!

Smoked Maple Syrup Thanksgiving Turkey

Servings: 8
Cooking Time: 375 Minutes

Ingredients:

- 1 Cup Butter, Room Temp
- 1/2 Cup Maple Syrup
- 2 Tablespoons Champion Chicken Seasoning
- 1, (Pre-Brined) Turkey, Whole

Directions:

1. Supply your smoker with wood pellets and follow the start-up procedure. Preheat the grill, with the lid closed, to 250° F.

2. Combine the melted butter and maple syrup in a bowl. With the Marinade Injector, fill with the butter and syrup mixture and pierce the meat with the needle while pushing on the plunger, injecting the flavor. You want to inject the marinade into the thickest part of the breast, thigh, and wings.

3. Next, combine the room temperature butter and Champion Chicken seasoning and spread all over the turkey, making sure that you get it under the skin as well.

4. Place the turkey in an aluminum pan to catch all the drippings (this makes incredible gravy) and place on the grill.

5. When the breast and thigh meat of the turkey reaches 165°F to 170°F, remove from grill and let rest 15 minutes before carving. Happy Thanksgiving!

Chicken Corn Fritters

Servings: 8
Cooking Time: 45 Minutes

Ingredients:

- 2 Tsp Baking Powder
- 1 Cup Cheddar Jack Cheese, Shredded
- 1 1/2 Lbs Chicken Breast, Bone-In
- 3/4 Cup Corn Kernels, Drained
- 2 Eggs
- 3/4 Cup Flour
- 1 1/2 Tsp Lemon Juice
- 3 Tbsp Mayonnaise
- Olive Oil
- 2 Tbsp Parsley, Chopped
- 2 Tsp Champion Chicken Seasoning, Divided
- 1 Tbsp Scallions, Chopped
- 2 Tbsp Sour Cream
- 1 Yellow Onion, Chopped
- 1/3 Cup Milk

Directions:

1. Supply your smoker with wood pellets and follow the start-up procedure. Preheat the grill, with the lid open, to 425° F. If using a gas or charcoal grill, set it up for medium-high heat.

2. Remove skin from chicken breast. Drizzle chicken with olive oil, then season with 1 teaspoon of Champion Chicken. Place directly on grill grate, over indirect heat and grill for 25 minutes, until internal temperature is 165° F. Remove from the grill and rest for 10 minutes, then pull chicken.

3. In a mixing bowl combine onion, corn, eggs, parsley, milk, cheese, and pulled chicken.

4. In a separate mixing bowl, whisk together remaining teaspoon of Champion Chicken, flour and baking powder. Combine with the wet ingredients, then cover with plastic wrap and refrigerate for 2 hours.

5. Prepare dip: whisk together mayonnaise, sour cream, scallions, parsley, and lemon juice. Refrigerate until fritters are ready to serve.

6. Preheat griddle over medium-low flame.

7. Drizzle vegetable oil on the griddle, then add ¼ cup of fritter mixture to the griddle and cook 3 to 4 minutes per side, adding additional oil if needed.

8. Transfer fritters to a wire rack lined sheet tray. Allow to cool for 2 minutes, then serve warm with dip.

Smoked Turkey Jerky

Servings: 6
Cooking Time: 240 Minutes

Ingredients:

- 1/2 Cup soy sauce
- 1/4 Cup water
- 2 Tablespoon honey
- 2 Tablespoon Asian chili garlic sauce
- 2 Tablespoon lime juice
- 1 Tablespoon Morton Tender Quick Home Meat Cure
- 2 Pound (4-5 lb) boneless turkey breast

Directions:

1. In a mixing bowl, combine the soy sauce, water, honey, chili-garlic paste, lime juice, and curing salt, if using. With a sharp knife, slice the turkey into 1/4" thick slices with the grain, which helps it hold together better as it dries. (This is easier if the meat is partially frozen.) Trim any fat, membrane, or connective tissue.

2. Put the turkey slices in a large resealable plastic bag. Pour the marinade mixture over the turkey, and massage the bag so that all the slices get coated with the marinade. Seal the bag and refrigerate for several hours, or overnight.

3. Supply your smoker with wood pellets and follow the start-up procedure. Preheat the grill, with the lid closed, to 180° F.

4. Remove the turkey from the marinade and discard the marinade. Dry the turkey slices between paper towels. Arrange in a single layer directly on the grill grate.

5. Smoke for 2 to 4 hours, or until the jerky is dry but still chewy and somewhat pliant when you bend a piece. Grill: 180 °F

6. Transfer to a resealable plastic bag while the jerky's still warm. Let the jerky rest for an hour at room temperature. Squeeze any air from the bag, and refrigerate the jerky. It will keep for several weeks. Enjoy!

Beer Can–smoked Chicken

Servings: 3-4
Cooking Time: 160 Minutes

Ingredients:

- 8 tablespoons (1 stick) unsalted butter, melted
- ½ cup apple cider vinegar
- ½ cup Cajun seasoning, divided
- 1 teaspoon garlic powder
- 1 teaspoon onion powder
- 1 (4-pound) whole chicken, giblets removed
- Extra-virgin olive oil, for rubbing
- 1 (12-ounce) can beer
- 1 cup apple juice
- ½ cup extra-virgin olive oil

Directions:

1. In a small bowl, whisk together the butter, vinegar, ¼ cup of Cajun seasoning, garlic powder, and onion powder.

2. Use a meat-injecting syringe to inject the liquid into various spots in the chicken. Inject

about half of the mixture into the breasts and the other half throughout the rest of the chicken.

3. Rub the chicken all over with olive oil and apply the remaining ¼ cup of Cajun seasoning, being sure to rub under the skin as well.

4. Drink or discard half the beer and place the opened beer can on a stable surface.

5. Place the bird's cavity on top of the can and position the chicken so it will sit up by itself. Prop the legs forward to make the bird more stable, or buy an inexpensive, specially made stand to hold the beer can and chicken in place.

6. Supply your smoker with wood pellets and follow the start-up procedure. Preheat, with the lid closed, to 250°F.

7. In a clean 12-ounce spray bottle, combine the apple juice and olive oil. Cover and shake the mop sauce well before each use.

8. Carefully put the chicken on the grill. Close the lid and smoke the chicken for 3 to 4 hours, spraying with the mop sauce every hour, until golden brown and a meat thermometer inserted in the thickest part of the thigh reads 165°F. Keep a piece of aluminum foil handy to loosely cover the chicken if the skin begins to brown too quickly.

9. Let the meat rest for 5 minutes before carving.

Cornish Game Hen

Servings: 4
Cooking Time: 180 Minutes

Ingredients:
- 4 Cornish game hens
- Extra-virgin olive oil, for rubbing
- 2 teaspoons salt
- 1 teaspoon freshly ground black pepper
- 1 teaspoon celery seeds

Directions:
1. Supply your smoker with wood pellets and follow the start-up procedure. Preheat, with the lid closed, to 275°F.

2. Rub the game hens over and under the skin with olive oil and season all over with the salt, pepper, and celery seeds.

3. Place the birds directly on the grill grate, close the lid, and smoke for 2 to 3 hours, or until a meat thermometer inserted in each bird reads 170°F.

4. Serve the Cornish game hens hot.

The Grilled Chicken Challenge

Servings: 4
Cooking Time: 60 Minutes

Ingredients:
- 1 (4 lb) whole chicken
- Chicken Rub

Directions:
1. Supply your smoker with wood pellets and follow the start-up procedure. Preheat the grill, with the lid closed, to 375° F.

2. Rinse and pat dry the whole chicken (remove and discard giblets, if any). Lightly season the entire chicken, including the cavity with Traeger Chicken Rub (or similar rub of choice).

3. Place the chicken on the grill grate and cook for about 1 hour and 10 minutes. Remove chicken from grill when internal temperature of breast reaches 160°F. The temperature will continue to rise to 165°F as the chicken rests. Check temperature periodically throughout as cook times will vary based on the weight of the chicken. Grill: 375 °F Probe: 160 °F

4. Allow bird to rest until internal temperature of breast reaches 165°F, 15 to 20 minutes. Enjoy!

Smoked Chicken Vermicelli Noodles

Servings: 4 – 6
Cooking Time: 120 Minutes

Ingredients:

- 2 Cup Broccoli
- ¼ Cup Chicken Stock
- 6 - 8 Chicken Thighs, Boneless, Skinless
- 1 Tbsp Chili Flakes
- 1 Tsp Cornstarch
- 4, Chopped Garlic Cloves
- 3 Tbsp Hoisin Sauce, Divided
- Knob Of Fresh Ginger, Grated
- 1, Thin Red Bell Peppers, Sliced
- 1 Tbsp Rice Wine Vinegar
- 8 Scallions, Sliced
- 1 ½ Tbsp Sesame Oil, Divided
- 1 Tbsp, Toasted Sesame Seeds
- 3.5 Oz Shitake Mushrooms, Sliced Thin
- 8 Oz Snow Peas
- 3 Tbsp Soy Sauce
- 2 Tbsp Sweet Chili Sauce
- 3 Tbsp Vegetable Oil
- 1 Lb Vermicelli Noodles, Or Linguini, Cooked And Drained

Directions:

1. In a large bowl, whisk together rice wine vinegar, 1 tablespoon of Hoisin sauce, and 1 tablespoon of sesame oil. Toss chicken to coat and allow to marinate for 1 hour.

2. Supply your smoker with wood pellets and follow the start-up procedure. Preheat the grill, with the lid open, to 225° F. If using a gas or charcoal grill, set it for low, indirect heat. Place chicken directly on the grill grate and smoke for 1 ½ to 2 hours, or until the internal temperature reaches 165° F. Remove it from the smoker, cover with foil, and rest for 10 minutes, then slice thin and set aside.

3. In a glass measuring cup whisk together 2 tablespoons of Hoisin sauce, soy sauce, sweet chili sauce, chicken stock, ½ tablespoon of sesame oil, and cornstarch. Set aside.

4. Preheat griddle to medium flame, then add oil. Working quickly, sauté ginger and garlic for 15 seconds, then add bell pepper and mushrooms and continue cooking for another minute, then add in snow peas and slaw. Toss in cooked pasta, chicken, scallions, and pour sauce over. Cook for one minute until sauce thickens and is well incorporated.

5. Transfer to platter and serve hot. Sprinkle with chili flakes and sesame seeds, if desired.

Smoked Chicken Fajita Quesadillas

Servings: 4
Cooking Time: 45 Minutes

Ingredients:

- 2 Chicken, Boneless/Skinless
- 1 Tsp Chilli, Powder
- 1 Tsp Garlic Powder
- 1/2 Green Bell Pepper, Sliced
- 1 Cup Mexican Cheese, Shredded
- 1/2 Onion, Sliced
- 1/2 Tsp Oregano
- 1 Tsp Paprika, Powder
- 1/4 Tsp Pepper
- 1/2 Red Bell Peppers
- Salsa
- Sour Cream
- 4 Tortilla
- 1/2 Yellow Bell Pepper, Sliced

Directions:

1. Supply your smoker with wood pellets and follow the start-up procedure. Preheat the grill, with the lid open, to 350° F.

2. Combine spices in a bowl and season chicken breasts. Leave a little bit of seasoning for the vegetables.

3. Place chicken on the grates and cook for 30 minutes, flipped halfway through.

4. In a Vegetable Basket, combine all vegetables and season with the remaining spice mixture.

5. Open up the flame broiler and saute over the open flame for about 15 minutes, or until the vegetables are cooked to your liking.

6. On a tortilla, layer cheese, vegetables, sliced chicken and more cheese. Fold the tortilla and place over the open flame on your Grill. Sear until the tortilla is nicely toasted and the cheese is melted. Cut and serve with salsa and sour cream.

Bbq Chicken Wings With Spicy Honey Glaze

Servings: 4

Cooking Time: 30 Minutes

Ingredients:

- 4 Pound chicken wings
- 6 Ounce Chicken Rub
- 2 Tablespoon corn starch
- 1 Cup honey
- 1 Cup Sriracha
- 1/2 Cup soy sauce
- 2 Tablespoon sesame oil
- 3 Tablespoon unsalted butter
- 2 Tablespoon sesame seeds

Directions:

1. Supply your smoker with wood pellets and follow the start-up procedure. Preheat the grill, with the lid closed, to 375° F.

2. While grill is preheating, dry off chicken wings with a paper towel. Mix the Traeger Chicken rub with the cornstarch and coat both sides of the chicken wings.

3. When the grill is heated, place the wings on the grill for 35 minutes flipping half way through. Grill: 375 °F

4. While the wings are cooking, mix the honey, Sriracha, soy sauce, sesame seed oil, and unsalted butter and heat on a stove top.

5. After the wings have cooked for 35 minutes, check the temperature. The minimum temperature must reach an internal temperature of 165 degrees F. An internal temperature between 175 to 180 degrees F may yield a better texture. Grill: 375 °F Probe: 177 °F

6. When wings are done, place in large bowl and toss with the warmed sauce.

7. Place wings on platter and sprinkle the sesame seeds. Enjoy!

Chicken Parmesan Sliders With Pesto Mayonnaise

Servings: 4

Cooking Time: 30 Minutes

Ingredients:

- 2 Pound Chicken, ground
- 1 Cup Parmesan cheese
- 1 Tablespoon Worcestershire sauce
- black pepper
- 1 Cup mayonnaise
- 2 Tablespoon Pesto Sauce
- 3 Roma tomatoes
- 1 red onion, sliced

- Baby Spinach

Directions:

1. Line a baking sheet with plastic wrap. In a large mixing bowl, combine the ground chicken, the Parmesan, the Worcestershire, and a few grinds of black pepper. Wet your hands with cold water, and use them to mix the ingredients.

2. Divide the meat mixture in half, then form six 2-inch patties out of each half. Place the patties on the baking sheet, cover with another sheet of plastic wrap, and refrigerate for at least 1 hour.

3. Combine the mayonnaise and pesto in a small bowl and whisk together. Cover and refrigerate until serving time.

4. Supply your smoker with wood pellets and follow the start-up procedure. Preheat the grill, with the lid closed, to 300° F.

5. Arrange the chicken patties on the grill grate and grill, turning once, until the patties are cooked through (165F), about 30 minutes. Grill: 300 °F Probe: 165 °F

6. To serve, put a chicken patty on the bottom of a slider bun and top with a dollop of the pesto mayonnaise. Add tomato, onion, and spinach as desired. Replace the top of the bun and skewer with a frilled toothpick, if desired.

Marinated Grilled Honey Chicken Wings

Servings: 4-6
Cooking Time: 30 Minutes

Ingredients:

- 1/2 Bottle Beer, Any Brand
- 2 Lbs Chicken Wings, Whole
- 2 Tablespoon Honey
- 1 Tablespoon Sweet Heat Rub
- 2 Tablespoon Rice Wine Vinegar

- 1/2 Tablesoon Sesame Oil
- 1/4 Cup Soy Sauce
- 1 Tablespoon Sriracha Hot Sauce

Directions:

1. In a large glass or plastic bowl, combine the beer, soy sauce, honey, rice wine vinegar, sriracha, sesame oil and   Sweet Heat Seasoning. Whisk well to combine.

2. Add the chicken wings to the marinade and toss well to combine. Cover with plastic wrap and refrigerate for 2 hours and up to 24 hours.

3. Remove chicken wings from refrigerator, drain marinade and pat dry. Supply your smoker with wood pellets and follow the start-up procedure. Supply your smoker with wood pellets and follow the start-up procedure. Preheat the grill, with the lid open, to 350° F. Place the wings on a grill pan and grill for 20-25 minutes, or until the wings' internal temperature is 165F. Remove from the grill, serve and enjoy!

Grilled Greek Chicken With Garlic & Lemon

Servings: 4
Cooking Time: 60 Minutes

Ingredients:

- 2 Whole Roasting Chicken, 3.5-4lbs, each cut into 8 pieces
- 2 Whole lemons, quartered
- Cup extra-virgin olive oil
- 4 Clove garlic, minced
- 1 1/2 Tablespoon Oregano, fresh
- 1 As Needed Chicken Rub
- 1 Cup Broth, chicken

Directions:

1. Arrange the chicken pieces in a single layer in a large roasting pan. Squeeze the juice from each piece of lemon over the chicken, catching any seeds in your fingers. Tuck the lemon rinds in with the chicken. Drizzle the olive oil over all.

2. Sprinkle the garlic over the chicken. Dust the chicken with the fresh oregano, and season it generously with the Traeger Chicken rub, or salt and black pepper. Pour the chicken broth into the pan.

3. Supply your smoker with wood pellets and follow the start-up procedure. Preheat the grill, with the lid closed, to 350° F.

4. Roast the chicken for an hour, or until the juices run clear or the internal temperature reaches 165°F on an instant-read meat thermometer. Grill: 350 °F Probe: 165 °F

5. Transfer to a platter or plates and spoon some of the juices on top. Let rest 3 minutes before serving. Enjoy!

Herb Roasted Turkey

Servings: 6
Cooking Time: 180 Minutes

Ingredients:
- 8 Tablespoon butter, room temperature
- 2 Tablespoon chopped mixed herbs, such as parsley, sage, rosemary and/or marjoram
- 1/4 Teaspoon black pepper
- 1 Teaspoon kosher salt
- 1 (12-14 lb) turkey, fresh or thawed
- 3 Tablespoon butter, melted
- Pork & Poultry Rub
- 2 Cup chicken or turkey broth

Directions:
1. In a small mixing bowl, combine the 8 tablespoons of softened butter, mixed herbs, salt

and black pepper and beat until fluffy with a wooden spoon. (You can make the herbed butter several days ahead: Cover and refrigerate, but bring to room temperature before using).

2. Remove any giblets from the turkey cavity and save them for gravy making, if desired. Wash the turkey, inside and out, under cold running water. Dry with paper towels.

3. Place the turkey on a roasting rack in a roasting pan. Tuck the wings behind the back, and tie the legs together with butcher's string.

4. Using your fingers or the handle of a wooden spoon, gently push some of the herbed butter underneath the turkey skin onto the breast halves, being careful not to tear the skin. Massage the skin to evenly distribute the herbed butter. Rub the outside of the turkey with the melted butter and sprinkle with the Traeger Pork and Poultry Rub.

5. Pour the chicken broth in the bottom of the roasting pan.

6. Supply your smoker with wood pellets and follow the start-up procedure. Preheat the grill, with the lid closed, to 325° F.

7. Put the roasting pan with the turkey directly on the grill grate. Roast the turkey for 3 hours. Insert the probe from the meat thermometer in the thickest part of the thigh, but not touching bone. Cook until internal temperature reaches 165°F. The turkey should also be beautifully browned with crisp skin. If the temperature is less than that, or if your turkey is not browned to your liking, let it roast for another 30 minutes, then check the temperature again. Repeat until the turkey is fully cooked. Grill: 325 °F Probe: 165 °F

8. When the turkey is done, carefully transfer it to a cutting board and let it rest for 20 to 30

minutes. Do not tent it with aluminum foil or the skin will lose its crispness. Use the drippings that have accumulated in the bottom of the roasting pan to make gravy, if desired. Carve the turkey and serve.

Whole Roasted Chicken

Servings: 4

Cooking Time: 60 Minutes

Ingredients:
- 1 Whole fresh young chicken
- 1 Bottle Chicken Rub
- water
- 1/2 Tablespoon kosher salt
- 1 Tablespoon chopped sage
- 1 Tablespoon chopped thyme
- 1/2 Cup butter, softened
- 1/2 Tablespoon coarse ground black pepper

Directions:

1. Remove whole chicken from packaging and wipe dry with a paper towel.

2. Mix water and chicken rub to create a brine. Place the chicken and brine in a container that's large enough to submerge the entire chicken.

3. Set in fridge for 4-12 hours.

4. Supply your smoker with wood pellets and follow the start-up procedure. Preheat the grill, with the lid closed, to 375° F.

5. Take chicken out of brine, do not rinse.

6. Mix together thyme, sage, salt, pepper and butter. Smear the outside of the chicken with the butter mixture. Put any of the remaining butter in the cavity of the chicken.

7. Place chicken directly on the grill grate. Cook chicken until it reaches an internal temperature of 165 degrees F (about 60 mins) with an instant-read thermometer between the leg and thigh joint. Grill: 375 ˚F Probe: 165 ˚F

8. Also check the internal temperature of the breast to ensure it registers at least 165 degrees F. Once chicken is done, let it rest for 15-20 minutes. Enjoy!

Bbq Pulled Turkey Sandwiches

Servings: 6

Cooking Time: 120 Minutes

Ingredients:
- 6 Whole Turkey Thighs
- Pork & Poultry Rub
- 1 1/2 Cup chicken broth
- 1 Cup 'Que BBQ Sauce
- 6 Whole Kaiser Buns, Split

Directions:

1. Season turkey thighs on both sides with the Traeger Pork & Poultry rub.

2. Supply your smoker with wood pellets and follow the start-up procedure. Preheat the grill, with the lid closed, to 180° F.

3. Arrange the turkey thighs directly on the grill grate and smoke for 30 minutes.

4. Transfer the thighs to a sturdy disposable aluminum foil or roasting pan. Pour the broth around the thighs. Cover the pan with foil or a lid.

5. Increase temperature to 325˚F and preheat, lid closed. Roast the thighs until they reach an internal temperature of 180˚F. Grill: 325 ˚F Probe: 180 ˚F

6. Remove pan from the grill, but leave grill on. Let the turkey thighs cool slightly until they can be comfortably handled.

7. Pour off the drippings and reserve. Remove the skin and discard.

8. Pull the turkey meat into shreds with your fingers and return the meat to the roasting pan.
9. Add 1 cup or more of your favorite Traeger BBQ Sauce along with some of the drippings.
10. Recover the pan with foil and reheat the BBQ turkey on the Traeger for 20 to 30 minutes.
11. Serve with toasted buns if desired. Enjoy!

Bbq Spatchcocked Chicken

Servings: 2
Cooking Time: 45 Minutes

Ingredients:
- 1 whole chicken
- 1/4 Cup Chicken Rub
- olive oil
- 1/2 Cup Sweet & Heat BBQ Sauce

Directions:
1. Supply your smoker with wood pellets and follow the start-up procedure. Preheat the grill, with the lid closed, to 375° F.
2. With a large knife or shears, cut the bird open along the backbone on both sides, through the ribs, and remove the backbone.
3. Brush chicken with olive oil and season both sides with Traeger Chicken rub.
4. Place the poultry on the Traeger, breast side up and cook for 35 to 40 minutes or until a thermometer inserted into the breast registers 160°F . Grill: 375 °F Probe: 160 °F
5. Remove from the grill and let rest 5 minutes before slicing. Enjoy!

Grilled Honey Chicken Kabobs

Servings: 4
Cooking Time: 14 Minutes

Ingredients:

- 1 pound boneless skinless chicken breasts (cut into 1 inch pieces)
- 1/4 cup olive oil
- 1/3 cup soy sauce
- 1/4 cup honey
- 1 teaspoon minced garlic
- salt and pepper to taste
- 1 red bell pepper (cut into 1 inch pieces)
- 1 yellow bell pepper (cut into 1 inch pieces)
- 2 small zucchini (cut into 1 inch slices)
- 1 red onion (cut into 1 inch pieces)
- 1 tablespoon chopped parsley

Directions:
1. In a large bowl combine the olive oil, soy sauce, honey, garlic and salt and pepper, and whisk.
2. Add the chicken, bell peppers, zucchini and red onion to the bowl,tossing to thoroughly coat.
3. Cover and refrigerate for 1 to 8 hours.
4. Soak wooden skewers in cold water for at least 30 minutes. Supply your smoker with wood pellets and follow the start-up procedure. Preheat the grill, with the lid closed, to high heat.
5. Thread the chicken and vegetables onto the skewers.
6. Cook for 5-7 minutes on each side or until chicken is cooked through.
7. To serve, sprinkle with parsley. Enjoy!

Green Goddess Chicken Legs

Servings: 4
Cooking Time: 40 Minutes

Ingredients:
- 2 Pound chicken legs
- 2 Cup Prepared "Green Goddess" Dressing
- 1/4 Cup parsley, chopped
- 1 Tablespoon paprika

Directions:

1. Place the chicken legs in a large resealable plastic bag. Combine the Green Goddess dressing as well as the parsley and paprika. Pour over the chicken legs. Refrigerate for 2 to 8 hours.

2. Supply your smoker with wood pellets and follow the start-up procedure. Preheat the grill, with the lid closed, to 350° F. Drain the chicken legs. Arrange the legs directly on the grill grate and grill, turning once, for 40 to 50 minutes, or until the legs are golden brown and cooked through. Serve at once. Grill: 350 °F

Smoked Wings

Servings: 6
Cooking Time: 50 Minutes

Ingredients:

- 24 chicken wings, flats and drumettes separated
- 12 Ounce Italian dressing
- 3 Ounce Chicken Rub
- 5 Ounce 'Que BBQ Sauce
- 3 Ounce chili sauce

Directions:

1. Wash all wings and place into resealable bag. Add Italian dressing to the resealable bag containing the wings. Place in refrigerator and allow to marinate for 6 to 12 hours.

2. Supply your smoker with wood pellets and follow the start-up procedure. Preheat the grill, with the lid closed, to 225° F.

3. Remove wings from marinade and shake off excess marinade. Season all sides of the wings with Traeger Chicken Rub and let sit for 15 minutes before putting wings on the Traeger.

4. In a small bowl, combine the BBQ and chili sauces. Set aside.

5. Cook wings to an internal temperature of 160°F. Remove the wings and toss in chili barbecue sauce. Grill: 225 °F Probe: 160 °F

6. Increase the grill temperature to 375°F and preheat. Once at temperature, place the wings on the Traeger and sear both sides until the internal temperature reaches 165°F. Grill: 375 °F Probe: 165 °F

7. Remove the wings from grill and let rest for 5 minutes. Serve with your favorite side wing dressing or sauce. Enjoy!

Crust Chicken Pizza

Servings: 4
Cooking Time: 35 Minutes

Ingredients:

- ½ Cup Alfredo Sauce
- 1 Tbsp Butter
- ¾ Lb. Shredded Chicken
- 2 Large Eggs
- 2 + 6 Divided Garlic Clove, Minced
- 1 ½ Cups Heavy Cream
- ¾ Cup Kale
- ¼ Cup Mushroom
- 1 Cup Grated Parmesan Cheese
- Champion Chicken Rub
- 2 Tbsp Red Onion, Diced
- ½ Tsp Salt

Directions:

1. Supply your smoker with wood pellets and follow the start-up procedure. Preheat the grill, with the lid open, to 400° F. If using a gas or charcoal grill, set heat to medium-high heat. Place pizza stone on grill grates and allow to preheat. Line a pizza peel with parchment paper and set aside.

2. In a medium bowl, stir together the shredded chicken, grated Parmesan cheese, minced garlic, and sea salt. Whisk the eggs lightly in a small bowl then add to chicken mixture. Mix until well combined.

3. Spread the chicken crust pizza "dough" onto the parchment paper on the pizza peel, as thinly as possible (about ¼" thick).

4. Using the pizza peel, transfer the parchment to the preheated pizza stone. Grill for 15 to 20 minutes, until firm and golden on the edges. Remove from the grill and let rest for 5-10 minutes.

5. Top pizza crust with alfredo sauce, kale, mushrooms, red onion and additional parmesan cheese. Return to the grill for 10 to 15 minutes, until the cheese is melted. Slice and serve!

Smoked Quarters

Servings: 2-4

Cooking Time: 120 Minutes

Ingredients:

- 4 chicken quarters
- 2 tablespoons olive oil
- 1 batch Chicken Rub
- 2 tablespoons butter

Directions:

1. Supply your smoker with wood pellets and follow the start-up procedure. Preheat the grill, with the lid closed, to 180°F.

2. Coat the chicken quarters all over with olive oil and season them with the rub. Using your hands, work the rub into the meat.

3. Place the quarters directly on the grill grate and smoke for 1½ hours.

4. Baste the quarters with the butter and increase the grill's temperature to 375°F.

Continue to cook until the chicken's internal temperature reaches 170°F.

5. Remove the quarters from the grill and let them rest for 10 minutes before serving.

Delicious Sweet And Sour Chicken Drumsticks

Servings: 4

Cooking Time: 150 Minutes

Ingredients:

- 3 Tbsp Brown Sugar
- 8 Chicken Drumsticks
- Garlic, Minced
- Ginger, Minced
- 2 Tbsp Honey
- 1 Cup Ketchup
- ½ Lemon Lemon, Juice
- 1/2 Lime, Juiced
- 2 Tbsp Rice Wine Vinegar
- ¼ Cup Soy Sauce
- 1 Tbsp Sweet Heat Rub

Directions:

1. In a mixing bowl, combine the ketchup, soy sauce, rice wine vinegar, brown sugar, honey, ginger, garlic, lemon, lime and Sweet Heat Rub. Reserve half of the mixture for dipping sauce and set aside. Use the remaining half and pour into a large resealable plastic bag. Add the drumsticks and seal bag. Refrigerate for at least 4-12 hours. Remove chicken from bag, discarding marinade.

2. Supply your smoker with wood pellets and follow the start-up procedure. Preheat the grill, with the lid open, to 225° F. If you're using a gas or charcoal grill, set it up for low-medium heat. Smoke the chicken over indirect heat with grill lid closed for 2 – 3 hours, turning once or twice,

until the chicken reaches 180°F. During the last half hour, feel free to brush more glaze on.

3. Remove from grill, and let stand for 10 minutes. Feel free to add more sauce if desired or use it as a dipping sauce for the drumsticks.

Smoked Cheesy Chicken Quesadilla

Servings: 4-8
Cooking Time: 180 Minutes

Ingredients:
- 2-3 Boneless, Skinless Chicken Breasts
- 1 Jalapeno, Chopped
- 1 Onion, Chopped
- Sweet Heat Rub
- 1, Chopped Red Bell Pepper
- 1-2 Cups Salsa
- 3 Cups Shredded Cheddar Cheese
- 3 Cups Shredded Monterey Or Pepper Jack Cheese
- Taco Sauce
- 20 Taco-Size Tortilla

Directions:
1. Supply your smoker with wood pellets and follow the start-up procedure. Preheat the grill, with the lid closed, to 350° F. If you're using a gas or charcoal grill, set it up for medium heat. Preheat with lid closed for 10-15 minutes.

2. Sprinkle chicken breasts generously in Sweet Heat Rub and rub to coat evenly. Place chicken breasts directly on preheated grill grates and cook for 45 minutes, or until the chicken is completely cooked (165°F internal temperature), tender, and falling apart. Remove from the grill and let cool slightly. Shred with meat claws and set aside. Turn grill up to 375°F.

3. In a large bowl, add the shredded chicken, onion, red bell pepper, jalapeno, and taco sauce. Mix to combine then set aside.

4. Cut each tortilla in half. Add about 2 tablespoons each of the cheddar cheese, Monterey Jack cheese, and chicken mixture to each tortilla half. Roll the tortillas into cones, starting from the cut edge, making sure not to push the ingredients out of the tortilla.

5. Place the small bowl in the center of the pizza plan and begin to stack quesadilla cones in a ring around the bowl. The points of each cone should be in the center just touching the bowl. Sprinkle cheese over the layer and repeat another layer with the remaining cones, finishing with a final sprinkle of cheese.

6. Remove bowl from the center of the ring and place the pizza pan directly on the grill grates. Cook with the lid closed for 15-20 minutes, or until the cheese is melted and the edges are browned and crispy.

7. Fill small bowl with salsa and return to the center of the ring. Serve immediately and enjoy!

Grilled Parmesan Chicken Wings

Servings: 4
Cooking Time: 25 Minutes

Ingredients:
- 4 Tbsp Butter
- 4 Lbs Chicken Wings, Trimmed And Patted Dry
- 4 Garlic Cloves, Chopped
- 2 Tbsp Olive Oil
- 1/2 Cup Parmesan Cheese, Grated
- 2 Tbsp Parsley, Chopped
- Champion Chicken Seasoning

Directions:

1. Lay chicken wings out on a sheet tray, blot with paper towel, then season with Champion Chicken.

2. Supply your smoker with wood pellets and follow the start-up procedure. Preheat the grill, with the lid open, to 400° F. If using a gas or charcoal grill, set it up for medium-high heat.

3. Transfer wings to grill and cook for 20 to 25 minutes, turning every 5 minutes, until lightly browned. Remove wings from the grill and set on a sheet tray. Place in the smoking cabinet to keep warm while preparing the garlic butter.

4. Melt butter and olive oil in a cast iron skillet, then add garlic and simmer until fragrant. Remove from the grill.

5. Transfer chicken wings to a large bowl and pour garlic butter over the wings. Add cheese and parsley, then toss well to coat. Serve warm with additional sprinkling of parmesan cheese.

Smoked Apple Chicken Leg Quarters

Servings: 8
Cooking Time: 120 Minutes

Ingredients:

- 8 leg quarters
- 1 bottle marinade
- Pork & chicken rub
- 1 cup of apple juice or water

Directions:

1. Rinse chicken and pat dry.

2. Marinade chicken in the fridge for at least 30 minutes or overnight (preferred).

3. Once the chicken is marinated, sprinkle both sides with the rub.

4. Supply your smoker with wood pellets and follow the start-up procedure. Preheat the grill, with the lid closed, to 225° F.

5. Place a small stainless steel pot of apple juice or water in the inside corner to help keep moist.

6. Place chicken on your grill, skin side up, with lid closed.

7. Smoke for 2 hours or until the internal temperature in the thickest part of a thigh is 165 °F.

8. Remove chicken from the grill and let it rest for 5 minutes before serving. Enjoy!

Oktoberfest Pretzel Mustard Chicken

Servings: 4
Cooking Time: 25 Minutes

Ingredients:

- 1/4 Pound pretzel sticks
- 3 Tablespoon Dijon mustard
- 3 Tablespoon apple cider or brown ale
- 1 Tablespoon honey
- 1 1/2 Teaspoon fresh thyme, plus more for garnish
- 4 boneless, skinless chicken breasts

Directions:

1. Pulse the pretzel sticks in a food processor or crush by hand in a resealable bag until they've turned into a powder the texture of panko breadcrumbs.

2. Transfer the crumbs to a wide, shallow bowl.

3. In separate shallow bowl, whisk mustard, beer or cider, honey and thyme together.

4. Spray a wire rack with cooking spray and place atop a sheet tray. Dip each chicken breast in the mustard mixture, then dredge in the pretzel crumbs to coat evenly and place on the wire rack.

Spray the top of each chicken breast lightly with cooking spray.

5. Supply your smoker with wood pellets and follow the start-up procedure. Preheat the grill, with the lid closed, to 375° F.

6. Place the pan on the Traeger and bake for about 20 to 25 minutes, until the chicken breasts are fully cooked and register 165°F on an instant-read thermometer. Grill: 375 °F Probe: 165 °F

7. Let chicken rest for 5 minutes. Garnish with fresh thyme if desired. Enjoy!

Spiced Cornish Hens With Cilantro Chutney

Servings: 2

Cooking Time: 60 Minutes

Ingredients:
- 2 Cornish game hens, each about 1 to 1¼lb (450 to 565g), thawed if frozen
- 1 small white onion, peeled and halved
- 4 slices of fresh ginger
- 4 garlic cloves, peeled
- 3 tbsp vegetable oil
- 2 tsp garam masala
- for the brine
- ½ gallon (1.9 liters) distilled water
- ½ cup kosher salt
- for the chutney
- 1 bunch of cilantro, washed and roughly chopped
- 4 scallions, trimmed and roughly chopped
- 2 garlic cloves, peeled and roughly chopped
- 2 small green chili peppers, deseeded and minced
- 1-inch (2.5cm) piece of fresh ginger, peeled and minced
- 1 tbsp dry-roasted peanuts
- 1 tsp coarse salt
- 1 tsp ground cumin
- ½ tsp ground coriander
- 3 tbsp freshly squeezed lemon juice
- ¼ cup extra virgin olive oil

Directions:

1. In a stockpot on the stovetop over medium-high heat, make the brine by bringing the water and salt to a boil. Stir until the salt dissolves. Remove the pot from the stovetop and let the brine cool to room temperature. Cover and refrigerate until cool.

2. Submerge the hens in the brine. If they float, place a resealable bag of ice on top. Cover and refrigerate for 4 hours or as long as 8 hours.

3. Supply your smoker with wood pellets and follow the start-up procedure. Preheat the grill, with the lid closed, to 350° F.

4. In a blender, make the chutney by combining all the ingredients except the olive oil. Blend until the ingredients begin to move, adding 1 tablespoon of water if they need help. When a paste has formed, add the olive oil in a thin stream until the chutney is smooth. If it seems too thick, add a small bit of water. If it's too thin, add a little more oil. Store in a covered container in the refrigerator until ready to use.

5. Remove the hens from the brine. Rinse inside and out under cold running water and pat dry with paper towels. Place half an onion, 2 slices of ginger, and 2 garlic cloves in the cavity of each hen. Tie the legs together with butcher's twine.

6. In a small bowl, combine the vegetable oil and garam masala. Rub the mixture thinly and evenly on the outside of the hens.

7. Place the hens on the grate and roast until they're nicely browned and the internal

temperature in the thickest part of a thigh reaches 165°F (74°C), about 1 hour.

8. Transfer the hens to a platter. Serve with the chutney.

Whole Smoked Honey Chicken

Servings: 4
Cooking Time: 40 Minutes

Ingredients:
- 1 Tablespoon Honey
- 1 ½ Lemon
- 4 Tablespoons Champion Chicken Seasoning
- 4 Tablespoons Unsalted Butter
- 1, 4 Pound Chicken, Giblets Removed And Patted Dry

Directions:
1. Supply your smoker with wood pellets and follow the start-up procedure. Preheat the grill, with the lid open, to 225° F.
2. In a small saucepan, melt together the butter and honey over low heat. Squeeze ½ lemon into the honey mixture and remove from the heat.
3. Smoke the chicken, skin side down until the chicken is lightly browned and the skin releases from the grate without ripping, about 6-8 minutes.
4. Turn the chicken over and baste with the honey butter mixture.
5. Continue to smoke the chicken, basting every 45 minutes, until the thickest part of the chicken reaches 160°F.

Smoke-roasted Chicken Thighs

Servings: 12-15
Cooking Time: 120 Minutes

Ingredients:

- 3 pounds chicken thighs
- 2 teaspoons salt
- 2 teaspoons freshly ground black pepper
- 2 teaspoons garlic powder
- 2 teaspoons onion powder
- 2 cups prepared Italian dressing

Directions:
1. Place the chicken thighs in a shallow dish and sprinkle with the salt, pepper, garlic powder, and onion powder, being sure to get under the skin.
2. Cover with the Italian dressing, coating all sides, and refrigerate for 1 hour.
3. Supply your smoker with wood pellets and follow the start-up procedure. Preheat, with the lid closed, to 250°F.
4. Remove the chicken thighs from the marinade and place directly on the grill, skin-side down. Discard the marinade.
5. Close the lid and roast the chicken for 1 hour 30 minutes to 2 hours, or until a meat thermometer inserted in the thickest part of the thighs reads 165°F. Do not turn the thighs during the smoking process.

Bacon-wrapped Chicken Breasts

Servings: 4 - 6
Cooking Time: 270 Minutes

Ingredients:
- 5 Oz Frozen Spinach, Thawed, Strained
- 8 Bacon Slices
- 1 Tbsp Butter
- 4 Chicken Breasts, Boneless, Skinless, Butterflied
- 2 Garlic Clove, Minced
- 1 Cup Italian Cheese Blend, Shredded
- 8 Oz Mushrooms, Sliced Thin
- 1 Tbsp Olive Oil

- 1 Tbsp Hickory Bacon Rub
- 1 Yellow Onion, Chopped

Directions:

1. Supply your smoker with wood pellets and follow the start-up procedure. Preheat the grill, with the lid open, to 375° F. If using a gas or charcoal grill, set heat to medium heat. For all other grills, preheat cast iron skillet on grill grates.

2. Heat olive oil and butter on griddle, then add mushrooms and cook for about 3 minutes, stirring frequently. Add chopped onion and garlic and cook for 2 minutes. Add spinach and sauté another minute, then transfer vegetables to a heat-safe bowl to cool slightly.

3. Season the butterflied chicken breasts with Hickory Bacon, coating both sides. Sprinkle half of cheese over each butterflied chicken breast, followed by the sautéed vegetables, and the remaining half of the cheese.

4. On a metal sheet tray, lay out two bacon slices. Gently fold chicken breast halves together and place on top of bacon slices, then wrap tightly with bacon. To secure, tuck ends of bacon underneath, or insert a toothpick to hold it together. Repeat with remaining breasts.

5. Arrange the chicken breasts, bacon seam down, directly on the grill grate and grill, turning once or twice, until the bacon is crisp and golden brown, about 25 to 30 minutes, or until internal temperature reaches 165°F.

6. Remove from grill, allow to rest for 5 minutes, remove any toothpicks, then serve hot.

BEEF LAMB AND GAME RECIPES

Steak Tips With Mashed Potatoes

Servings: 4-6
Cooking Time: 60 Minutes

Ingredients:

- 1 Cup Beef Broth
- 1 Stick (Room Temperature) Butter, Unsalted
- 2 Tablespoon Flour, All-Purpose
- 1 Tablespoon Java Chophouse Seasoning
- 4 Tablespoon Java Chophouse Seasoning, Divided
- 2 Pounds Medium Russet Potatoes, Peeled And Cut (Large Chunks)
- 2 Pounds Strip Sirloin
- 1/2 To 1 Cup Whole Milk, Warm

Directions:

1. For the mashed potatoes: add the potatoes to a large pot and add enough cold water to cover the potatoes. Bring to a simmer over medium heat until the potatoes are tender enough to be pierced with a fork, about 40 minutes. Drain the potatoes.

2. Add the potatoes to a large mixing bowl. Add the butter, 1 tablespoon of Java Chop House and ½ cup of warm milk. Mash until smooth and lump free. If potatoes are too thick, add more milk, a tablespoon at a time, until you reach your desired consistency.

3. For the steak tips: Supply your smoker with wood pellets and follow the start-up procedure. Preheat the grill, with the lid closed, to 350° F. Season the steaks generously on both sides with 2 tablespoons of Java Chop House seasoning and grill for 8-10 minutes per side. When steaks are done, remove from grill, allow to rest for 15 minutes, then cut into chunks.

4. While the steak is resting, add the butter to a small saucepan over low heat. Once the butter is melted, whisk in the flour and cook for 2 minutes until the flour smells toasted. Slowly whisk in the beef broth and remaining 2 tablespoons of Java Chop House seasoning and cook the gravy over low heat until thickened. Remove from heat and toss the steak tips in the gravy.

5. Serve steak tips over mashed potatoes. Enjoy!

The Perfect T-bones

Servings: 4
Cooking Time: 30 Minutes

Ingredients:

- 4 (1½- to 2-inch-thick) T-bone steaks
- 2 tablespoons olive oil
- 1 batch Espresso Brisket Rub or Chili-Coffee Rub

Directions:

1. Supply your smoker with wood pellets and follow the start-up procedure. Preheat the grill, with the lid closed, to 500°F.

2. Coat the steaks all over with olive oil and season both sides with the rub. Using your hands, work the rub into the meat.

3. Place the steaks directly on a grill grate and smoke until their internal temperature reaches 135°F for rare, 145°F for medium-rare, and 155°F for well-done. Remove the steaks from the grill and serve hot.

Salt-crusted Prime Rib

Servings: 8
Cooking Time: 180 Minutes

Ingredients:

- 1 1/2 Cup Jacobsen Salt Co. Pure Kosher Sea Salt
- 3/4 Cup coarse ground black pepper
- 1 Head garlic, peeled
- 1/2 Cup rosemary
- 2 Tablespoon chile powder
- 3/4 Cup extra-virgin olive oil
- 1 (15-16 lb) 6-bone prime rib roast

Directions:

1. In a food processor, combine salt, pepper, garlic cloves, rosemary and chile powder and process until fine. Add the olive oil and pulse to form a paste.
2. Place the prime rib roast on a cutting board, bone-side up and rub with 1 tablespoon of the salt paste.
3. Transfer the meat to a large roasting pan and place bone-side down. Pack the salt paste all over the fatty surface, pressing to help it adhere. Let the prime rib stand at room temperature for 1 hour.
4. Supply your smoker with wood pellets and follow the start-up procedure. Preheat the grill, with the lid closed, to 450° F.
5. Roast the prime rib for 1 hour, or until the crust is slightly darkened. Lower the Traeger temperature to 300°F and roast for about 2 hours and 15 minutes longer, or until an instant-read thermometer inserted into the center of the roast (not touching the bone) registers 125°F for medium-rare. Grill: 450 °F
6. Transfer the roast to a large carving board and let the meat rest for 30 minutes. Grill: 300 °F Probe: 135 °F
7. Carefully lift the salt crust off the meat and transfer to a bowl. Brush away any excess salt.
8. To remove the roast in one piece while keeping the rib rack intact, run a long sharp carving knife along the bones, using them as your guide. Leave on 1/2 inch of meat, or more if reserving for leftovers.
9. Carve the prime rib roast 1/2 inch thick and serve, using some of the crumbled salt crust as a condiment.

Reverse Seared Rib-eye Caps

Servings: 4
Cooking Time: 45 Minutes

Ingredients:

- 1 1/2 Pound rib-eye cap
- 2 Tablespoon Coffee Rub
- 2 Tablespoon Beef Rub

Directions:

1. Trim the rib-eye cap of excess silverskin and fat, if needed. Cut the cap into 4 equal portions and roll into steaks. Tie with butcher's twine to secure.
2. In a small bowl, combine both rubs. Season the steaks liberally with the rub mixture and set aside while the grill heats up.
3. Supply your smoker with wood pellets and follow the start-up procedure. Preheat the grill, with the lid closed, to 225° F.
4. Place the steaks directly on the grill grate, and smoke for 30 to 45 minutes until the internal temperature reaches 120°F. Grill: 225 °F Probe: 120 °F
5. Remove from the grill and set aside to rest.

6. Increase the grill temperature to 450°F. Grill: 450 °F

7. Place the steaks directly on the grill grate and cook 3 to 4 minutes per side, or until the internal temperature reaches 130°F. Grill: 450 °F Probe: 130 °F

8. Remove from grill and let rest 5 minutes before serving. Enjoy!

Spicy Beer Beef Jerky

Servings: 4-6
Cooking Time: 240 Minutes

Ingredients:

- 1 12 Oz Bottle Dark Beer
- 1/4 Cup Brown Sugar
- 2 Tbsp Coarse Black Pepper
- 4 Tbsp Garlic Salt
- 2 Tbsp Hot Sauce
- 2 Tablespoons, Divided Sweet Heat Rub
- 1 Tablespoon Quick Curing Salt
- 1 Cup Soy Sauce
- 2 Pounds Trimmed Flank Steak
- ¼ Worcestershire Sauce

Directions:

1. When you are ready to smoke your jerky, remove the beef from the marinade and discard the marinade.

2. Supply your smoker with wood pellets and follow the start-up procedure. Preheat the grill, with the lid closed, to 200° F. If using a sawdust or charcoal smoker, set it up for medium low heat.

3. Arrange the meat in a single layer directly on the smoker grate. Smoke the beef for 4-5 hours, or until the jerky is dry but still chewy and still bends somewhat.

4. Remove the jerky from the grill with tongs and transfer to a resealable plastic bag while still warm. Let the jerky rest for 1 hour at room temperature.

5. Squeeze any air out of the resealable plastic bag and refrigerate the jerky. It will keep for several weeks. Enjoy!

Smoked Tomato Brisket Chili

Servings: 6-8
Cooking Time: 120 Minutes

Ingredients:

- 4 Tablespoon Chipotles In Adobo, Diced
- 1 Cup Cooked Bacon, Chopped
- 1 (12 Oz) Beer, Any Brand
- 1 (Drained And Rinsed) Black Beans, Can
- 3 Cups Diced Cooked, Fat Trimmed Brisket
- 2 Tablespoon Chili Powder
- 1/2 Can Corn Kernels, Drained
- 1/2 (Drained) Corn, Can
- 1 Tablespoon Cumin
- 1 Green Hatch Chilies, Can
- 1 Can Kidney Beans, Drained And Rinsed
- 1 Red Onion, Diced
- 1 Tablespoon Beef And Brisket Seasoning
- 1 (15 Oz) Tomato Sauce

Directions:

1. In a sauce pan, sauté the red onion, bacon, and 2 tablespoons of the beer in oil or butter on medium heat until the onions are caramelized, and the bacon is cooked.

2. Supply your smoker with wood pellets and follow the start-up procedure. Preheat the grill, with the lid closed, to 250° F. Grill for 2 hours, or until the chili is bubbling and brisket is tender.

3. Remove from the grill and serve.

Grilled Loco Moco Burger

Servings: 4
Cooking Time: 10 Minutes

Ingredients:

- Ounce ground beef, 80% lean
- 3 Tablespoon kosher salt
- 2 Tablespoon black pepper
- Cup Beef Gravy
- 2 Cup Rice, Cooked
- 4 eggs
- burger buns
- 2 Cup Hawaiian Pasta Salad

Directions:

1. Supply your smoker with wood pellets and follow the start-up procedure. Preheat the grill, with the lid closed, to 375° F.
2. Divide the ground beef into four, 6 oz portions and shape into patties. Season the patties with salt and pepper.
3. Place the patties on the grill and flip after six minutes cook time.
4. Check the internal temperature of the patties. Burgers are done when they reach an internal temperature of 165°F. Probe: 165 °F
5. While the patties are cooking, heat the gravy and the rice. Cook the eggs over easy.
6. To assemble the burger: Start with the bottom of the bun, 1/4 cup rice, 1/4 cup pasta salad, a hamburger patty, gravy, a fried egg, and the top of the bun.
7. Serve while hot. Enjoy!

Potato Asoaragus Lamb

Servings: 2
Cooking Time: 180 Minutes

Ingredients:

- 1 Bunch Asparagus
- 1/2 Cup Butter
- 1 Rack Lamb, Rib
- 2 Tbsp Olive Oil
- Pepper
- 1 Dozen Potato, Baby
- 2 Rosemary, Springs
- Salt

Directions:

1. Supply your smoker with wood pellets and follow the start-up procedure. Preheat the grill, with the lid closed, to 225° F.
2. Remove the membrane from the back side of the ribs. Drizzle olive oil over both sides of the ribs and sprinkle rosemary.
3. In a deep baking dish, mix the potatoes with butter.
4. Place the rack of ribs directly on the grates of your grill alongside the dish of potatoes. Smoke for 3 hours or until the internal temperature of the lamb reaches 145F. During the last 20 minutes of smoking, add the asparagus to the potatoes to cook until tender.
5. Slice the lamb and serve with potatoes and asparagus.

Grilled Lemon Skirt Steak

Servings: 1-2
Cooking Time: 5 Minutes

Ingredients:

- 2 Cloves Garlic, Chopped
- 1 Lemon, Juice
- 2 Tablespoons Mustard, Grainy
- 1/4 Cup Olive Oil
- 2 Tablespoons   Java Chophouse Seasoning
- 2 Pounds Skirt Steak, Trimmed
- 1 Tablespoon Worcestershire Sauce

Directions:

1. In a small bowl, mix together the Java Chophouse Seasoning, oil, garlic, lemon juice, and Worcestershire. Generously rub the mixture all over the skirt steak and allow to marinate for 45 minutes.

2. Supply your smoker with wood pellets and follow the start-up procedure. Preheat the grill, with the lid closed, to 400° F.

3. Grill the skirt steaks for 3-5 minutes on each side or until the steak is done to the desired degree of doneness.

4. Remove the steaks from the grill and allow to rest for 5 minutes before slicing and serving.

Smoked Chuck Roast Tater Tot Casserole

Servings: 6
Cooking Time: 635 Minutes

Ingredients:

- 2 cups beef stock, divided
- 1 cup cheddar cheese, shredded
- 2 lbs chuck roast
- 1 tbsp cilantro, chopped
- 1 tsp cumin, ground
- 2 jalapeños, chopped
- to taste, lone star brisket rub
- 14 oz tater tots, miniature
- 1 lb white American cheese, cubed
- 1 yellow onion
- 1 cup milk

Directions:

1. Supply your smoker with wood pellets and follow the start-up procedure. Preheat the grill, with the lid closed, to 225° F. If using a gas or charcoal grill, set it up for low, indirect heat.

2. Set the chuck roast on a sheet tray, then season with Lonestar Brisket.

3. Place the chuck roast directly on the grill grate. Close the lid and smoke for 3 hours, spraying with ½ cup of beef stock after the 1st and 2nd hours.

4. Slice the onion and place in a cast iron skillet/Dutch oven with a lid, or aluminum pan. Pour the remaining 1 ½ cups of stock over the onions and set roast on top of onions.

5. Increase the temperature to 275° F and cook an additional 2 ½ to 3 hours, or until internal temperature reaches 165° F.

6. Once 165 F internal temperature is reached, cover the roast with a lid or aluminum foil, and cook another 2 ½ to 3 hours, or until the internal temperature reaches 200° F.

7. Remove the lid then pull the chuck roast apart with tongs. Remove from the grill and set aside.

8. Heat another cast iron skillet on the grill. Open the sear slide, then to the skillet add the cubed cheese, milk, jalapeño, milk, cumin, and cilantro. Stir occasionally, for 5 minutes, until the cheese melts. Close the lid and allow the cheese to smoke for 30 to 45 minutes, then remove from the grill and set aside for casserole assembly.

9. Assemble the casserole: In a deep cast iron skillet, layer the smoked chuck roast, smoked queso, and tater tots.

10. Increase the temperature of the grill to 375° F. If using a gas or charcoal grill, set it to medium heat.

11. Place the skillet on the grill, over indirect heat. Bake for 25 to 30 min, until tater tots begin to brown. Add shredded cheese, then continue baking on the grill for 5 minutes, until the cheese has melted.

12. Remove the casserole from the grill, rest for 10 minutes, then serve warm with additional cilantro, if desired.

Cheeseburger Hand Pies

Servings: 4

Cooking Time: 10 Minutes

Ingredients:

- ½ pound lean ground beef
- 1 tablespoon minced onion
- 1 tablespoon steak seasoning
- 1 cup shredded Monterey Jack and Colby cheese blend
- 8 slices white American cheese, divided
- 2 (14-ounce) refrigerated prepared pizza dough sheets, divided
- 2 eggs, beaten with 2 tablespoons water (egg wash), divided
- 24 hamburger dill pickle chips
- 2 tablespoons sesame seeds
- 6 slices tomato, for garnish
- Ketchup and mustard, for serving

Directions:

1. Supply your smoker with wood pellets and follow the start-up procedure. Preheat, with the lid closed, to 325°F.

2. On your stove top, in a medium sauté pan over medium-high heat, brown the ground beef for 4 to 5 minutes, or until cooked through. Add the minced onion and steak seasoning.

3. Toss in the shredded cheese blend and 2 slices of American cheese, and stir until melted and fully incorporated.

4. Remove the cheeseburger mixture from the heat and set aside.

5. Make sure the dough is well chilled for easier handling. Working quickly, roll out one prepared pizza crust on parchment paper and brush with half of the egg wash.

6. Arrange the remaining 6 slices of American cheese on the dough to outline 6 hand pies.

7. Top each cheese slice with ¼ cup of the cheeseburger mixture, spreading slightly inside the imaginary lines of the hand pies.

8. Place 4 pickle slices on top of the filling for each pie.

9. Top the whole thing with the other prepared pizza crust and cut between the cheese slices to create 6 hand pies.

10. Using kitchen scissors, cut the parchment to further separate the pies, but leave them on the paper.

11. Using a fork dipped in egg wash, seal the edges of the pies on all sides. Baste the tops of the pies with the remaining egg wash and sprinkle with the sesame seeds.

12. Remove the pies from the parchment paper and gently place on the grill grate. Close the lid and smoke for 5 minutes, then carefully flip and smoke with the lid closed for 5 more minutes, or until browned.

13. Top with the sliced tomato and serve with ketchup and mustard.

Traditional Tomahawk Steak

Servings: 4-6

Cooking Time: 120 Minutes

Ingredients:

- 1 tomahawk ribeye steak (2 1/2 to 3 1/2 lbs)
- 5 garlic cloves, minced
- 2 tbsp kosher salt
- 1 bundle fresh thyme
- 2 tbsp ground black pepper
- 8 oz butter stick
- 1 tbsp garlic powder
- 1/8 cup olive oil

Directions:

1. Mix rub ingredients (salt, black pepper, and garlic powder) in a small bowl. Use this mixture to season all sides of the ribeye steak generously. You can also substitute your favorite steak seasoning. After applying seasoning, let the steak rest at room temperature for at least 30 minutes.

2. While the steak rests, preheat your pellet grill to 450°F - 550°F for searing

3. Sear the steak for 5 minutes on each side. Halfway through each side (so after 2 1/2 minutes), rotate the steak 90° to form grill marks on the tomahawk

4. After the tomahawk steak has seared for 5 minutes on each side (10 minutes total), move the steak to a raised rack

5. Adjust your pellet grill's temperature to 250°F and turn up smoke setting if applicable. Leave the lid open for a moment to help allow some heat to escape

6. Stick your probe meat thermometer into the very center of the cut to measure internal temperature.

7. Place butter stick, garlic cloves, olive oil, and thyme in the aluminum pan. Then place the aluminum pan under the steak to catch drippings. After a few minutes, the steak drippings and ingredients will mix together

8. Baste the steak with the aluminum pan mixture every 10 minutes until the tomahawk steak reaches your desired doneness

9. Once the steak reaches its desired doneness, remove from the grill and place on a cutting board or serving dish. The steak should rest for 10-15 minutes before cutting/serving.

Garlic Leg Of Lamb Roast

Servings: 4

Cooking Time: 70 Minutes

Ingredients:
- 1/3 Cup Beef Stock
- 1 Tsp Black Pepper
- 2 Tsp Brown Sugar
- 1 Tsp Coriander, Ground
- 1 Tbsp Dijon Mustard
- 2 Tbsp Fresh Mint Leaves, Chopped
- 4 Garlic Cloves, Chopped
- 2 Leg Of Lamb Roasts, Bone-In (2 Lbs. Each)
- 1 Lemon, Juice
- 1/2 Cup Olive Oil
- 1/2 Red Onion, Chopped (For Marinade)
- 1 Red Onion, Sliced
- 1/4 Cup Red Wine
- 1 1/2 Tbsp Rosemary Leaves
- To Taste, Rosemary Sprigs
- 1 1/2 Tbsp Sage Leaves, Chopped
- 2 Tsp Salt
- To Taste, Thyme Sprigs
- 2 Tsp Worcestershire Sauce

Directions:
1. Blot lamb legs dry with paper towel, then place in a resealable plastic bag.

2. In the bowl of a food processor, combine olive oil, beef stock, red wine, lemon, mint, rosemary, sage, red onion, garlic, Dijon, Worcestershire sauce, brown sugar, salt, pepper, and coriander. Process for 1 minute, then pour the marinade over the lamb. Seal the bag and refrigerate for 4 hours.

3. Remove the lamb from the refrigerator 30 minutes prior to roasting,

4. Supply your smoker with wood pellets and follow the start-up procedure. Preheat the grill,

with the lid opened, to 375° F. If using a gas or charcoal grill, set it up for medium-high heat.

5. Place sliced red onion, rosemary and thyme sprigs in a cast iron skillet [preferably oblong], then set the lamb on top. Add 1 cup of water to the skillet.

6. Roast on the grill for 55 to 70 minutes, until an internal temperature of 135° to 140° F is reached.

7. Remove the lamb and let it rest for 15 minutes on a cutting board, then slice lamb and serve warm.

Texas Seared Beef

Servings: 4
Cooking Time: 150 Minutes

Ingredients:

- 1 cup beef stock
- 1/2 tsp black pepper
- 1/3 cup chili powder
- 1/2 tsp chipotle powder
- 2 1/2 lbs chuck roast, cut in 2-inch cubes
- to taste, cilantro
- 15 oz crushed tomatoes
- 1 tbsp cumin, ground
- 2 tbsp diced green chili peppers
- 3 garlic cloves, minced
- to taste, jalapeño
- 1 jalapeño, minced
- 1 1/2 tsp kosher salt
- 1 lime, zest & juice
- 1 tbsp olive oil
- 1 1/2 tsp oregano, dried
- to taste, red onion
- 1 red onion, diced
- to taste, sour cream

Directions:

1. Supply your smoker with wood pellets and follow the start-up procedure. Preheat the grill, with the lid closed, to 400° F. If using a gas or charcoal grill, set it up for medium-high heat. Set a deep cast iron skillet or Dutch oven on the grill and allow to preheat.

2. Place cubed chuck roast in a shallow pan then season with salt and pepper.

3. Add the oil to the Dutch oven then sear the beef on all sides. Remove seared beef and set aside.

4. Add the onions, garlic, and jalapeño to the pot. Stir then season with salt and pepper. Sauté for 3 minutes, then push all onions to the sides of the pot, creating a hole in the center. Add the chili powder, cumin, oregano, and green chilis. Cook for 1 minute, until the spices are fragrant, then reincorporate the onions. Stir in the beef stock, then bring to a hard simmer.

5. Return the seared beef to the Dutch oven, and stir to coat. Pour the crushed tomatoes in a single layer over the top of the beef. Cover the pot and reduce the grill temperature to 300 F. Braise the beef chili for 2 to 2 ½ hours, until beef is fork-tender.

6. Remove from the grill, then stir in lime zest and juice. Allow chili to sit for 10 minutes, then serve warm with your favorite chili toppings.

Georgia Smoked Onion Brisket Sandwich

Servings: 4
Cooking Time: 450 Minutes

Ingredients:

- ½ Cup Barbecue Sauce
- ¼ Cup Beef Broth
- 2 Tablespoons Bourbon

- 1, 3 Pound Brisket Flat, Trimmed
- 4 Kaiser Rolls
- ½ Cup Peach Preserves
- Sliced Pickles
- 4 Tablespoons Pulled Pork Rub
- Sliced White Onions

Directions:

1. Supply your smoker with wood pellets and follow the start-up procedure. Preheat the grill, with the lid closed, to 225° F.

2. Generously rub the brisket with the Pulled Pork Rub. Set aside.

3. In a bowl, mix together the barbecue sauce, peach preserves and bourbon. Set aside.

4. Place the brisket in the smoker and smoke for 5 hours, or until the internal temperature reaches 170°F. Once the brisket reaches temperature, remove from the smoker, place the brisket in foil and pour the beef broth over the top. Wrap the brisket tightly in aluminum foil and return to the smoker for another 2 hours, or until the internal temperature reaches 190°F.

5. Remove the brisket from the grill, unwrap the brisket, discard the foil, and brush the brisket generously with the peach glaze mixture. Place the brisket back on the smoker and smoke for 30 minutes, or until the brisket is shiny and glazed. Remove the brisket from the grill and rest for 10 minutes, covered in foil.

6. Once the brisket has rested, slice thickly against the grain and top the Kaiser rolls with the brisket slices, onion slices and pickle slices. Serve immediately.

Traeger Filet Mignon

Servings: 2
Cooking Time: 10 Minutes

Ingredients:
- 1 Teaspoon salt
- 1 Teaspoon pepper
- 2 Clove garlic, minced
- 3 Tablespoon butter, softened
- 2 filet mignon steaks

Directions:

1. In a small bowl, combine salt, pepper, garlic and softened butter. Rub on both sides of filets. Let rest 10 minutes.

2. Supply your smoker with wood pellets and follow the start-up procedure. Preheat the grill, with the lid closed, to 450° F.

3. Place steaks directly on the grill and cook for 5 to 8 minutes on each side, or until the filets reach an internal temperature of 130°F to 135°F for medium-rare. Enjoy! Pro Tip: With filets there will not be much marbling, so look for a rich, red color. Grill: 450 °F Probe: 140 °F

Traeger Smoked Salami

Servings: 8
Cooking Time: 480 Minutes

Ingredients:
- Pound Ground Sirloin
- 1 Tablespoon Morton Tender Quick Home Meat Cure
- Tablespoon Worcestershire sauce
- 1 Tablespoon ground black pepper
- 2 Teaspoon mustard seeds
- 1 Teaspoon red pepper flakes
- 1 Teaspoon black peppercorn
- Teaspoon honey

Directions:

1. Plan ahead! This recipe requires overnight time. In a large glass bowl combine the beef, curing salt, Worcestershire, pepper, mustard, red

pepper flakes, and peppercorns. Gently distribute the ingredients through the meat.

2. Cover with plastic wrap and refrigerate for 1 day.

3. After the meat has cured for 1 day, lay two pieces of long plastic wrap on top of each other on your work surface. Overturn the meat directly into the middle of the plastic wrap. Form the meat into a long log shape.

4. Pull the plastic wrap around one side and smooth out the edges of the log. Use even pressure across the length to work out any bubbles. Pull the plastic wrap tightly around the other side and overlap the edges of the wrap to create a tight seal. Roll the sausage forward and back with both hands. Once you have the sausage fairly uniform in width, tightly twist the ends of the plastic wrap. Return to the refrigerator for 1 day.

5. Supply your smoker with wood pellets and follow the start-up procedure. Preheat the grill, with the lid closed, to 180° F.

6. Unwrap the sausage and drizzle with the honey. Place directly on the grill grate, close the lid and smoke for 6-8 hours or until the internal temperature of the sausage reads 170℉ with a meat thermometer. Probe: 170 ℉

7. Allow the sausage to cool completely before slicing and serving. Enjoy!

Grilled Bell Pepper Flank Steak Fajitas

Servings: 1
Cooking Time: 30 Minutes

Ingredients:
- 1 Green Bell Pepper, Sliced
- 3 Tbsp Olive Oil
- 1 Onion, Diced
- Sweet Heat Rub
- 1 Red Bell Peppers, Sliced
- 1 -16Oz Steak, Flank
- 8 Tortilla, Corn
- 1 Yellow Bell Pepper, Sliced

Directions:
1. Rub flank steak with 1 tbsp olive oil and Sweet Heat Rub Grill seasoning. Cover and marinate in the refrigerator for 1 hour.

2. Lightly brush peppers and onion with olive oil.

3. Supply your smoker with wood pellets and follow the start-up procedure. Preheat the grill, with the lid closed, to 400° F. Place pepper and onion on grill and cook 5 minutes per side. Watch carefully to ensure the peppers and onion do not burn.

4. Remove peppers and onion from grill and toss lightly with remaining olive oil in a medium sized bowl. Transfer peppers and onions to a cutting board and slice into strips. Set aside.

5. Place flank steak directly on grill. Cook until medium rare (an internal temperature of 165°F).

6. Remove flank steak from the grill and transfer to cutting board. Let meat rest for 5 minutes, then slice against the grain into strips.

7. Place flank steak, peppers, and onions in a platter and serve immediately with warm tortillas, salsa, guacamole, sour cream, shredded cheese, thinly sliced iceberg lettuce, or your favorite fajita toppings.

Venison Bbq Burger By Nikki Boxler

Servings: 4
Cooking Time: 12 Minutes

Ingredients:
- 5 Slices bacon
- 1 Pound Venison, ground
- 1/2 Cup 'Que BBQ Sauce
- 1/2 Cup shredded cheddar cheese

Directions:
1. Supply your smoker with wood pellets and follow the start-up procedure. Preheat the grill, with the lid closed, to 350° F.
2. Place bacon slices directly on the grill grate and cook 15 minutes until fat is rendered and bacon is crispy. Remove from grill and let cool. When bacon is cool, break it into pieces.
3. Combine the venison, barbecue sauce, bacon and cheese into a large bowl. Then mix carefully so that the ingredients are spread evenly.
4. Once mixed, press the ground venison into burger patties.
5. Place patties directly on the grill grate and cook until the internal temperature reaches 165 degrees F, flipping halfway through.
6. Once the burgers are done, pair it with your favorite bun and top with your choice of toppings. I personally don't add a bun or condiments as the burger is so good, you don't need them. Enjoy!

Cheesy Egg Beef Rib Burger

Servings: 4
Cooking Time: 30 Minutes

Ingredients:
- 1/4 Cup Barbecue Sauce
- 4 Cheddar Cheese, Slices
- 4 Eggs
- 1 Pound Ground Chuck
- 1/2 Tablespoon Olive Oil
- 1 Tablespoon Beef And Brisket Rub
- 1/2 Cup Cooked Shredded Beef Rib(S)

Directions:
1. Supply your smoker with wood pellets and follow the start-up procedure. Preheat the grill, with the lid closed, to 350° F.
2. In a large bowl, mix the ground chuck and, Beef and Brisket Rub until evenly combined. Shape into patties.
3. Grill the patties for 7-10 minutes, flipping halfway and topping with a slice of cheddar cheese. When the burgers are to the desired degree of doneness, remove from the grill and set aside.
4. In a small bowl, mix the short rib and barbecue sauce.
5. In a small frying pan, heat the olive oil over medium-low heat and fry the eggs until the white is firm and the yolk is runny.
6. Assemble the burgers: top each bun with a burger patty, a spoonful of the short rib mixture, and a fried egg. Serve and enjoy

Bbq Beef Sandwich

Servings: 4
Cooking Time: 360 Minutes

Ingredients:
- 1 (4-6 lb) chuck roast
- 1/4 Cup Coffee Rub
- 1 Cup beef broth
- 6 hamburger buns
- 1 white onion, sliced
- dill pickles
- 1/2 Cup Special Sauce

- Sweet & Heat BBQ Sauce

Directions:

1. Supply your smoker with wood pellets and follow the start-up procedure. Preheat the grill, with the lid closed, to 250° F.

2. Trim excess fat from chuck roast. Rub roast with Traeger Coffee Rub. Place roast on Traeger and cook for 3-1/2 hours or until roast reaches an internal temperature of 160°F. Grill: 250 °F Probe: 160 °F

3. Remove roast from grill and wrap in a double layer of aluminum foil, add beef broth and place roast back in grill. Continue to cook for 1-1/2 hours while checking the temperature. The roast is done when the internal temperature reaches 204°F. Check every 30 minutes if internal temperature has not been reached. Grill: 250 °F Probe: 204 °F

4. Remove roast from grill and pull or shred the meat. Add the drippings back into the meat to help keep it moist.

5. Serve pulled roast in buns and top with sliced onions, pickles Traeger Special Sauce and Traeger Sweet & Heat BBQ Sauce.

Venison Steaks

Servings: 4
Cooking Time: 80 Minutes

Ingredients:
- 4 (8-ounce) venison steaks
- 2 tablespoons extra-virgin olive oil
- 4 garlic cloves, minced
- 1 tablespoon ground sage
- 2 teaspoons sea salt
- 2 teaspoons freshly ground black pepper

Directions:

1. Supply your smoker with wood pellets and follow the start-up procedure. Preheat, with the lid closed, to 225°F.

2. Rub the venison steaks well with the olive oil and season with the garlic, sage, salt, and pepper.

3. Arrange the venison steaks directly on the grill grate, close the lid, and smoke for 1 hour and 20 minutes, or until a meat thermometer inserted in the center reads 130°F to 140°F, depending on desired doneness. If you want a better sear, remove the steaks from the grill at an internal temperature of 125°F, crank up the heat to 450°F, or the "High" setting, and cook the steaks on each side for an additional 2 to 3 minutes.

Texas Shoulder Clod

Servings: 16-20
Cooking Time: 960 Minutes

Ingredients:
- ½ cup sea salt
- ½ cup freshly ground black pepper
- 1 tablespoon red pepper flakes
- 1 tablespoon minced garlic
- 1 tablespoon cayenne pepper
- 1 tablespoon smoked paprika
- 1 (13- to 15-pound) beef shoulder clod

Directions:

1. In a small bowl, combine the salt, pepper, red pepper flakes, minced garlic, cayenne pepper, and smoked paprika to create a rub. Generously apply it to the beef shoulder.

2. Supply your smoker with wood pellets and follow the start-up procedure. Preheat, with the lid closed, to 250°F.

3. Put the meat on the grill grate, close the lid, and smoke for 12 to 16 hours, or until a meat thermometer inserted deeply into the beef reads

195°F. You may need to cover the clod with aluminum foil toward the end of smoking to prevent over-browning.

4. Let the meat rest for about 15 minutes before slicing against the grain and serving.

Crusted Prime Rib With Rosemary

Servings: 4-6
Cooking Time: 180 Minutes

Ingredients:

- 4-6 garlic, cloves
- 1/3 cup olive oil
- chop house steak seasoning
- 7 pound, boned tied and rolled prime rib roast
- 3 tablespoon rosemary, fresh
- 3 tablespoon thyme, fresh sprigs

Directions:

1. In a food processor, blend together the garlic, rosemary, thyme, sage, and oil until a rough paste forms. Place the prime rib on a sheet pan over a wire rack and rub the prime rib generously with the herb paste on all sides.

2. Season the prime rib with   Chop House Steak Seasoning generously on all sides, then chill uncovered in the refrigerator overnight, or for 12 hours.

3. Once the prime rib has chilled for 12 hours, supply your smoker with wood pellets and follow the start-up procedure. Preheat the grill, with the lid closed, to 250° F, and grill for 2 hours or until the internal temperature of the roast reaches 110°F, then increase the temperature to 400 and grill for an additional 15-30 minutes, or until the internal temperature reaches 125 - 140°F.

4. Remove the prime rib from the grill, cover tightly in foil and allow to rest for 30 minutes.

The final temperature of the prime rib should be 125 - 140°F after resting. Serve and enjoy!

Smoked Chicken Steak Sandwiches

Servings: 6
Cooking Time: 270 Minutes

Ingredients:

- 1 1/2 tsp black pepper, ground
- 3 lbs brisket flat
- 1 tbsp butter
- 1 1/2 cups chicken stock
- 1/4 cup chop house steak rub
- for topping, dill pickles
- 2 tsp garlic powder
- 8 oz maple cure
- 2 tsp mustard powder
- 1 onion, sliced
- 1 1/2 tbsp pickling spice
- pumpernickel rye, sliced
- to taste, sauerkraut
- to taste, spicy brown mustard
- 6 swiss cheese, sliced
- 2 qts water, cold

Directions:

1. Set the brisket flat on a cutting board, then trim off excess fat and silver skin.

2. Whisk together water and maple cure, until dissolved.

3. Lay brisket in a large container, season with pickling spice, then cover with brine/cure. The meat must be completely immersed. Cover and place in the refrigerator for 3 to 4 days.

4. Remove brisket flat from brine/cure. It will be pale grey in color, which is normal. Discard the cure and replace with plain water. Allow brisket to soak 1-2 hours.

5. Combine all ingredients for the rub in a bowl. Remove the brisket from the water and blot dry with paper towel.

6. Season the brisket well with the rub, pushing and massaging it into the surface. Place the brisket back into the refrigerator, uncovered, overnight.

7. Supply your smoker with wood pellets and follow the start-up procedure. Preheat the grill, with the lid closed, to 250° F. If using a gas or charcoal grill, set it up for low, indirect heat.

8. Transfer the brisket flat directly on the grill grate, fat side down, over indirect heat. Smoke for 2 hours, flipping after 1 hour.

9. Remove the brisket from the grill and place it in a cast iron skillet, or foil-lined aluminum pan with chicken stock and onions. Cover with a lid, or foil and return to the grill.

10. Increase temperature to 275° F, and cook an additional 1 hour, then check the brisket to see if enough liquid remains. If reducing too quickly, add 1 cup of water. Cook the brisket for another 1 hour, or until the brisket is probe tender

11. Remove from the grill and rest for at least 30 minutes, prior to slicing thin.

12. Preheat the griddle over low flame.

13. Grease griddle with 1 tablespoon of butter, then spread mustard on 4 slices of rye, then set on griddle. Add 2 portions of sliced pastrami. Warm pastrami 1 to 2 minutes, then flip. Top pastrami with sauerkraut and cheese, then close the griddle lid for 1 minute to crisp up the underside of the pastrami and melt the cheese.

14. Brush rye with mustard then set pastrami on every other slice. Set remaining toasted rye on top complete the smoked pastrami sandwich.

15. Remove from the griddle, then repeat. Slice each sandwich on the bias and serve warm with dill pickles.

Smoked Tri-tip

Servings: 4
Cooking Time: 300 Minutes

Ingredients:
- 1½ pounds tri-tip roast
- Salt
- Freshly ground black pepper
- 2 teaspoons garlic powder
- 2 teaspoons lemon pepper
- ½ cup apple juice

Directions:
1. Supply your smoker with wood pellets and follow the start-up procedure. Preheat the grill, with the lid closed, to 180°F.

2. Season the tri-tip roast with salt, pepper, garlic powder, and lemon pepper. Using your hands, work the seasoning into the meat.

3. Place the roast directly on the grill grate and smoke for 4 hours.

4. Pull the tri-tip from the grill and place it on enough aluminum foil to wrap it completely.

5. Increase the grill's temperature to 375°F.

6. Fold in three sides of the foil around the roast and add the apple juice. Fold in the last side, completely enclosing the tri-tip and liquid. Return the wrapped tri-tip to the grill and cook for 45 minutes more.

7. Remove the tri-tip roast from the grill and let it rest for 10 to 15 minutes, before unwrapping, slicing, and serving.

Braised Short Ribs

Servings: 2-4

Cooking Time: 240 Minutes

Ingredients:

- 4 beef short ribs
- Salt
- Freshly ground black pepper
- ½ cup beef broth

Directions:

1. Supply your smoker with wood pellets and follow the start-up procedure. Preheat the grill, with the lid closed, to 180°F.
2. Season the ribs on both sides with salt and pepper.
3. Place the ribs directly on the grill grate and smoke for 3 hours.
4. Pull the ribs from the grill and place them on enough aluminum foil to wrap them completely.
5. Increase the grill's temperature to 375°F.
6. Fold in three sides of the foil around the ribs and add the beef broth. Fold in the last side, completely enclosing the ribs and liquid. Return the wrapped ribs to the grill and cook for 45 minutes more. Remove the short ribs from the grill, unwrap them, and serve immediately.

Reverse-seared Tri-tip

Servings: 4

Cooking Time: 180 Minutes

Ingredients:

- 1½ pounds tri-tip roast
- 1 batch Espresso Brisket Rub

Directions:

1. Supply your smoker with wood pellets and follow the start-up procedure. Preheat the grill, with the lid closed, to 180°F.
2. Season the tri-tip roast with the rub. Using your hands, work the rub into the meat.
3. Place the roast directly on the grill grate and smoke until its internal temperature reaches 140°F.
4. Increase the grill's temperature to 450°F and continue to cook until the roast's internal temperature reaches 145°F. This same technique can be done over an open flame or in a cast-iron skillet with some butter.
5. Remove the tri-tip roast from the grill and let it rest 10 to 15 minutes, before slicing and serving.

Cheddar Bacon Beef Burgers

Servings: 12

Cooking Time: 30 Minutes

Ingredients:

- Bacon Cheddar Burger Seasoning
- 3/4 Cup Bacon, Chopped
- 3 Lbs Beef, Ground
- 1 Jalapeno, Chopped
- Pepper
- 1/2 Cup Ranch Dressing
- Salt
- 1 1/2 Cups Shredded Cheddar Cheese

Directions:

1. Supply your smoker with wood pellets and follow the start-up procedure. Preheat the grill, with the lid closed, to 350° F.
2. In a small bowl, combine cheese, bacon, jalapeno and ranch dressing.
3. In a clean, large bowl, combine ground beef with enough salt and pepper to taste.
4. Form meat into patties and place on a pan. A good rule of thumb is for each patty to be about the size of the palm of your hand.

5. Using a clean glass, press into each patty, leaving the imprint of the bottom of the glass in the patty. Stuff the filling into the indent. Grill for 25 minutes or until the ground beef reaches an internal temperature of 160°F. Serve hot.

Cornish Game In Mandarin Glaze

Servings: 4
Cooking Time: 45 Minutes

Ingredients:

- 2 Tablespoon onion powder
- 1 Tablespoon granulated garlic
- 1 Tablespoon Jacobsen Salt Co. Pure Kosher Sea Salt
- 1 Tablespoon ground ginger
- 5 Whole Cornish game hens
- 15 Sprig fresh thyme
- 2 Large oranges, quartered
- 2 Tablespoon olive oil
- 1 Bottle (12 oz) mandarin orange sauce

Directions:

1. Supply your smoker with wood pellets and follow the start-up procedure. Preheat the grill, with the lid closed, to 375° F.
2. Combine onion powder, granulated garlic, Jacobsen Salt and ground ginger.
3. Remove the hens from the packaging. Remove any giblets from each cavity and pat them dry with a paper towel.
4. Place 4 to 5 sprigs fresh thyme into each cavity, along with 1 orange wedge.
5. Sprinkle each bird with the spice mixture, then rub with olive oil. Tie the legs together with butcher's twine.
6. Place the game hens on the Traeger and cook for 20 minutes. Grill: 375 °F

7. After 20 minutes, brush each hen with mandarin glaze. Let them cook an additional 20 minutes and brush again with the glaze. Grill: 375 °F
8. Cook until hens have reached an internal temperature of 160°F. Enjoy! Grill: 375 °F Probe: 160 °F

Smoked Burgers

Servings: 8
Cooking Time: 120 Minutes

Ingredients:

- 2 Pound ground beef
- 1 Tablespoon Worcestershire sauce
- 2 Tablespoon Beef Rub

Directions:

1. Mix ground beef with Worcestershire sauce and Traeger Beef rub.
2. Form beef mixture into 8 hamburger patties.
3. Supply your smoker with wood pellets and follow the start-up procedure. Preheat the grill, with the lid closed, to 180° F.
4. Place patties directly on the grill grate and smoke for 2 hours. Grill: 180 °F
5. After 2 hours, remove from grill and serve with your favorite toppings. Enjoy!

Bacon-swiss Cheesesteak Meatloaf

Servings: 4
Cooking Time: 120 Minutes

Ingredients:

- 1 tablespoon canola oil
- 2 garlic cloves, finely chopped
- 1 medium onion, finely chopped

- 1 poblano chile, stemmed, seeded, and finely chopped
- 2 pounds extra-lean ground beef
- 2 tablespoons Montreal steak seasoning
- 1 tablespoon A.1. Steak Sauce
- ½ pound bacon, cooked and crumbled
- 2 cups shredded Swiss cheese
- 1 egg, beaten
- 2 cups breadcrumbs
- ½ cup Tiger Sauce

Directions:

1. On your stove top, heat the canola oil in a medium sauté pan over medium-high heat. Add the garlic, onion, and poblano, and sauté for 3 to 5 minutes, or until the onion is just barely translucent

2. Supply your smoker with wood pellets and follow the start-up procedure. Preheat, with the lid closed, to 225°F.

3. In a large bowl, combine the sautéed vegetables, ground beef, steak seasoning, steak sauce, bacon, Swiss cheese, egg, and breadcrumbs. Mix with your hands until well incorporated, then shape into a loaf.

4. Put the meatloaf in a cast iron skillet and place it on the grill. Close the lid and smoke for 2 hours, or until a meat thermometer inserted in the loaf reads 165°F.

5. Top with the meatloaf with the Tiger Sauce, remove from the grill, and let rest for about 10 minutes before serving.

Philly Cheese Onion Steaks

Servings: 6
Cooking Time: 45 Minutes

Ingredients:

- 2 Green Bell Pepper, Sliced
- 6 Hot Dog Bun(S)
- 2 Cups Mozzarella Cheese, Shredded
- 1 Quart Mushroom
- 1 Onion, Sliced
- Pepper
- Salt
- 2 Thick Steak, Flank

Directions:

1. Supply your smoker with wood pellets and follow the start-up procedure. Preheat the grill, with the lid closed, to 250° F.

2. Season both sides of your steaks with salt and pepper to your liking. We're going to reverse sear these steaks, so place on the grates of your preheated Grill. You'll want to cook the steaks until the internal temperature reaches 130°F (for medium-rare). Follow these internal temperatures if you'd like to cook your steak more/less done:

3. Rare: 125°F

4. Medium Rare: 130°F

5. Medium: 140°F

6. Well Done: 160°F

7. If you're cooking your steaks medium rare, it will take around 45 minutes depending on how thick the steaks are.

8. While the steaks are cooking, slice up the onion, mushrooms, and peppers thinly and sauté until soft.

9. When the steaks have reached your desired internal temperature, remove steaks from the grill and let them rest for 15 minutes. In the meantime, open up your flame broiler and crank up the grill to HIGH. Sear each side of the steak for about 1 minutes each.

10. Rest steaks again for 10 minutes.

11. Slice steak thinly, combine with the sautéed vegetables and fill a hot dog bun generously with the mixture.

Bison Tomahawk Steak

Servings: 2

Cooking Time: 15 Minutes

Ingredients:

- 2 1/2 Whole Thick Bone-in Buffalo Rib-eye Steak
- 2 Teaspoon Jacobsen Salt Co. Cherrywood Smoked Salt
- 1 1/2 Tablespoon black pepper

Directions:

1. Supply your smoker with wood pellets and follow the start-up procedure. Preheat the grill, with the lid closed, to 450° F.

2. Combine salt and pepper and evenly coat steak with seasoning. Place steak directly on grill grate.

3. Grill for 6 minutes on one side, then flip steak and continue cooking until the internal temperature reaches 140 degrees for medium rare, 145 for medium. Enjoy!

Beef Tenderloin With Tomato Vinaigrette

Servings: 6

Cooking Time: 40 Minutes

Ingredients:

- 1 Whole (1-1/4 to 1-1/2 inch thick) beef tenderloin steaks
- 1 Bottle Prime Rib Rub
- 2/3 Cup extra-virgin olive oil
- salt and pepper
- 1 Teaspoon fresh thyme
- 6 Whole plum tomatoes
- 1 Teaspoon Thyme, minced
- 2 Tablespoon balsamic vinegar

Directions:

1. Supply your smoker with wood pellets and follow the start-up procedure. Preheat the grill, with the lid closed, to 450° F.

2. Tuck the thin end of the tenderloin underneath the roast and secure it with butcher's string. Rub the meat with olive oil and season it with the Prime Rib Rub or salt and pepper. Place the meat on a rack in a shallow roasting pan.

3. Roast in the preheated Traeger for 20 minutes. Adjust the heat to 350F. Roast 20 minutes longer, or to desired degree of doneness (130F for rare; 145F for medium; 155F or higher for well-done). Grill: 350 °F

4. Let rest for 5 minutes before slicing thinly. (If serving cold, thoroughly chill the tenderloin before slicing.) Garnish with sprigs of thyme.

5. To make the vinaigrette, combine the tomatoes, olive oil, balsamic vinegar, and thyme leaves in a blender jar or food processor; puree until smooth. Season to taste with Traeger Prime Rib Rub or salt and pepper.

6. Transfer to a gravy boat and serve with the tenderloin. (Best served the day it's made.)

Smoked Cheese Beef Burgers

Servings: 4

Cooking Time: 66 Minutes

Ingredients:

- 1 ½ pounds ground beef chuck 80/20
- 4 slices cheddar cheese optional
- 4 burger buns
- Assorted burger toppings
- Smoked Burger Seasoning
- 1 Tablespoon Kosher salt
- 1 Tablespoon coarse ground black pepper
- 1 Tablespoon garlic powder

Directions:

1. Supply your smoker with wood pellets and follow the start-up procedure. Preheat the grill, with the lid closed, to 225 °F.

2. Shape your ground beef into 4 patties, about 1/2 inch larger in diameter than your burger buns.

3. In a small bowl combine the burger seasoning and sprinkle on both sides of your burger patties.

4. Place the seasoned patties on the grill and smoke for up to 1 hour, or until the internal temperature of your burgers reads 135 °F.

5. Increase the heat of your grill to the high setting (at least 400 °F). Sear the burger patties for about 2-3 minutes on both sides. Add cheese after the first flip, if desired.

6. Check the temperature of your burger patties for desired doneness. The FDA recommends 165 °F for a well done burger.

7. Remove the burger patties and toast the buns over high heat. Assemble your smoked burgers on your toasted buns with any desired toppings and serve immediately.

Savory Chili Mac And Cheese

Servings: 4
Cooking Time: 25 Minutes

Ingredients:
- 4 Cups Beef Stock
- 2 Teaspoons Chili Powder
- 2 Tbsp Chopped Fresh Parsley Leaves
- 2 Cloves Garlic, Minced
- 1 1/2 Teaspoon Cumin
- 10 Oz. Elbow Macaroni / Noodles
- 8 Oz Ground Beef
- 3/4 Cup Kidney Beans, Drained And Rinsed
- And Freshly Ground Black Pepper Kosher Salt
- 1 Tbs Olive Oil

- 1 Onion, Diced
- 1 Tbs Sweet Heat Rub
- 3/4 Cup Shredded Cheddar Cheese
- 1 (14.5-Ounce) Tomatoes, Canned And Diced

Directions:
1. Supply your smoker with wood pellets and follow the start-up procedure. Preheat the grill, with the lid open, to 350° F. If you're using a gas or charcoal grill, set it up for medium heat.

2. Heat olive oil in a Dutch oven or cast iron pan over medium-high heat. Add garlic, onion and ground beef, and cook until browned, about 3-5 minutes. Break up the beef as it cooks with a large wooden spoon or fork.

3. Stir in beef broth, tomatoes, beans, Sweet Heat, chili powder and cumin. Add salt and pepper to taste. Bring to a simmer and stir in pasta.

4. Transfer pot to the preheated grill and cover. Cook until pasta is cooked through, about 15-20 minutes. Remove from heat and top generously with shredded cheese, replace the cover to allow cheese to melt, about 2 minutes. Garnish with fresh parsley and serve immediately!

Smoked Garlic Prime Rib Roast

Servings: 12
Cooking Time: 60 Minutes

Ingredients:
- 1 10 pounds Prime Rib Roast (the bones cut off and tied back on)
- 1/2 cup horseradish mustard
- 2 tablespoons Worcestershire sauce
- 4 cloves garlic (minced)
- Coarse ground salt and black pepper (to taste)

Directions:

1. Supply your smoker with wood pellets and follow the start-up procedure. Preheat the grill, with the lid closed, to 225 °F.

2. Prepare your roast while the grill is heating. Trim any excess fat from the top of the roast down to 1/4 inch thick.

3. In a small bowl, combine the mustard, Worcestershire sauce,and garlic. Slather the entire roast with the mustard mixture and season liberally with salt and pepper.

4. Place the roast on the grill grate and close the lid. Smoke until the internal temperature of the roast reaches 120 °F for Rare or 130 °F for Medium. For a rare, bone-in roast, plan on 35 minutes per pound of prime rib.

5. Remove the roast to a cutting board, cover the roast with foil, and allow it to rest for 20 minutes.

6. While the roast is resting, increase the temperature of your grill to 400 °F.

7. Once the grill temperature reaches 400 °F, return the roast to the grill and sear until it reaches your desired internal temperature. Pull the roast off at 130 °F for rare, 135 °F for medium rare, 140 °F for medium. This process should go quickly, so keep an eye on your temperature.

8. Remove your roast to the cutting board and let the meat rest for at least 15 minutes.

9. Slice and serve.

Braised Onion Chuck Roast Beef Sandwiches

Servings: 4

Cooking Time: 540 Minutes

Ingredients:

- 3 cups beef stock, divided
- 2 lbs chuck roast
- 4 hoagie rolls, sliced lengthwise
- to taste, lone star brisket rub
- 1 yellow onion

Directions:

1. Place chuck roast in a glass baking dish. Season with Lone Star Brisket Rub, then cover with plastic wrap and refrigerate overnight.

2. The next day, remove chuck roast from the refrigerator. Supply your smoker with wood pellets and follow the start-up procedure. Preheat the grill, with the lid closed, to 225° F. If using a gas or charcoal grill, set it up for low, indirect heat.

3. Place chuck roast directly on the grill grate, then close the lid and smoke for 3 hours, spraying with 1 cup of beef stock every hour.

4. Slice the onion and place in a cast iron skillet, then pour the remaining cup of stock over the onions and set roast on top of onions.

5. Increase temperature to 275° F and cook an additional 2 ½ to 3 hours, or until internal temperature reaches 165° F.

6. Cover the roast with a cast iron lid or aluminum foil, and cook for another 2 ½ to 3 hours, or until the internal temperature reaches 200° F.

7. Remove chuck roast from the grill. Allow the roast to rest for 10 minutes, then remove from the skillet and shred.

8. Serve pulled roast beef in a hoagie roll with braised onions and pan jus.

Chicken Wings With Teriyaki Glaze

Servings: 4
Cooking Time: 50 Minutes

Ingredients:

* 16 large chicken wings, about 3lb (1.4kg) total
* 1 to 1½ tbsp toasted sesame oil
* for the glaze
* ½ cup light soy sauce or tamari
* ¼ cup sake or sugar-free dark-colored soda
* ¼ cup light brown sugar or low-carb substitute
* 2 tbsp mirin or 1 tbsp honey
* 1 garlic clove, peeled, minced or grated
* 2 tsp minced fresh ginger
* 1 tsp cornstarch mixed with 1 tbsp distilled water (optional)
* for serving
* 1 tbsp toasted sesame seeds
* 2 scallions, trimmed, white and green parts sliced sharply diagonally

Directions:

1. Supply your smoker with wood pellets and follow the start-up procedure. Preheat the grill, with the lid closed, to 350° F.
2. Place the chicken wings in a large bowl, add the sesame oil, and turn the wings to coat thoroughly.
3. Place the wings on the grate at an angle to the bars. Grill for 20 minutes and then turn. Continue to cook until the wings are nicely browned and the meat is no longer pink at the bone, about 20 minutes more.
4. To make the glaze, in a saucepan on the stovetop over medium-high heat, combine the ingredients and bring the mixture to a boil. Reduce the glaze by 1/3, about 6 to 8 minutes. If you prefer your glaze to be glossy and thick, add the cornstarch and water mixture to the glaze and cook until it coats the back of a spoon, about 1 to 2 minutes more.
5. Transfer the wings to an aluminum foil roasting pan. Pour the glaze over them, turning to coat thoroughly. Place the pan on the grate and cook the wings until the glaze sets, about 5 to 10 minutes.
6. Transfer the wings to a platter. Scatter the sesame seeds and scallions over the top. Serve with plenty of napkins.

Bacon-wrapped Jalapeño Poppers

Servings: 12
Cooking Time: 30 Minutes

Ingredients:

* 8 ounces cream cheese, softened
* ½ cup shredded Cheddar cheese
* ¼ cup chopped scallions
* 1 teaspoon chipotle chile powder or regular chili powder
* 1 teaspoon garlic powder
* 1 teaspoon salt
* 18 large jalapeño peppers, stemmed, seeded, and halved lengthwise
* 1 pound bacon (precooked works well)

Directions:

1. Supply your smoker with wood pellets and follow the start-up procedure. Preheat, with the

lid closed, to 350°F. Line a baking sheet with aluminum foil.

2. In a small bowl, combine the cream cheese, Cheddar cheese, scallions, chipotle powder, garlic powder, and salt.

3. Stuff the jalapeño halves with the cheese mixture.

4. Cut the bacon into pieces big enough to wrap around the stuffed pepper halves.

5. Wrap the bacon around the peppers and place on the prepared baking sheet.

6. Put the baking sheet on the grill grate, close the lid, and smoke the peppers for 30 minutes, or until the cheese is melted and the bacon is cooked through and crisp.

7. Let the jalapeño poppers cool for 3 to 5 minutes. Serve warm.

Bacon Pork Pinwheels (kansas Lollipops)

Servings: 4-6
Cooking Time: 20 Minutes

Ingredients:
- 1 Whole Pork Loin, boneless
- To Taste salt and pepper
- To Taste Greek Seasoning
- 4 Slices bacon
- To Taste The Ultimate BBQ Sauce

Directions:
1. When ready to cook, start the smoker and set temperature to 500F. Preheat, lid closed, for 10 to 15 minutes.

2. Trim pork loin of any unwanted silver skin or fat. Using a sharp knife, cut pork loin length wise, into 4 long strips.

3. Lay pork flat, then season with salt, pepper and Cavender's Greek Seasoning.

4. Flip the pork strips over and layer bacon on unseasoned side. Begin tightly rolling the pork strips, with bacon being rolled up on the inside.

5. Secure a skewer all the way through each pork roll to secure it in place. Set the pork rolls down on grill and cook for 15 minutes.

6. Brush BBQ Sauce over the pork. Turn each skewer over, then coat the other side. Let pork cook for another 5-10 minutes, depending on thickness of your pork. Enjoy!

Bayou Wings With Cajun Rémoulade

Servings: 8
Cooking Time: 40 Minutes

Ingredients:
- 16 large whole chicken wings or 32 drumettes and flats, about 3lb (1.4kg) total
- for the rub
- 1 tbsp kosher salt
- 1 tsp freshly ground black pepper
- 1 tsp paprika
- ½ tsp ground cayenne, plus more
- ½ tsp garlic powder
- ½ tsp celery salt
- ½ tsp dried thyme
- 2 tbsp vegetable oil
- for the rémoulade
- 1¼ cups reduced-fat mayo
- ¼ cup Creole-style or whole grain mustard
- 2 tbsp horseradish
- 2 tbsp pickle relish
- 1 tbsp freshly squeezed lemon juice
- 1 tsp paprika, plus more
- 1 tsp hot sauce, plus more
- 1 tsp Worcestershire sauce
- coarse salt

- for serving
- lemon wedges
- pickled okra (optional)

Directions:

1. Supply your smoker with wood pellets and follow the start-up procedure. Preheat the grill, with the lid closed, to 350° F.

2. If using whole wings, cut through the two joints, separating them into drumettes, flats, and wing tips. (Discard the wing tips or save them for chicken stock.) Alternatively, leave the wings whole. Place the chicken in a resealable plastic bag.

3. In a small bowl, make the rub by combining the ingredients. Mix well. Pour the rub over the wings and toss them to thoroughly coat. Refrigerate for 2 hours.

4. In a small bowl, make the Cajun rémoulade by whisking together the mayo, mustard, horseradish, pickle relish, lemon juice, paprika, hot sauce, and Worcestershire. Season with salt to taste. The mixture should be highly seasoned. Transfer to a serving bowl and lightly dust with paprika. Cover and refrigerate until ready to serve.

5. Remove the wings from the refrigerator and allow the excess marinade to drip off. Place the wings on the grate at an angle to the bars. Grill for 20 minutes and then turn. (They'll brown more evenly but will also have less of a tendency to stick.) Continue to cook until the wings are nicely browned and the meat is no longer pink at the bone, about 20 minutes more.

6. Remove the wings from the grill and pile them on a platter. Serve with the Cajun rémoulade, lemon wedges, and pickled okra (if using).

Pulled Pork Loaded Nachos

Servings: 4

Cooking Time: 10 Minutes

Ingredients:

- 2 cups leftover smoked pulled pork
- 1 small sweet onion, diced
- 1 medium tomato, diced
- 1 jalapeño pepper, seeded and diced
- 1 garlic clove, minced
- 1 teaspoon salt
- 1 teaspoon freshly ground black pepper
- 1 bag tortilla chips
- 1 cup shredded Cheddar cheese
- ½ cup The Ultimate BBQ Sauce, divided
- ½ cup shredded jalapeño Monterey Jack cheese
- Juice of ½ lime
- 1 avocado, halved, pitted, and sliced
- 2 tablespoons sour cream
- 1 tablespoon chopped fresh cilantro

Directions:

1. Supply your smoker with wood pellets and follow the start-up procedure. Preheat, with the lid closed, to 375°F.

2. Heat the pulled pork in the microwave.

3. In a medium bowl, combine the onion, tomato, jalapeño, garlic, salt, and pepper, and set aside.

4. Arrange half of the tortilla chips in a large cast iron skillet. Spread half of the warmed pork on top and cover with the Cheddar cheese. Top with half of the onion-jalapeño mixture, then drizzle with ¼ cup of barbecue sauce.

5. Layer on the remaining tortilla chips, then the remaining pork and the Monterey Jack cheese. Top with the remaining onion-jalapeño mixture

and drizzle with the remaining ¼ cup of barbecue sauce.

6. Place the skillet on the grill, close the lid, and smoke for about 10 minutes, or until the cheese is melted and bubbly. (Watch to make sure your chips don't burn!)

7. Squeeze the lime juice over the nachos, top with the avocado slices and sour cream, and garnish with the cilantro before serving hot.

Citrus-infused Marinated Olives

Servings: 6

Cooking Time: 30 Minutes

Ingredients:

- 1½ cups mixed brined olives, with pits
- ½ cup extra virgin olive oil
- 1 tbsp freshly squeezed lemon juice
- 1 garlic clove, peeled and thinly sliced
- 1 tsp smoked Spanish paprika
- 2 sprigs of fresh rosemary
- 2 sprigs of fresh thyme
- 2 bay leaves, fresh or dried
- 1 small dried red chili pepper, deseeded and flesh crumbled, or ¼ tsp crushed red pepper flakes
- 3 strips of orange zest
- 3 strips of lemon zest

Directions:

1. Supply your smoker with wood pellets and follow the start-up procedure. Preheat the grill, with the lid closed, to 180° F.

2. Drain the olives, reserving 1 tablespoon of brine. Spread the olives in a single layer in an aluminum foil roasting pan. Place the pan on the grate and cook the olives for 30 minutes, stirring the olives or shaking the pan once or twice.

3. In a small saucepan on the stovetop over low heat, warm the olive oil. Whisk in the lemon juice

and the reserved 1 tablespoon of brine. Stir in the garlic and paprika. Add the rosemary, thyme, bay leaves, chili pepper, and orange and lemon zests. Warm over low heat for 10 minutes. Remove the saucepan from the heat.

4. Transfer the olives and olive oil mixture to a pint jar. Tuck the aromatics around the sides of the jar. Let cool and then cover and refrigerate for up to 5 days. Let the olives come to room temperature before serving.

Chorizo Queso Fundido

Servings: 4-6

Cooking Time: 20 Minutes

Ingredients:

- 1 poblano chile
- 1 cup chopped queso quesadilla or queso Oaxaca
- 1 cup shredded Monterey Jack cheese
- ¼ cup milk
- 1 tablespoon all-purpose flour
- 2 (4-ounce) links Mexican chorizo sausage, casings removed
- ⅓ cup beer
- 1 tablespoon unsalted butter
- 1 small red onion, chopped
- ½ cup whole kernel corn
- 2 serrano chiles or jalapeño peppers, stemmed, seeded, and coarsely chopped
- 1 tablespoon minced garlic
- 1 tablespoon freshly squeezed lime juice
- 1 teaspoon ground cumin
- 1 teaspoon salt
- 1 teaspoon freshly ground black pepper
- 1 tablespoon chopped fresh cilantro
- 1 tablespoon chopped scallions
- Tortilla chips, for serving

Directions:

1. Supply your smoker with wood pellets and follow the start-up procedure. Preheat, with the lid closed, to 350°F.

2. On the smoker or over medium-high heat on the stove top, place the poblano directly on the grate (or burner) to char for 1 to 2 minutes, turning as needed. Remove from heat and place in a closed-up lunch-size paper bag for 2 minutes to sweat and further loosen the skin.

3. Remove the skin and coarsely chop the poblano, removing the seeds; set aside.

4. In a bowl, combine the queso quesadilla, Monterey Jack, milk, and flour; set aside.

5. On the stove top, in a cast iron skillet over medium heat, cook and crumble the chorizo for about 2 minutes.

6. Transfer the cooked chorizo to a small, grill-safe pan and place over indirect heat on the smoker.

7. Place the cast iron skillet on the preheated grill grate. Pour in the beer and simmer for a few minutes, loosening and stirring in any remaining sausage bits from the pan.

8. Add the butter to the pan, then add the cheese mixture a little at a time, stirring constantly.

9. When the cheese is smooth, stir in the onion, corn, serrano chiles, garlic, lime juice, cuvmin, salt, and pepper. Stir in the reserved chopped charred poblano.

10. Close the lid and smoke for 15 to 20 minutes to infuse the queso with smoke flavor and further cook the vegetables.

11. When the cheese is bubbly, top with the chorizo mixture and garnish with the cilantro and scallions.

12. Serve the chorizo queso fundido hot with tortilla chips.

Grilled Guacamole

Servings: 6

Cooking Time: 30 Minutes

Ingredients:

- 3 large avocados, halved and pitted
- 1 lime, halved
- ½ jalapeño, deseeded and deveined
- ½ small white or red onion, peeled
- 2 garlic cloves, peeled and skewered on a toothpick
- 1 tsp coarse salt, plus more
- 1½ tbsp reduced-fat mayo
- 2 tbsp chopped fresh cilantro
- 2 tbsp crumbled queso fresco (optional)
- tortilla chips

Directions:

1. Supply your smoker with wood pellets and follow the start-up procedure. Preheat the grill, with the lid closed, to 225° F.

2. Place the avocados, lime, jalapeño, and onion cut sides down on the grate. Use the toothpicks to balance the garlic cloves between the bars. Smoke for 30 minutes. (You want the vegetables to retain most of their rawness.)

3. Transfer everything to a cutting board. Remove the garlic cloves from the toothpick and roughly chop. Sprinkle with the salt and continue to mince the garlic until it begins to form a paste. Scrape the garlic and salt into a large bowl.

4. Scoop the avocado flesh from the peels into the bowl. Squeeze the juice of ½ lime over the avocado. Mash the avocados but leave them somewhat chunky. Finely dice the jalapeño. Dice 2 tablespoons of onion. (Reserve the remaining

onion for another use.) Add the jalapeño, onion, mayo, and cilantro to the bowl. Stir gently to combine. Taste for seasoning, adding more salt, lime juice, and jalapeño as desired.

5. Transfer the guacamole to a serving bowl. Top with the queso fresco (if using). Serve with tortilla chips.

Pigs In A Blanket

Servings: 4-6
Cooking Time: 15 Minutes

Ingredients:
- 2 Tablespoon Poppy Seeds
- 1 Tablespoon Dried Minced Onion
- 2 Teaspoon garlic, minced
- 2 Tablespoon Sesame Seeds
- 1 Teaspoon salt
- 8 Ounce Original Crescent Dough
- 1/4 Cup Dijon mustard
- 1 Large egg, beaten

Directions:
1. When ready to cook, start your smoker at 350 degrees F, and preheat with lid closed, 10 to 15 minutes.
2. Mix together poppy seeds, dried minced onion, dried minced garlic, salt and sesame seeds. Set aside.
3. Cut each triangle of crescent roll dough into thirds lengthwise, making 3 small strips from each roll.
4. Brush the dough strips lightly with Dijon mustard. Put the mini hot dogs on 1 end of the dough and roll up.
5. Arrange them, seam side down, on a greased baking pan. Brush with egg wash and sprinkle with seasoning mixture.

6. Bake in smoker until golden brown, about 12 to 15 minutes.
7. Serve with mustard or dipping sauce of your choice. Enjoy!

Simple Cream Cheese Sausage Balls

Servings: 5
Cooking Time: 30 Minutes

Ingredients:
- 1 pound ground hot sausage, uncooked
- 8 ounces cream cheese, softened
- 1 package mini filo dough shells

Directions:
1. Supply your smoker with wood pellets and follow the start-up procedure. Preheat, with the lid closed, to 350°F.
2. In a large bowl, using your hands, thoroughly mix together the sausage and cream cheese until well blended.
3. Place the filo dough shells on a rimmed perforated pizza pan or into a mini muffin tin.
4. Roll the sausage and cheese mixture into 1-inch balls and place into the filo shells.
5. Place the pizza pan or mini muffin tin on the grill, close the lid, and smoke the sausage balls for 30 minutes, or until cooked through and the sausage is no longer pink.
6. Plate and serve warm.

Deviled Eggs With Smoked Paprika

Servings: 6
Cooking Time: 30 Minutes

Ingredients:

- 6 large eggs
- 3 tbsp reduced-fat mayo, plus more
- 1 tsp Dijon or yellow mustard
- ½ tsp Spanish smoked paprika or regular paprika, plus more
- dash of hot sauce
- coarse salt
- freshly ground black pepper
- for garnishing
- small sprigs of fresh parsley, dill, tarragon, or cilantro
- chopped chives
- minced scallions
- Mustard Caviar
- sliced green or black olives
- celery leaves
- sliced radishes
- diced bell peppers
- sliced cherry tomatoes
- fresh or pickled jalapeños
- sliced or diced pickles
- slivers of sun-dried tomatoes
- bacon crumbles
- smoked salmon
- Hawaiian black salt
- Caviar

Directions:

1. Supply your smoker with wood pellets and follow the start-up procedure. Preheat the grill, with the lid closed, to 180° F.

2. On the stovetop over medium-high heat, bring a saucepan of water to a boil. (Make sure there's enough water in the saucepan to cover the eggs by 1 inch [5cm].) Use a slotted spoon to gently lower the eggs into the water. Lower the heat to maintain a simmer. Set a timer for 13 minutes.

3. Prepare an ice bath by combining ice and cold water in a large bowl. Carefully transfer the eggs to the ice bath when the timer goes off.

4. When the eggs are cool enough to handle, gently tap them all over to crack the shell. Carefully peel the eggs. Rinse under cold running water to remove any clinging bits of shell, but don't dry the eggs. (A damp surface will help the smoke adhere to the egg whites.)

5. Place the eggs on the grate and smoke until the eggs take on a light brown patina from the smoke, about 25 minutes. Transfer the eggs to a cutting board, handling them as little as possible.

6. Slice each egg in half lengthwise with a sharp knife. Wipe any yolk off the blade before slicing the next egg. Gently remove the yolks and place them in a food processor. Pulse to break up the yolks. Add the mayo, mustard, paprika, and hot sauce. Season with salt and pepper to taste. Pulse until the filling is smooth. Add additional mayo 1 teaspoon at a time if the mixture is a little dry. (It shouldn't be too loose either.)

7. Spoon the filling into each egg half or pipe it in using a small resealable plastic bag. You can also use a pastry bag fitted with a fluted tip.

8. Place the eggs on a platter and lightly dust with paprika. Accompany with one or more of the suggested garnishes.

Smoked Cashews

Servings: 6
Cooking Time: 60 Minutes

Ingredients:

- 1 pound roasted, salted cashews

Directions:

1. Supply your smoker with wood pellets and follow the start-up procedure. Preheat the grill, with the lid closed, to 120°F.
2. Pour the cashews onto a rimmed baking sheet and smoke for 1 hour, stirring once about halfway through the smoking time.
3. Remove the cashews from the grill, let cool, and store in an airtight container for as long as you can resist.

Pig Pops (sweet-hot Bacon On A Stick)

Servings: 24
Cooking Time: 30 Minutes

Ingredients:

- Nonstick cooking spray, oil, or butter, for greasing
- 2 pounds thick-cut bacon (24 slices)
- 24 metal skewers
- 1 cup packed light brown sugar
- 2 to 3 teaspoons cayenne pepper
- ½ cup maple syrup, divided

Directions:

1. Supply your smoker with wood pellets and follow the start-up procedure. Preheat, with the lid closed, to 350°F.
2. Coat a disposable aluminum foil baking sheet with cooking spray, oil, or butter.
3. Thread each bacon slice onto a metal skewer and place on the prepared baking sheet.

4. In a medium bowl, stir together the brown sugar and cayenne.
5. Baste the top sides of the bacon with ¼ cup of maple syrup.
6. Sprinkle half of the brown sugar mixture over the bacon.
7. Place the baking sheet on the grill, close the lid, and smoke for 15 to 30 minutes.
8. Using tongs, flip the bacon skewers. Baste with the remaining ¼ cup of maple syrup and top with the remaining brown sugar mixture.
9. Continue smoking with the lid closed for 10 to 15 minutes, or until crispy. You can eyeball the bacon and smoke to your desired doneness, but the actual ideal internal temperature for bacon is 155°F
10. Using tongs, carefully remove the bacon skewers from the grill. Let cool completely before handling.

Chuckwagon Beef Jerky

Servings: 6
Cooking Time: 300 Minutes

Ingredients:

- 2½lb (1.2kg) boneless top or bottom round steak, sirloin tip, flank steak, or venison
- 1 cup sugar-free dark-colored soda
- 1 cup cold brewed coffee
- ½ cup light soy sauce
- ¼ cup Worcestershire sauce
- 2 tbsp whiskey (optional)
- 2 tsp chili powder
- 1½ tsp garlic salt
- 1 tsp onion powder
- 1 tsp pink curing salt

Directions:

1. Slice the meat into ¼-inch-thick (.5cm) strips, trimming off any visible fat or gristle. (Slice against the grain for more tender jerky and with the grain for chewier jerky.) Place the meat in a large resealable plastic bag.

2. In a small bowl, whisk together the soda, coffee, soy sauce, Worcestershire sauce, whiskey (if using), chili powder, garlic salt, onion powder, and curing salt (if using). Whisk until the salt dissolves. Pour the mixture over the meat and reseal the bag. Refrigerate for 24 to 48 hours, turning the bag several times to redistribute the brine.

3. Supply your smoker with wood pellets and follow the start-up procedure. Preheat the grill, with the lid closed, to 150° F.

4. Drain the meat and discard the brine. Place the strips of meat in a single layer on paper towels and blot any excess moisture.

5. Place the meat in a single layer on the grate and smoke for 4 to 5 hours, turning once or twice. (If you're aware of hot spots on your grate, rotate the strips so they smoke evenly.) To test for doneness, bend one or two pieces in the middle. They should be dry but still somewhat pliant. Or simply eat a piece to see if it's done to your liking.

6. For the best texture, when you remove the meat from the grill, place the still-warm jerky in a resealable plastic bag and let rest for 30 minutes. (You might see condensation form on the inside of the bag, but the moisture will be reabsorbed by the meat.) Or let the meat cool completely and then store in a resealable plastic bag or covered container. The jerky will last a few days at room temperature but will last longer (up to 2 weeks) if refrigerated.

Smoked Cheese

Servings: 4
Cooking Time: 150 Minutes

Ingredients:
- 1 (2-pound) block medium Cheddar cheese, or your favorite cheese, quartered lengthwise

Directions:
1. Supply your smoker with wood pellets and follow the start-up procedure. Preheat the grill, with the lid closed, to 90°F.

2. Place the cheese directly on the grill grate and smoke for 2 hours, 30 minutes, checking frequently to be sure it's not melting. If the cheese begins to melt, try flipping it. If that doesn't help, remove it from the grill and refrigerate for about 1 hour and then return it to the cold smoker.

3. Remove the cheese, place it in a zip-top bag, and refrigerate overnight.

4. Slice the cheese and serve with crackers, or grate it and use for making a smoked mac and cheese.

Roasted Red Pepper Dip

Servings: 8
Cooking Time: 45 Minutes

Ingredients:
- 4 red bell peppers, halved, destemmed, and deseeded
- 1 cup English walnuts, divided
- 1 small white onion, peeled and coarsely chopped
- 2 garlic cloves, peeled and smashed with a chef's knife
- ¼ cup extra virgin olive oil, plus more
- 1 tbsp balsamic vinegar or balsamic glaze
- 1 tsp honey (eliminate if using balsamic glaze)

- 1 tsp coarse salt, plus more
- 1 tsp ground cumin
- 1 tsp smoked paprika
- ½ to 1 tsp Aleppo red pepper flakes, plus more
- ¼ cup fresh white breadcrumbs (optional)
- distilled water (optional)
- assorted crudités or wedges of pita bread

Directions:

1. Supply your smoker with wood pellets and follow the start-up procedure. Preheat the grill, with the lid closed, to 400° F.

2. Place the peppers skin side down on the grate and grill until the skins blister and the flesh softens, about 30 minutes. Transfer the peppers to a bowl and cover with plastic wrap. Let cool to room temperature. Remove the skins with a paring knife or your fingers. Coarsely chop or tear the peppers.

3. Place ¾ cup of walnuts in an aluminum foil roasting pan. Place the pan on the grate and toast for 10 to 15 minutes, stirring twice. Remove the pan from the grill and let the walnuts cool.

4. Place the peppers, onion, garlic, and walnuts in a food processor fitted with the chopping blade. Pulse several times. Add the olive oil, balsamic vinegar, honey, salt, cumin, paprika, and red pepper flakes. Process until the mixture is fairly smooth. Taste for seasoning, adding more salt or red pepper flakes (if desired). (If the mixture is too loose, add breadcrumbs until the texture is to your liking. If it's too thick, add olive oil or water 1 tablespoon at a time.)

5. Transfer the dip to a serving bowl. Use the back of a spoon to make a shallow depression in the center. Top with the remaining ¼ cup of walnuts and drizzle olive oil in the depression. Serve with crudités or pita bread.

Delicious Deviled Crab Appetizer

Servings: 30
Cooking Time: 10 Minutes

Ingredients:

- Nonstick cooking spray, oil, or butter, for greasing
- 1 cup panko breadcrumbs, divided
- 1 cup canned corn, drained
- ½ cup chopped scallions, divided
- ½ red bell pepper, finely chopped
- 16 ounces jumbo lump crabmeat
- ¾ cup mayonnaise, divided
- 1 egg, beaten
- 1 teaspoon salt
- 1 teaspoon freshly ground black pepper
- 2 teaspoons cayenne pepper, divided
- Juice of 1 lemon

Directions:

1. Supply your smoker with wood pellets and follow the start-up procedure. Preheat, with the lid closed, to 425°F.

2. Spray three 12-cup mini muffin pans with cooking spray and divide ½ cup of the panko between 30 of the muffin cups, pressing into the bottoms and up the sides. (Work in batches, if necessary, depending on the number of pans you have.)

3. In a medium bowl, combine the corn, ¼ cup of scallions, the bell pepper, crabmeat, half of the mayonnaise, the egg, salt, pepper, and 1 teaspoon of cayenne pepper.

4. Gently fold in the remaining ½ cup of breadcrumbs and divide the mixture between the prepared mini muffin cups.

5. Place the pans on the grill grate, close the lid, and smoke for 10 minutes, or until golden brown.

6. In a small bowl, combine the lemon juice and the remaining mayonnaise, scallions, and cayenne pepper to make a sauce.

7. Brush the tops of the mini crab cakes with the sauce and serve hot.

Smoked Turkey Sandwich

Servings: 1
Cooking Time: 15 Minutes

Ingredients:
- 2 slices sourdough bread
- 2 tablespoons butter, at room temperature
- 2 (1-ounce) slices Swiss cheese
- 4 ounces leftover Smoked Turkey
- 1 teaspoon garlic salt

Directions:
1. Supply your smoker with wood pellets and follow the start-up procedure. Preheat the grill, with the lid closed, to 375°F.

2. Coat one side of each bread slice with 1 tablespoon of butter and sprinkle the buttered sides with garlic salt.

3. Place 1 slice of cheese on each unbuttered side of the bread, and then put the turkey on the cheese.

4. Close the sandwich, buttered sides out, and place it directly on the grill grate. Cook for 5 minutes. Flip the sandwich and cook for 5 minutes more. Remove the sandwich from the grill, cut it in half, and serve.

Sriracha & Maple Cashews

Servings: 10
Cooking Time: 60 Minutes

Ingredients:
- 2 tbsp unsalted butter
- 3 tbsp pure maple syrup
- 1 tbsp sriracha
- 1 tsp coarse salt (use only if nuts are unsalted)
- 2½ cups unsalted cashews

Directions:
1. Supply your smoker with wood pellets and follow the start-up procedure. Preheat the grill, with the lid closed, to 250° F.

2. In a small saucepan on the stovetop over low heat, melt the butter. Add the maple syrup, sriracha, and salt (if using). Stir until combined. Add the nuts and stir gently to coat thoroughly.

3. Spread the nuts in a single layer in an aluminum foil roasting pan coated with cooking spray. Place the pan on the grate and smoke the nuts until they're lightly toasted, about 1 hour, stirring once or twice.

4. Remove the pan from the grill and let the nuts cool for 15 minutes. They'll be sticky at first but will crisp up. Break them up with your fingers and store at room temperature in an airtight container, such as a lidded glass jar.

Jalapeño Poppers With Chipotle Sour Cream

Servings: 8
Cooking Time: 45 Minutes

Ingredients:
- 3 strips of thin-sliced bacon
- 12 large jalapeños, red, green, or a mix
- 8oz (225g) light cream cheese, at room temperature
- 1 cup shredded pepper Jack, Monterey Jack, or Cheddar cheese
- 1 tsp chili powder
- ½ tsp garlic salt

- smoked paprika
- for the sour cream
- 1¼ cups light sour cream
- juice of ½ lime
- ½ to 1 canned chipotle peppers in adobo sauce, finely minced, plus 1 tsp of sauce, plus more
- 1 tbsp minced fresh cilantro leaves
- ½ tsp coarse salt, plus more

Directions:

1. Supply your smoker with wood pellets and follow the start-up procedure. Preheat the grill, with the lid closed, to 375° F.

2. Line a rimmed sheet pan with aluminum foil and place a wire rack on top. Place the bacon in a single layer on the wire rack. Place the pan on the grate and grill until the bacon is crisp and golden brown, about 20 minutes. Transfer the bacon to paper towels to cool and then crumble. Set aside.

3. In a small bowl, make the chipotle sour cream by whisking together the ingredients. Add more salt, chipotle peppers, or adobe sauce to taste. Cover and refrigerate.

4. Slice the jalapeños lengthwise through their stems. Scrape out the veins and seeds with the edge of a small metal spoon.

5. In a small bowl, beat together the cream cheese, shredded cheese, chili powder, and garlic salt. Stir in the crumbled bacon. Mound the cream cheese mixture in the jalapeño halves. Line another rimmed sheet pan with aluminum foil and place a wire rack on top. Place the jalapeños filled side up in a single layer on the wire rack.

6. Place the sheet pan on the grate and roast the jalapeños until the filling has melted and the peppers have softened, about 20 to 25 minutes. (They should no longer look bright in color.)

Remove the pan from the grill and let the peppers rest for 5 minutes.

7. Transfer the poppers to a platter and lightly dust with paprika. Serve with the chipotle sour cream.

Cold-smoked Cheese

Servings: 6
Cooking Time: 180 Minutes

Ingredients:

- 2lb (1kg) well-chilled hard or semi-hard cheese, such as:
- Edam
- Gouda
- Cheddar
- Monterey Jack
- pepper Jack
- goat cheese
- fresh mozzarella
- Muenster
- aged Parmigiano-Reggiano
- Gruyère
- blue cheese

Directions:

1. Unwrap the cheese and remove any protective wax or coating. Cut into 4-ounce (110g) portions to increase the surface area.

2. If possible, move your smoker to a shady area. Place 1 resealable plastic bag filled with ice on top of the drip pan. This is especially important on a warm day because you want to keep the interior temperature of the grill between 70 and 90°F (21 and 32°C) or below.

3. Place a grill mat on one side of the grate. Place the cheese on the mat and allow space between each piece.

4. Fill your smoking tube or pellet maze (see Cast Iron Skillets and Grill Pans) with pellets or sawdust and light according to the manufacturer's instructions. Place the smoking tube on the grate near—but not on—the grill mat. When the tube is smoking consistently, close the grill lid.

5. Smoke the cheese for 1 to 3 hours, replacing the pellets or sawdust and ice if necessary. Monitor the temperature and make sure the cheese isn't beginning to melt. Carefully lift the mat with the cheese to a rimmed baking sheet and let the cheese cool completely before handling.

6. Package the smoked cheese in cheese storage paper or bags or vacuum-seal the cheese, labeling each. (While you can wrap the cheese tightly in plastic wrap, the cheese will spoil faster.) Let the cheese rest for at least 2 to 3 days before eating. It will be even better after 2 weeks.

COCKTAILS RECIPES

A Smoking Classic Cocktail

Servings: 2

Cooking Time: 60 Minutes

Ingredients:

- 2 Bottle Angostura orange bitters
- 10 sugar cubes
- 8 Ounce Champagne
- lemon twist

Directions:

1. Supply your smoker with wood pellets and follow the start-up procedure. Preheat the grill, with the lid closed, to 180° F.

2. For the Smoked Orange Bitters: In a small skillet, combine 1 bottle of Angostura orange bitters with a splash of water and 4 sugar cubes.

3. Place skillet on the grill grate and smoke for 60 minutes. Cool the smoked bitters and put back into the bottle. Grill: 180 °F

4. Add a sugar cube to each Champagne flute and soak the sugar cubes with the smoked bitters.

5. Add champagne and a lemon twist in a flute glass. Enjoy!

Zombie Cocktail Recipe

Servings: 2

Cooking Time: 45 Minutes

Ingredients:

- fresh squeezed orange juice
- pineapple juice
- 2 Ounce light rum
- 2 Ounce dark rum
- 2 Ounce lime juice
- 1 Ounce Smoked Simple Syrup
- 6 Ounce smoked orange and pineapple juice
- 2 grilled orange peel, for garnish
- 2 grilled pineapple chunks, for garnish

Directions:

1. Supply your smoker with wood pellets and follow the start-up procedure. Preheat the grill, with the lid closed, to 180° F.

2. Smoked Orange and Pineapple Juice: Pour equal parts fresh squeezed orange juice and pineapple juice into a shallow sheet pan and smoke for 45 minutes. Remove and let cool. Measure out 3 ounces of juice and reserve any remaining juice in the refrigerator for future use. Grill: 180 °F

3. Add dark and light rums, 3 ounces smoked orange and pineapple juice, lime juice and Traeger Smoked Simple Syrup to a mixing glass.

4. Add ice, shake and strain over clean ice into a Tiki glass.

5. Garnish with a grilled orange peel and grilled pineapple. Enjoy!

Smoked Mulled Wine

Servings: 10

Cooking Time: 60 Minutes

Ingredients:

- 2 Bottle red wine
- 1/2 Cup whiskey
- 1/2 Cup white rum
- 1/2 Cup honey
- 1 cinnamon stick
- 2 pods star anise
- 4 whole cloves
- 1 (3 in) orange peel

Directions:

1. Supply your smoker with wood pellets and follow the start-up procedure. Preheat the grill, with the lid closed, to 180° F.

2. In a shallow baking dish, combine wine, whiskey, rum, honey, cinnamon stick, star anise, cloves and orange peel. Stir well until combined.

3. Place the dish directly on the grill grate and smoke for one hour until the mixture is warm. Grill: 180 °F

4. Remove from grill and ladle into mugs leaving the mulling spices behind. Garnish with fresh cinnamon sticks, anise, orange zest or a combination. Enjoy!

Smoked Sangria

Servings: 6
Cooking Time: 45 Minutes

Ingredients:
- 1 (750 ml) medium-bodied red wine
- 1/4 Cup Grand Marnier
- 1/4 Cup Smoked Simple Syrup
- 1 Cup fresh cranberries
- 1 Whole apple, sliced
- 2 Whole limes, sliced
- 4 cinnamon stick
- soda water

Directions:
1. Supply your smoker with wood pellets and follow the start-up procedure. Preheat the grill, with the lid closed, to 180° F.

2. In a shallow dish, combine red wine, Grand Marnier, Traeger Smoked Simple Syrup and cranberries, and place directly on the grill grate.

3. Smoke for 30 to 45 minutes or until the liquid picks up desired amount of smoke. Remove from grill and place in the fridge to cool. Grill: 180 °F

4. When the mixture has cooled, place in a large pitcher. Add sliced apples, limes, cinnamon sticks and ice to pitcher.

5. Top with soda water, if desired. Enjoy!

Traeger Gin & Tonic

Servings: 2
Cooking Time: 45 Minutes

Ingredients:
- 1/2 Cup berries
- 2 orange, sliced
- 4 Tablespoon granulated sugar
- 3 Ounce gin
- 1 Cup tonic water
- 2 Sprig fresh mint, for garnish

Directions:
1. Supply your smoker with wood pellets and follow the start-up procedure. Preheat the grill, with the lid closed, to 180° F.

2. For the Smoked Berries: Spread mixed fresh berries on a sheet pan and place directly on the grill grate. Smoke for 30 minutes then remove from grill. Grill: 180 °F

3. For the Orange Slices: Increase the grill temperature to 450°F and preheat, lid closed for 15 minutes. Grill: 450 °F

4. Toss the orange slices with granulated sugar and place directly on grill grate. Cook for about 5 minutes, turning once or until the slices have developed grill marks. Grill: 450 °F

5. Pour gin into a glass, add ice and berries, then top with tonic water. Garnish with a fresh mint sprig and grilled orange wheel. Enjoy!

Smoked Apple Cider

Servings: 2

Cooking Time: 30 Minutes

Ingredients:

- 32 Ounce apple cider
- 2 cinnamon sticks
- 4 whole cloves
- 3 star anise
- 2 Pieces orange peel
- 2 Pieces lemon peel

Directions:

1. Supply your smoker with wood pellets and follow the start-up procedure. Preheat the grill, with the lid closed, to 225° F.

2. Combine the cider, cinnamon stick, star anise, clove, lemon and orange peel in a shallow baking dish.

3. Place directly on the grill grate and smoke for 30 minutes. Remove from grill, strain and transfer to four mugs. Grill: 225 ˚F

4. Finish with a slice of apple and a cinnamon stick to serve. Enjoy!

Grilled Peach Smash Cocktail

Servings: 2

Cooking Time: 10 Minutes

Ingredients:

- 2 peach, sliced and grilled
- 10 fresh mint leaves
- 1 1/2 Ounce Smoked Simple Syrup
- 4 Ounce bourbon
- 2 mint sprig, for garnish

Directions:

1. Supply your smoker with wood pellets and follow the start-up procedure. Preheat the grill, with the lid closed, to 375° F.

2. Cut the peach into 6 slices and brush with Traeger Smoked Simple Syrup. Place directly on the grill grate and cook 10 to 12 minutes or until peaches soften and get grill marks. Grill: 375 ˚F

3. In a mixing glass, add 3 slices of grilled peaches, 5 mint leaves and Traeger Smoked Simple Syrup.

4. Muddle ingredients to release oils of the mint and juices from the grilled peaches. Add bourbon and crushed ice.

5. Shake and pour into a stemless wine glass. Top off with more crushed ice. Garnish with a grilled peach and mint sprig. Enjoy!

Sunset Margarita

Servings: 2

Cooking Time: 55 Minutes

Ingredients:

- 4 oranges
- 2 Cup plus 1 teaspoon agave
- 1/2 Cup water
- 1 Ounce burnt orange agave
- 3 Ounce reposado tequila
- 1 1/2 Ounce fresh squeezed lime juice
- Jacobsen Salt Co. Cherrywood Smoked Salt

Directions:

1. Supply your smoker with wood pellets and follow the start-up procedure. Preheat the grill, with the lid closed, to 350° F.

2. For the Burnt Orange Agave Syrup: Cut one orange in half and brush cut side with agave. Place cut side down directly on the grill grate and grill for 15 minutes or until grill marks develop. Grill: 350 ˚F

3. While the orange halves are grilling, slice the other orange and brush both sides of the slices with agave. Place slices directly on the grill grate

next to the halves and cook for 15 minutes or until grill marks develop. Grill: 350 °F

4. Remove orange halves from grill grate and let cool. After they have cooled, juice halves and strain. Set aside.

5. Combine 1/4 cup water and agave in a shallow dish and mix well. Remove orange slices from the grill and place in the agave mixture, reserving a few for garnish.

6. Reduce the grill temperature to 180 degrees F and place the shallow dish with agave and oranges directly on the grill grate. Smoke for 40 minutes. Remove from heat and strain. Set aside. Grill: 180 °F

7. To Mix Drink: Rim glass with Jacobsen Smoked Salt. Combine tequila, fresh lime juice, grilled orange juice and burnt orange agave syrup in a glass. Add ice and shake well.

8. Strain into a rimmed glass over clean ice. Garnish with a grilled orange slice. Enjoy!

Traeger Boulevardier Cocktail

Servings: 2
Cooking Time: 60 Minutes

Ingredients:
- 4 oranges
- 1/2 Cup honey
- 1500 mL rye whiskey
- 1 1/2 Ounce Campari
- 1 1/2 Ounce sweet vermouth
- 2 Tablespoon granulated sugar
- 3 Ounce grilled orange infused rye

Directions:
1. Supply your smoker with wood pellets and follow the start-up procedure. Preheat the grill, with the lid closed, to 350° F.

2. Slice 2 oranges in half and coat cut side with honey. Peel remaining orange and place peels on the grill. Cook 20 to 25 minutes. Grill: 350 °F

3. Remove from grill and let cool. Place orange halves cut side down directly on the grill grate and cook 20 to 30 minutes or until dark grill marks appear. Remove orange halves and allow to cool. Grill: 350 °F

4. Place orange halves into a bottle of rye whiskey and let steep for 10 to 12 hours. The longer they steep, the sweeter and more pronounced the orange flavor will be.

5. Add all ingredients into a mixing glass and stir until diluted. Strain into a fresh coupe glass and serve neat.

6. Garnish with grilled orange peel. Enjoy!

Smoked Salted Caramel White Russian

Servings: 4
Cooking Time: 20 Minutes

Ingredients:
- 16 Ounce half-and-half
- salted caramel sauce
- 6 Ounce vodka
- 6 Ounce Kahlúa

Directions:
1. Supply your smoker with wood pellets and follow the start-up procedure. Preheat the grill, with the lid closed, to 180° F.

2. Pour the half-and-half in a shallow baking dish and place directly on the grill grate. In another shallow baking dish, pour 2 to 3 cups of water and place on the grill next to the half-and-half.

3. Smoke both the half-and-half and water for 20 minutes. Remove from the grill and let cool. Grill: 180 °F

4. Place the half-and-half in the fridge until ready to use. Pour the smoked water into ice cube trays and transfer to the freezer until completely frozen.

5. Separate the smoked ice cubes into four glasses. Drizzle the salted caramel sauce around the inside of the glass.

6. Pour 1-1/2 ounce vodka and 1-1/2 ounce Kahlúa into each of the glasses and top with the smoked half-and-half. Enjoy!

Dublin Delight Cocktail

Servings: 2
Cooking Time: 20 Minutes

Ingredients:

- 2 orange, sliced
- 3 Fluid Ounce Teeling Whiskey
- 1 1/2 Fluid Ounce Smoked Simple Syrup
- 6 Dash aromatic bitters
- 6 Fluid Ounce Guinness beer
- 2 Amarena cherry, for garnish

Directions:

1. Supply your smoker with wood pellets and follow the start-up procedure. Preheat the grill, with the lid closed, to 450° F.

2. Place orange slices directly on the grill grate and cook 20 to 25 minutes. Remove from grill and let cool. Grill: 450 °F

3. In a mixing glass, add whiskey, Traeger Smoked Simple Syrup and bitters. Add ice and shake. Pour over a beer glass filled with ice and top off with cold Guinness.

4. Garnish with a grilled orange slice and Amarena cherry. Enjoy!

Cran-apple Tequila Punch With Smoked Oranges

Servings: 2
Cooking Time: 15 Minutes

Ingredients:

- 6 Cup apple juice, chilled
- 6 Cup light cranberry cocktail
- 1 Cup cranberries, fresh or thawed
- 3 Large oranges, halved
- 1 Cup sugar, for rimming glasses
- 2 Tablespoon lemon juice
- 2 Cup reposado tequila
- 1 Cup orange-flavored liqueur, such as Grand Marnier or Cointreau
- 2 Bottle sparkling wine (such as prosecco) or sparkling water

Directions:

1. Combine 1 cup each of the apple and cranberry juices, then pour into ice cube trays. If the cube molds are big enough, place a few cranberries into each cube. Freeze for 6 hours to overnight.

2. Supply your smoker with wood pellets and follow the start-up procedure. Preheat the grill, with the lid closed, to 180° F.

3. Place the orange halves cut-side down on the grill and smoke for 15 minutes. Remove from the grill and juice oranges. Reserve smoked orange juice. Grill: 180 °F

4. When ready to serve, place the sugar on a flat plate. Pour the lemon juice into a bowl that will fit the rim of each glass.

5. Carefully dip the rim of each glass in the lemon juice, then dip in the sugar to create a 1/8" sugar rim. Turn the glass right-side up and allow to dry for a few minutes before using.

6. Just before serving, mix the remaining apple juice, cranberry cocktail and smoked orange juice with the tequila, orange liqueur, and sparkling wine in a large bowl or pitcher. Taste, adding more of any ingredient to meet your preference.

7. When ready to serve, place a few ice cubes in each glass, then pour a cup of the punch over the top. Alternatively, place all of the ice cubes in the punch bowl and allow guests to help themselves. Enjoy!

Grilled Blood Orange Mimosa

Servings: 4

Cooking Time: 15 Minutes

Ingredients:
- 3 blood orange, halved
- 2 Tablespoon granulated sugar
- 1 Bottle sparkling wine
- thyme sprigs, for garnish

Directions:

1. Supply your smoker with wood pellets and follow the start-up procedure. Preheat the grill, with the lid closed, to 375° F.

2. When the grill is hot, dip the cut side of the orange halves in sugar and place cut side down directly on the grill grate. Grill: 375 °F

3. Grill the oranges for 10-15 minutes or until grill marks develop. Grill: 375 °F

4. Remove from the grill and let cool at room temperature.

5. When cool enough to handle, juice the oranges and strain through a fine strainer removing any pulp.

6. Pour 5 oz of sparkling wine into each glass and top with 1 oz blood orange juice.

7. Garnish with a sprig of thyme. Enjoy!

Garden Gimlet Cocktail

Servings: 2

Cooking Time: 45 Minutes

Ingredients:
- 2 Cup honey
- 4 lemons, zested
- 4 Sprig rosemary, plus more for garnish
- 1/2 Cup water
- 4 Slices cucumber
- 1 1/2 Ounce lime juice
- 3 Ounce vodka

Directions:

1. Supply your smoker with wood pellets and follow the start-up procedure. Preheat the grill, with the lid closed, to 180° F.

2. To make smoked lemon and rosemary honey syrup, thin 1 cup honey by adding 1/4 cup water to a shallow pan. Add lemon zest and 2 sprigs rosemary.

3. Place the pan directly on the grill grate and smoke 45 minutes to an hour. Remove from heat, strain and cool. Grill: 180 °F

4. In a cocktail shaker, muddle the cucumbers and 1oz of the smoked lemon and rosemary honey syrup.

5. After muddling, add lime juice, vodka, and ice. Shake and double strain into a coup glass.

6. Garnish with a sprig of rosemary. Enjoy!

Grilled Rabbit Tail Cocktail

Servings: 2

Cooking Time: 25 Minutes

Ingredients:
- 1 1/2 Ounce lemon juice
- 4 Ounce Apple Brandy
- 1 Ounce orange juice

- 1 Ounce Smoked Simple Syrup

Directions:

1. Supply your smoker with wood pellets and follow the start-up procedure. Preheat the grill, with the lid closed, to 350° F.

2. Place lemon halves directly on the grill grate and cook for 20-25 minutes or until grill marks appear. Remove from grill and let cool. Once cool enough to handle, juice the lemons then chill and reserve the juice. Grill: 350 ˚F

3. Using the proportions listed above and considering the size and consumption rate of your tailgate crew or party, mix all the above ingredients in a large thermos and top with a bit of ice.

4. Using 6-8 oz glasses or cups, guests can serve themselves from the thermos and garnish each drink with a grilled apple slice. Enjoy!

Smoked Hot Buttered Rum

Servings: 4
Cooking Time: 30 Minutes

Ingredients:
- 2 Cup water
- 1/4 Cup brown sugar
- 1/2 Stick butter, melted
- 1 Teaspoon ground cinnamon
- 1/4 Teaspoon ground nutmeg
- ground cloves
- salt
- 6 Ounce Rum

Directions:

1. Supply your smoker with wood pellets and follow the start-up procedure. Preheat the grill, with the lid closed, to 180° F.

2. In a shallow baking dish, combine 2 cups water with all ingredients except for the rum and place directly on the grill grate. Smoke for 30 minutes. Grill: 180 ˚F

3. Remove from the grill and pour into the pitcher of a blender. Process until somewhat frothy.

4. Pour 1.5 ounces of rum each into 4 glasses. Split hot butter mixture evenly between the four glasses.

5. Garnish with a cinnamon stick and freshly grated nutmeg. Enjoy!

Smoky Mountain Bramble Cocktail

Servings: 2
Cooking Time: 15 Minutes

Ingredients:
- 16 Ounce blackberries
- 2 Cup sugar
- 10 smoked blackberries
- 3 Ounce vodka
- 1 1/2 Ounce Alpine Distilling Preserve Liqueur
- 1 1/2 Ounce lemon juice
- 1 Ounce smoked blackberry syrup

Directions:

1. Supply your smoker with wood pellets and follow the start-up procedure. Preheat the grill, with the lid closed, to 180° F.

2. To make Smoked Blackberry Simple Syrup: Place blackberries on a grill mat and smoke for 15 to 20 minutes. Grill: 180 ˚F

3. Combine 1 cup water and sugar in a small sauce pan and warm over medium heat until sugar dissolves. Remove from heat and place 2/3 of blackberries in the simple syrup and macerate.

4. Strain through a fine mesh strainer and store for up to 14 days.

5. To make the cocktail: Muddle 4 to 5 smoked blackberries in a cocktail shaker. Add vodka, Preserve Liqueur, lemon and smoked blackberry syrup. Add ice and shake vigorously. Double strain into an old fashioned glass.

6. Garnish with a smoked blackberry and lemon twist. Enjoy!

Smoked Cold Brew Coffee

Servings: 8
Cooking Time: 120 Minutes

Ingredients:
- 12 Ounce coarse ground coffee
- heavy cream or milk
- sugar

Directions:

1. Place half the coffee grounds in a plastic container and slowly pour 3-1/2 cups water over the top of the grounds. Add remaining grounds and pour another 3-1/2 cups water over the top in a circular motion.

2. Press the grounds down into the water using the back of a spoon. Cover and transfer to the refrigerator and let sit for 18 to 24 hours.

3. Remove from refrigerator and strain into a clean container through a fine mesh strainer or double layer of cheese cloth.

4. Supply your smoker with wood pellets and follow the start-up procedure. Preheat the grill, with the lid closed, to 180° F.

5. Pour cold brew into a shallow baking dish and place directly on the grill grate. Smoke for 1 to 2 hours depending on desired level of smoke. Grill: 180 ℉

6. Remove from grill and place over an ice bath to cool. Drink as is over ice, with cream or sugar or use in your favorite coffee recipes. Enjoy!

Fig Slider Cocktail

Servings: 2
Cooking Time: 15 Minutes

Ingredients:
- 2 peach, halved
- 4 oranges
- honey
- sugar
- 2 Teaspoon orange fig spread
- 1 Ounce fresh lemon juice
- 4 Ounce bourbon
- 3 Ounce honey glazed grilled orange juice

Directions:

1. Supply your smoker with wood pellets and follow the start-up procedure. Preheat the grill, with the lid closed, to 325° F.

2. Pit the peach and cut in half. Cut one of the oranges in half. Glaze the peach and orange cut sides with honey and set directly on the grill grate until the honey caramelizes and fruit has grill marks. Grill: 325 ℉

3. Cut the second orange into wheels and coat with granulated sugar on both sides. Place directly on the grill grate and cook 15 minutes each side or until grill marks form. Grill: 325 ℉

4. In a mixing tin, add grilled peaches, bourbon, orange fig spread, fresh lemon juice and honey glazed orange juice.

5. Shake vigorously to blend the juices and fig spread. Strain over clean ice. Garnish with grilled orange wheel. Enjoy!

Smoked Texas Ranch Water

Servings: 4
Cooking Time: 60 Minutes

Ingredients:
- 3 Whole limes
- 1 Tablespoon Blackened Saskatchewan Rub
- 12 Ounce blanco tequila
- 24 Ounce Topo Chico or other sparkling mineral water
- 8 Slices jalapeño, optional

Directions:
1. Supply your smoker with wood pellets and follow the start-up procedure. Preheat the grill, with the lid closed, to 225° F.
2. Cut two of the limes in half and sprinkle with Traeger Blackened Saskatchewan Rub. Place the four lime halves on the edge of the grill grate and smoke for 1 hour. Remove from grill and set aside to cool. Grill: 225 ˚F
3. Pour some of the rub onto a small plate. Cut the third lime into 1/4 wedges and use the lime to rub the rim of 4 cocktail glasses, turn the glasses upside down, and into the rub to salt the rim.
4. Place several ice cubes into your rimmed glasses and pour 3 ounces tequila, 6 ounces Topo Chico, squeeze the juice of one smoked lime (discard after squeezing), and add one fresh lime wedge to each. If using the jalapeño, add one or two slices to each glass (muddle if desired).
5. Stir to combine and enjoy!

Smoky Scotch & Ginger Cocktail

Servings: 2
Cooking Time: 60 Minutes

Ingredients:
- 1 Ounce ginger syrup
- 1/2 Ounce brandied cherry juice
- 1/2 Ounce agave nectar
- 4 Ounce scotch
- 1 1/2 Ounce lemon juice
- 2 Slices grilled lemon, for garnish
- 2 cherry, for garnish

Directions:
1. Supply your smoker with wood pellets and follow the start-up procedure. Preheat the grill, with the lid closed, to 180° F.
2. For the smoked ginger cherry syrup: Place ginger syrup, cherry juice and agave nectar in a shallow dish and place the dish directly on the grill grate.
3. Smoke for 60 minutes, or until the mixture has picked up the smoke flavor. Remove from grill and allow to cool for 30 minutes. Grill: 180 ˚F
4. Place smoked ginger cherry syrup, scotch and lemon juice into a shaker tin and shake with ice. Strain into a glass over fresh ice and garnish with a grilled lemon wheel and cherry. Enjoy!

Smoked Raspberry Bubbler Cocktail

Servings: 2
Cooking Time: 45 Minutes

Ingredients:
- 2 Cup fresh raspberries
- Smoked Simple Syrup
- 8 Ounce sparkling wine

Directions:
1. Supply your smoker with wood pellets and follow the start-up procedure. Preheat the grill, with the lid closed, to 180° F.

2. Smoked Raspberry Syrup: Place 1 cup fresh raspberries on a grill mat and smoke for 30 minutes. Grill: 180 °F

3. After the raspberries have been smoked, set a few aside for garnish. Place the remainder into a shallow sheet pan with Traeger Smoked Simple Syrup. Place back on the grill grate and let smoke for 45 minutes. Remove from heat and allow to cool. Strain and refrigerate until ready to use. Grill: 180 °F

4. Place 1 ounce of the smoked raspberry syrup in the bottom of a champagne flute and top off with sparkling white wine or champagne.

5. Garnish with smoked raspberries. Enjoy!

Smoked Hibiscus Sparkler

Servings: 4
Cooking Time: 30 Minutes

Ingredients:
- 1/2 Cup sugar
- 2 Tablespoon dried hibiscus flowers
- 1 Bottle sparkling wine
- crystallized ginger, for garnish

Directions:
1. Supply your smoker with wood pellets and follow the start-up procedure. Preheat the grill, with the lid closed, to 180° F.

2. Place water in a shallow baking dish and place directly on the grill grate. Smoke the water for 30 minutes or until desired smoke flavor is achieved. Grill: 180 °F

3. Pour water into a small saucepan and add sugar and hibiscus flowers. Bring to a simmer over medium heat and cook until sugar is dissolved.

4. Strain out the hibiscus flowers and transfer your simple syrup to a small container and refrigerate until chilled.

5. Pour 1/2 ounce smoked hibiscus simple syrup in the bottom of a champagne glass and top with sparkling wine.

6. Drop in a few pieces of crystallized ginger to garnish. Enjoy!

Ryes And Shine Cocktail

Servings: 2
Cooking Time: 30 Minutes

Ingredients:
- 2 lemon, cut into wheels for garnish
- 6 Tablespoon granulated sugar
- 2 Ounce rye
- 1 Ounce bourbon
- 3 Ounce lemon juice
- 1 Ounce Smoked Simple Syrup
- 6 Dash Fernet-Branca

Directions:
1. Supply your smoker with wood pellets and follow the start-up procedure. Preheat the grill, with the lid closed, to 325° F.

2. Toss lemon wheels with granulated sugar to coat on both sides. Place wheels directly on the grill grate and cook for 15 minutes on each side or until grill marks form. Grill: 325 °F

3. Add rye, bourbon, lemon juice, Traeger Smoked Simple Syrup and Fernet-Branca to a shaker and shake until slightly diluted (about 10 to 15 seconds).

4. Pour into a fresh glass, serve neat and garnish with a grilled lemon wheel. Enjoy!

Smoked Irish Coffee

Servings: 2

Cooking Time: 15 Minutes

Ingredients:

- 10 Ounce hot coffee
- 1/2 Cup heavy cream
- 1 Tablespoon sugar
- 2 Ounce Irish whiskey
- freshly grated nutmeg, for garnish (optional)

Directions:

1. Supply your smoker with wood pellets and follow the start-up procedure. Preheat the grill, with the lid closed, to 180° F.

2. Place the coffee and cream in separate shallow baking dishes and place both directly on the grill grate. Smoke for 10 to 15 minutes until the liquids pick up a slight smoke flavor. Grill: 180 ˚F

3. Remove from the grill and cool the cream. When the cream is cool, add sugar and whip in a stand mixer or by hand to soft peaks.

4. Pour the hot coffee into two mugs then add 2 ounces of whiskey to each.

5. Top with smoked whipped cream and finish with freshly grated nutmeg, if desired. Enjoy!

Smoked Pumpkin Spice Latte

Servings: 4

Cooking Time: 45 Minutes

Ingredients:

- 1 Small sugar pumpkin
- olive oil
- 1 Can sweetened condensed milk
- 1 Cup whole milk
- 2 Tablespoon Smoked Simple Syrup
- 1 Teaspoon pumpkin pie spice
- pinch of salt
- cinnamon
- whipped cream
- shaved nutmeg
- 8 Ounce smoked cold brew coffee

Directions:

1. Supply your smoker with wood pellets and follow the start-up procedure. Preheat the grill, with the lid closed, to 325° F.

2. Cut the sugar pumpkin in half, scoop out the seeds and discard. Place the pumpkin halves cut side up on a baking sheet and brush lightly with olive oil.

3. Place the sheet tray directly on the grill grate and cook 45 minutes or until the flesh is tender. Remove from heat and place on the counter to cool. Grill: 325 ˚F

4. When the pumpkin is cool enough to handle, scoop out the flesh and mash until smooth.

5. Place 3 Tbsp of the pumpkin puree in a separate bowl and reserve the remaining for another use.

6. Add the sweetened condensed milk, whole milk, Traeger Smoked Simple Syrup, pumpkin pie seasoning and salt to the pumpkin puree. Whisk to combine.

7. Pour the cold brew over ice, add desired amount of pumpkin spice creamer and top with whipped cream, cinnamon, and shaved nutmeg if desired. Enjoy!

Strawberry Mule Cocktail

Servings: 2

Cooking Time: 15 Minutes

Ingredients:

- 8 grilled strawberries, plus more for serving
- 3 Ounce vodka
- 1 Ounce Smoked Simple Syrup

- 1 Ounce lemon juice
- 6 Ounce ginger beer
- fresh mint leaves

Directions:

1. Supply your smoker with wood pellets and follow the start-up procedure. Preheat the grill, with the lid closed, to 400° F.

2. Place strawberries directly on the grill grate and cook 15 minutes or until grill marks appear. Grill: 400 °F

3. For the cocktail: Add vodka, grilled strawberries, Traeger Smoked Simple Syrup and lemon juice to a shaker. Shake vigorously.

4. Double strain into a fresh glass or copper mug with crushed ice.

5. Top with ginger beer and garnish with extra grilled strawberries and fresh mint. Enjoy!

Smoking Gun Cocktail

Servings: 2

Cooking Time: 45 Minutes

Ingredients:

- 2 Jar vermouth soaked cocktail onions
- 3 Ounce vodka
- 1 Ounce dry vermouth

Directions:

1. Supply your smoker with wood pellets and follow the start-up procedure. Preheat the grill, with the lid closed, to 180° F.

2. To make the smoked onion vermouth: Pour jar of vermouth soaked cocktail onions onto a shallow sheet pan. Smoke for 45 minutes. Remove from grill and set aside to chill. Grill: 180 °F

3. To make the cocktail: Add vodka, 1 teaspoon liquid from the smoked onions and dry vermouth to a mixing glass. Shake and strain into a chilled martini glass.

4. Garnish with smoked cocktail onions on a skewer. Enjoy!

Grilled Hawaiian Sour

Servings: 2

Cooking Time: 15 Minutes

Ingredients:

- 2 Whole pineapple, trimmed and sliced
- 1/2 Cup palm sugar
- 3 Ounce bourbon
- 2 Ounce grilled pineapple juice
- 2 Ounce Smoked Simple Syrup
- 10 Ounce lemon juice
- 2 grilled pineapple chunk, for garnish
- 2 pineapple leaf, for garnish

Directions:

1. Supply your smoker with wood pellets and follow the start-up procedure. Preheat the grill, with the lid closed, to 350° F.

2. For the Grilled Pineapple Juice: Dust pineapple slices with palm sugar. Place directly on the grill grate and cook for 8 minutes per side. Grill: 350 °F

3. Remove from grill and let cool. Reserve a few pieces for garnish. Run remaining pineapple pieces through centrifugal juicer to extract juice.

4. To Make the Drink: Add bourbon, grilled pineapple juice, simple syrup and lemon juice to a cocktail strainer with ice. Shake vigorously. Double strain into a chilled coupe glass. Garnish with grilled pineapple chunk and pineapple leaf. Enjoy!

Smoked Pineapple Hotel Nacional Cocktail

Servings: 2
Cooking Time: 20 Minutes

Ingredients:

- 2 pineapple
- 1/2 Cup water
- 1/2 Cup sugar
- 3 Fluid Ounce white rum
- 1 1/2 Fluid Ounce lime juice
- 1 1/2 Fluid Ounce Pineapple Syrup
- 1 Fluid Ounce apricot brandy
- 2 Dash Angostura bitters

Directions:

1. For the Syrup: Supply your smoker with wood pellets and follow the start-up procedure. Preheat the grill, with the lid closed, to 180° F.

2. Trim both ends of the pineapple, discard the ends. Cut the pineapple into slices about 3/4" thick. Don't worry about the skin, it doesn't hurt to leave it on. Place the pineapple slices on the grill and smoke for about 15 minutes on each sideTrim both ends of the pineapple and discard the ends. Cut the pineapple into slices about 3/4 inch thick. Don't worry about the skin, it doesn't hurt to leave it on. Place the pineapple slices on the grill and smoke for about 15 minutes per side. Grill: 180 °F

3. While the pineapple is smoking, combine 1/4 cup water and sugar in a saucepan over low heat, stirring constantly, until sugar is dissolved. Pour syrup into a large bowl and set aside.

4. When the pineapple is done cooking, cut each slice into eight or so wedges and add the wedges to the bowl with the simple syrup, tossing to coat and cover.

5. Leave the mixture to macerate for at least 4 hours (or up to 24) in the refrigerator, stirring from time to time.

6. Strain the syrup into a clean bowl through a fine-mesh strainer and press on the pineapple with a ladle to extract as much liquid as possible. You can bottle and refrigerate the syrup for up to 4 days.

7. To make the cocktail: Combine the rum, lime juice, pineapple syrup, apricot brandy, and bitters in a cocktail shaker or mixing glass. Fill with ice cubes and shake until cold.

8. Strain into a chilled cocktail glass. Garnish with a lime wheel and serve. Enjoy!

Traeger Old Fashioned

Servings: 2
Cooking Time: 60 Minutes

Ingredients:

- 2 orange
- 2 Cup cherries
- 3 Ounce bourbon
- 1 Ounce Smoked Simple Syrup
- 8 Dash Bitters Lab Apricot Vanilla Bitters

Directions:

1. Supply your smoker with wood pellets and follow the start-up procedure. Preheat the grill, with the lid closed, to 180° F.

2. While Traeger preheats, slice whole orange into wheels.

3. Place cherries on a small sheet pan and place in the Traeger. Place orange slices directly on the grill grate.

4. Smoke cherries for 1 hour and oranges for 25 minutes, depending on taste, before removing from the grill. Let oranges and cherries cool. Grill: 180 °F

5. Pour bourbon into glass, followed by Traeger Smoked Simple Syrup and bitters. Add ice and stir for 45 seconds or until drink is well-diluted.

6. Strain contents into new glass over fresh ice. Skewer orange wheel and add cherry for garnish. Enjoy!

Smoked Eggnog

Servings: 4

Cooking Time: 60 Minutes

Ingredients:

- 2 Cup whole milk
- 1 Cup heavy cream
- 4 egg yolk
- Cup sugar
- 3 Ounce bourbon
- 1 Teaspoon vanilla extract
- 1 Teaspoon nutmeg
- 4 egg white
- whipped cream

Directions:

1. Plan ahead, this recipe requires chill time.

2. Supply your smoker with wood pellets and follow the start-up procedure. Preheat the grill, with the lid closed, to 180° F.

3. Pour the milk and the cream into a baking pan and smoke on the Traeger for 60 minutes. Grill: 180 °F

4. Meanwhile, in the bowl of a stand mixer, beat the egg yolks until they lighten in color. Gradually add 1/3 cup sugar and continue to beat until sugar completely dissolves.

5. After the milk and cream have smoked, add them along with the bourbon, vanilla and nutmeg into the egg mixture and stir to combine.

6. Place the egg whites in the bowl of a stand mixer and beat to soft peaks. When you lift the beaters the whites will make a peak that slightly curls down.

7. With the mixer still running, gradually add 1 tablespoon of sugar and beat until stiff peaks form.

8. Gently fold the egg whites into the cream mixture and then whisk to thoroughly combine.

9. Chill eggnog for a couple hours to let the flavors meld. Garnish with a dash of nutmeg and whipped cream on top. Enjoy!

Smoked Plum And Thyme Fizz Cocktail

Servings: 2

Cooking Time: 60 Minutes

Ingredients:

- 6 fresh plums
- 4 Fluid Ounce vodka
- 1 1/2 Fluid Ounce fresh lemon juice
- 2 Ounce smoked plum and thyme simple syrup
- 4 Fluid Ounce club soda
- 2 Slices smoked plum, for garnish
- 2 Sprig fresh thyme, for garnish
- 8 Sprig thyme
- 2 Cup Smoked Simple Syrup

Directions:

1. Supply your smoker with wood pellets and follow the start-up procedure. Preheat the grill, with the lid closed, to 180° F.

2. Cut plums in half and remove the pit. Place the plum halves directly on the grill grate and smoke for 25 minutes. Grill: 180 °F

3. For the Plum and Thyme Simple Syrup: After 25 minutes, remove plums from the grill and cut into quarters. Add plums and thyme sprigs to 1 cup of Traeger Smoked Simple Syrup.

Smoke the mixture for 45 minutes. Remove from grill, strain and let cool. Grill: 180 °F

4. Add vodka, fresh lemon juice and smoked plum and thyme simple syrup to a mixing glass.

5. Add ice and shake. Strain over clean ice, top off with club soda and garnish with a piece of thyme and slice of smoked plum. Enjoy!

Grilled Peach Sour Cocktail

Servings: 2
Cooking Time: 15 Minutes

Ingredients:

- 2 peach, sliced
- 2 Tablespoon sugar
- 1 1/2 Ounce Smoked Simple Syrup
- 4 Ounce bourbon
- 6 Dash Bitters Lab Apricot Vanilla Bitters
- 2 Sprig fresh thyme, for garnish

Directions:

1. Supply your smoker with wood pellets and follow the start-up procedure. Preheat the grill, with the lid closed, to 325° F.

2. Toss peach slices with granulated sugar and place directly on grill grate. Cook for 20 minutes or until grill marks form. Remove from grill and let cool. Grill: 325 °F

3. Place peaches and Traeger Smoked Simple Syrup into tin and muddle. Peaches should form about an ounce of juice during the muddling. Once completed, add remaining ingredients and shake.

4. Pour contents into glass over fresh ice and garnish with fresh thyme. Enjoy!

Smoked Jacobsen Salt Margarita

Servings: 2
Cooking Time: 1 Day

Ingredients:

- kosher sea salt
- 3 Cup Jacobsen Co. Honey
- 6 Ounce tequila
- 4 Ounce fresh squeezed lime juice
- 1/2 Cup Jacobsen Salt Co. Cherrywood Smoked Salt or smoked kosher salt
- 2 Ounce simple syrup
- 2 Teaspoon orange liqueur

Directions:

1. If making your own smoked salt, take kosher sea salt (however much you want to smoke) and spread it out on a tray.

2. Supply your smoker with wood pellets and follow the start-up procedure. Preheat the grill, with the lid closed, to 165° F.

3. Place tray of salt directly on the grill grate and smoke for about 24 hours, stirring the salt every 8 hours. Once it has smoked for 24 hours, take off grill and use in all your favorite dishes. Note: If you want to skip the long smoke session, use Jacobsen Salt Co. Cherrywood Smoked Salt. Grill: 165 °F

4. Simple Syrup: Put the honey and 1 cup water in a small saucepan. Cook over low heat, stirring, for about 20 min.

5. Fill a cocktail shaker with ice. Add tequila, lime juice, simple syrup and orange liqueur. Cover and shake until mixed and chilled, about 30 seconds.

6. Place smoked salt on a plate. Press the rim of a chilled rocks glass into the salt to rim the edge. Strain margarita into the glass. Enjoy!

Honey Glazed Grapefruit Shandy Cocktail

Servings: 2
Cooking Time: 20 Minutes

Ingredients:

- 4 grapefruits
- 4 Tablespoon honey
- granulated sugar
- 2 Ounce bourbon
- 1 Ounce Smoked Simple Syrup
- 4 Ounce honey glazed grilled grapefruit, juiced
- 2 Bottle Ballast Point Grapefruit Sculpin

Directions:

1. Supply your smoker with wood pellets and follow the start-up procedure. Preheat the grill, with the lid closed, to 375° F.
2. For the honey glazed grapefruit: Slice one grapefruit in half and coat with 2 tablespoons honey.
3. Take the other grapefruit and slice into wheels. Toss the wheels in granulated sugar until well coated.
4. Place the grapefruit halves and wheels directly on the grill grate, cut side down, and cook for 20 to 30 minutes. Remove from grill and set the wheels aside. Grill: 375 °F
5. Squeeze the grapefruit halves into a measuring cup. It should yield about 2 oz juice.
6. Pour the grapefruit juice into a shaker and add bourbon and Traeger Smoked Simple Syrup then top with ice. Shake for 10-15 seconds.
7. Strain into glass, add ice and fill with beer. Garnish with the grilled grapefruit wheel. Enjoy!

Smoked Pomegranate Lemonade Cocktail

Servings: 2
Cooking Time: 45 Minutes

Ingredients:

- 32 Ounce POM Juice
- 2 Cup pomegranate seeds
- 3 Ounce vodka
- 8 Ounce lemonade
- lemon wheel, for garnish
- fresh mint, for garnish

Directions:

1. Supply your smoker with wood pellets and follow the start-up procedure. Preheat the grill, with the lid closed, to 225° F.
2. For the Smoked Pomegranate Ice Cubes: Pour one small container of POM juice and 1 cup of pomegranate seeds into a shallow sheet pan. Smoke on the Traeger for 45 minutes. Pull off grill and let sit until cooled. Grill: 180 °F
3. Pour smoked POM juice into ice molds of your choice and put into freezer.
4. When ready to serve, place the frozen pomegranate cubes into a mason jar. Pour vodka and lemonade over the ice cubes.
5. Garnish with a lemon wheel and fresh mint. Enjoy!

In Traeger Fashion Cocktail

Servings: 2
Cooking Time: 20 Minutes

Ingredients:

- 2 Whole orange peel
- 2 Whole lemon peel
- 3 Ounce bourbon
- 1 Ounce Smoked Simple Syrup

- 6 Dash Bitters Lab Charred Cedar & Currant Bitters

Directions:

1. Supply your smoker with wood pellets and follow the start-up procedure. Preheat the grill, with the lid closed, to 350° F.

2. Place the lemon and orange peel directly on the grill grate and cook 20 to 25 minutes or until lightly browned. Grill: 350 °F

3. Add bourbon, Traeger Smoked Simple Syrup and bitters to a mixing glass and stir over ice. Stir until glass is chilled and contents are well diluted.

4. Strain into a new glass over fresh ice and garnish with grilled lemon and orange peel. Enjoy!

Smoked Barnburner Cocktail

Servings: 2

Cooking Time: 45 Minutes

Ingredients:

- 16 Ounce fresh raspberries
- 1/2 Cup Smoked Simple Syrup
- 1 1/2 Ounce smoked raspberry syrup
- 3 Ounce reposado tequila
- 1 Ounce lime juice
- 1 Ounce lemon juice
- 2 grilled lime wheel, for garnish

Directions:

1. Supply your smoker with wood pellets and follow the start-up procedure. Preheat the grill, with the lid closed, to 180° F.

2. For Smoked Raspberry Syrup: Place fresh raspberries on a grill mat and smoke for 30 minutes. After the raspberries have been smoked, reserve a few for garnish and place the remainder into a shallow sheet pan with Traeger Smoked Simple Syrup. Grill: 180 °F

3. Place sheet pan on the grill grate and smoke for 45 minutes. Remove from grill and let cool. Strain through a fine mesh sieve discarding solids. Transfer the syrup to the refrigerator until ready to use. Makes about 1/2 cup of smoked raspberry syrup. Grill: 180 °F

4. For cocktail: Add 3/4 ounce smoked raspberry syrup, tequila, lime juice and lemon juice with ice into a mixing glass. Shake and pour over clean ice. Garnish with smoked raspberries and a grilled lime wheel. Enjoy!

Smoke And Bubz Cocktail

Servings: 2

Cooking Time: 45 Minutes

Ingredients:

- 16 Ounce POM Juice
- 2 Cup pomegranate seeds
- 6 Ounce sparkling white wine
- 2 lemon twist, for garnish
- 2 Teaspoon pomegranate seeds

Directions:

1. Supply your smoker with wood pellets and follow the start-up procedure. Preheat the grill, with the lid closed, to 180° F.

2. For the Smoked Pomegranate Juice: Pour POM juice and a cup of pomegranate seeds into a shallow sheet pan. Smoke on the Traeger for 45 minutes. Pull off grill, strain, discard seeds and let sit until chilled. Grill: 180 °F

3. Add 1-1/2 ounces of the smoked pomegranate juice to the bottom of a champagne flute.

4. Add sparkling white wine, a few fresh pomegranate seeds and a lemon twist to garnish. Enjoy!

Grilled Peach Mint Julep

Servings: 2

Cooking Time: 45 Minutes

Ingredients:

- 2 Whole peach
- 4 Ounce whiskey
- 2 Cup sugar
- 4 Tablespoon pink peppercorns
- 20 Whole fresh mint leaves, plus more for garnish
- 2 lime wedge, for garnish
- 4 Ounce bourbon

Directions:

1. For the Grilled Whiskey Peaches: cut peach into slices, then soak peach slices in whiskey in the refrigerator for 4 to 6 hours.

2. For the Pink Peppercorn Simple Syrup: In a shallow pan, combine sugar, 1 cup water and pink peppercorns.

3. Supply your smoker with wood pellets and follow the start-up procedure. Preheat the grill, with the lid closed, to 180° F.

4. Cook syrup down on the grill for 30 minutes, or until desired smoke flavor has been reached. Remove from the grill. Grill: 180 ˚F

5. Increase Traeger temperature to 350˚F and preheat. Place the whiskey peach slices directly on the grill grate and cook 10 to 12 minutes or until peaches soften and get grill marks. Grill: 350 ˚F

6. To make the Julep: Muddle 1/2 ounce Pink Peppercorn Simple Syrup with 10 fresh mint leaves and 4 slices of grilled whiskey peaches.

7. Add crushed ice over the rim of the glass. Pour bourbon over the crushed ice and stir. Garnish with 1 large sprig of mint and fresh lime. Enjoy!

Traeger Paloma Cocktail

Servings: 2

Cooking Time: 25 Minutes

Ingredients:

- 4 grapefruit, halved
- Smoked Simple Syrup
- 10 Stick cinnamon
- 3 Ounce reposado tequila
- 1 Ounce lime juice
- 1 Ounce Smoked Simple Syrup
- grilled lime, for garnish
- cinnamon stick, for garnish

Directions:

1. Supply your smoker with wood pellets and follow the start-up procedure. Preheat the grill, with the lid closed, to 350° F.

2. Grilled Grapefruit Juice: Cut 2 grapefruits in half. Place a cinnamon stick in each grapefruit half and glaze with Traeger Smoked Simple Syrup. Place on grill grate and cook for 20 minutes or until edges start to burn and it acquires grill marks. Remove from heat and let cool. Grill: 350 ˚F

3. After grapefruits have cooled, squeeze and strain juice. It should yield 10 to 12 ounces of juice.

4. In a mixing glass, add tequila, lime juice, Traeger Smoked Simple Syrup and 2 ounces of the grilled grapefruit juice.

5. Add ice and shake. Strain over ice in an old fashioned glass.

6. Add a grilled lime slice and cinnamon stick to garnish. Enjoy!

Grilled Frozen Strawberry Lemonade

Servings: 4
Cooking Time: 15 Minutes

Ingredients:
- 1 Pound fresh strawberries
- 1/2 Cup turbinado sugar
- 8 lemon, halved
- 1/4 Cup Cointreau
- 1/4 Cup simple syrup
- 2 Cup ice
- 1 Cup Titos Vodka

Directions:
1. Supply your smoker with wood pellets and follow the start-up procedure. Preheat the grill, with the lid closed, to High heat.
2. Dip the lemon halves in turbinado sugar and place directly on the grill grate. Toss the strawberries with remaining sugar and place next to the lemons.
3. Cook until grill marks develop on both, about 15 min for lemons and 10 min for strawberries.
4. Remove from heat and let cool.
5. Juice grilled lemons straining out any seeds or pulp. Pour into a blender pitcher.
6. Remove stems from grilled strawberries and place in blender pitcher with lemon juice. Add simple syrup, vodka, cointreau, and 2 cups of ice.
7. Puree until smooth and transfer to 4-6 glasses. Garnish with grilled strawberries and grilled lemon slices if desired. Enjoy!

Smoked Berry Cocktail

Servings: 2
Cooking Time: 15 Minutes

Ingredients:
- 1/2 Cup strawberries, stemmed
- 1/2 Cup blackberries
- 1/2 Cup blueberries
- 8 Ounce bourbon or iced tea
- 2 Ounce lime juice
- 3 Ounce simple syrup
- soda water
- fresh mint, for garnish

Directions:
1. Supply your smoker with wood pellets and follow the start-up procedure. Preheat the grill, with the lid closed, to 180° F.
2. Wash berries well, spread them on a clean cookie sheet and place on the grill. Smoke berries for 15 minutes. Grill: 180 °F
3. Remove berries from grill and transfer to a blender. Puree berries until smooth then pass through a fine mesh strainer to remove seeds.
4. To create a layered cocktail, pour 2 ounces of berry puree in the bottom of a glass. Next, pour 2 ounces of bourbon or iced tea over the back of a spoon into the glass, then 1/2 ounce lime juice and 1/2 ounce simple syrup, top with soda water and ice. Finish with mint or extra berries for garnish.
5. Repeat the same process for 3 more servings. Enjoy!

Smoked Ice Mojito Slurpee

Servings: 2
Cooking Time: 30 Minutes

Ingredients:
- water
- 1 Cup white rum
- 1/2 Cup lime juice
- 1/4 Cup Smoked Simple Syrup
- 12 Whole fresh mint leaves

- 4 Sprig mint
- 4 Whole lime wedge, for garnish

Directions:

1. Supply your smoker with wood pellets and follow the start-up procedure. Preheat the grill, with the lid closed, to 180° F.

2. For optimal flavor, use Super Smoke if available. Grill: 180 ˚F

3. Remove water from grill and pour smoked water into ice cube trays. Place in freezer until frozen.

4. Add rum, lime juice, Traeger Smoked Simple Syrup, mint and smoked ice to a blender.

5. Blend until a slushy consistency and pour into glasses.

6. Garnish with a mint sprig and lime wedge. Enjoy!

Bacon Old-fashioned Cocktail

Servings: 2

Cooking Time: 20 Minutes

Ingredients:

- 16 Slices bacon
- 1/2 Cup warm water (110°F to 115°F)
- 1500 mL bourbon
- 1/2 Fluid Ounce maple syrup
- 4 Dash Angostura bitters
- 2 fresh orange peel

Directions:

1. Smoke bacon prior to making Old Fashioned using this recipe for Applewood Smoked Bacon.

2. To Make Bacon: Supply your smoker with wood pellets and follow the start-up procedure. Preheat the grill, with the lid closed, to 325° F.

3. Place bacon in a single layer on a cooling rack that fits inside a baking sheet pan. Cook in Traeger for 15-20 minutes or until bacon is browned and crispy. Reserve bacon for later. Let the fat cool slightly; you'll use the fat to infuse the bourbon. Grill: 325 ˚F

4. Combine 1/4 cup of warm (not hot) liquid bacon fat with the entire contents of a 750ml bottle of bourbon in a glass or heavy plastic container.

5. Use a fork to stir well. Let it sit on the counter for a few hours, stirring every so often.

6. After about four hours, put bourbon fat mixture into the freezer. After about an hour, the fat will congeal and you can simply scoop it out with a spoon. You can fine-strain the mixture through a sieve to remove all fat if desired.

7. Combine ingredients with ice and stir until cold. Strain over fresh ice in an Old Fashioned glass and garnish with reserved bacon and orange peel. Enjoy!

RECIPE INDEX

Grilled Rabbit Tail Cocktail 151
Grilled Raspberry Chipotle Pork Ribs 60
Grilled Ratatouille Salad 20
Grilled Trout With Citrus & Basil 74
Grilled Whole Steelhead Fillet 74

H
Hawaiian Pineapple Pork Butt 64
Hawaiian Pulled Pig 66
Herb Roasted Turkey 103
Honey Balsamic Salmon 82
Honey Glazed Grapefruit Shandy Cocktail 161
Honey Pork Belly Burnt Ends 71
Honey-soy Garlic Salmon 78

I
In Traeger Fashion Cocktail 161

J
Jalapeño Poppers With Chipotle Sour Cream 143
Jalapeño-bacon Pork Tenderloin 62

L
Lemon Herb Grilled Salmon 85
Lemon Scallops Wrapped In Bacon 76
Lemon Shrimp Scampi 89
Lemon Strawberry Rhubarb Pie 39
Lip-smackin' Pork Loin 69
Lobster Tail 87

M
Maple Baby Backs 69
Marinated Grilled Honey Chicken Wings 102
Mashed Red Potatoes 26
Mexican Mahi Mahi With Baja Cabbage Slaw 80
Mezcal Shrimp With Salsa De Molcajete 91
Mint Butter Chocolate Chip Cookies 41

O
Oktoberfest Pretzel Mustard Chicken 109
Oysters In The Shell 82

Oysters Margarita 76

P
Parmesan Roasted Cauliflower 32
Philly Cheese Onion Steaks 129
Pig Pops (sweet-hot Bacon On A Stick) 140
Pigs In A Blanket 138
Pineapple-pepper Pork Kebabs 59
Pizza Bites 49
Pork Belly Burnt Ends 70
Pork Loin Porchetta 57
Potato Asoaragus Lamb 116
Potluck Salad With Smoked Cornbread 24
Pound Cake 34
Pretzel Rolls 46
Pull-apart Dinner Rolls 49
Pulled Pork Loaded Nachos 135

R
Reverse Seared Rib-eye Caps 114
Reverse-seared Tri-tip 127
Roasted Artichokes With Garlic Butter 31
Roasted Beet & Bacon Salad 29
Roasted Fall Vegetables 19
Roasted Garlic Herb Fries 29
Roasted Jalapeno Cheddar Deviled Eggs 17
Roasted New Potatoes 22
Roasted Pickled Beets 27
Roasted Potato Poutine 19
Roasted Pumpkin Seeds 18
Roasted Red Pepper Dip 141
Roasted Red Pepper White Bean Dip 21
Roasted Sheet Pan Vegetables 24
Roasted Vegetable Napoleon 22
Ryes And Shine Cocktail 155

S
S'mores Dip Skillet 46
Salt-crusted Prime Rib 114

Savory Cheesecake With Bourbon Pecan Topping 44

Savory Chili Mac And Cheese 131

Scalloped Potatoes With Ham, Corn And Bacon 56

Seared Ahi Tuna Steak With Soy Sauce 85

Shrimp Cabbage Tacos With Lime Cream 79

Simple Cream Cheese Sausage Balls 138

Smoke And Bubz Cocktail 162

Smoked Airline Chicken 93

Smoked Apple Chicken Leg Quarters 109

Smoked Apple Cider 148

Smoked Avocado Turkey Tamale Pie 94

Smoked Barnburner Cocktail 162

Smoked Berry Cocktail 164

Smoked Burgers 128

Smoked Cashews 140

Smoked Cheese 141

Smoked Cheese Beef Burgers 130

Smoked Cheesy Chicken Quesadilla 108

Smoked Chicken Fajita Quesadillas 100

Smoked Chicken Leg & Thigh Quarters 96

Smoked Chicken Steak Sandwiches 125

Smoked Chicken Vermicelli Noodles 100

Smoked Chuck Roast Tater Tot Casserole 117

Smoked Cold Brew Coffee 153

Smoked Curry Ketchup Pork Ribs 72

Smoked Eggnog 159

Smoked Garlic Prime Rib Roast 131

Smoked Hibiscus Sparkler 155

Smoked Hot Buttered Rum 152

Smoked Ice Mojito Slurpee 164

Smoked Irish Coffee 156

Smoked Jacobsen Salt Margarita 160

Smoked Jalapeño Poppers 25

Smoked Lemon Cheesecake 48

Smoked Macaroni Salad 26

Smoked Mango Shrimp 81

Smoked Maple Syrup Thanksgiving Turkey 97

Smoked Mulled Wine 146

Smoked Mushrooms 23

Smoked Parmesan Herb Popcorn 31

Smoked Pineapple Hotel Nacional Cocktail 158

Smoked Plum And Thyme Fizz Cocktail 159

Smoked Pomegranate Lemonade Cocktail 161

Smoked Pork Tenderloin 58

Smoked Pumpkin Spice Latte 156

Smoked Quarters 107

Smoked Raspberry Bubbler Cocktail 154

Smoked Rendezvous Ribs 54

Smoked Salted Caramel White Russian 149

Smoked Sangria 147

Smoked Texas Ranch Water 154

Smoked Tomato Brisket Chili 115

Smoked Tri-tip 126

Smoked Turkey Jerky 98

Smoked Turkey Sandwich 143

Smoked Wings 106

Smoked, Salted Caramel Apple Pie 35

Smoke-roasted Chicken Thighs 111

Smokin' Lemon Bars 52

Smoking Gun Cocktail 157

Smoky Mountain Bramble Cocktail 152

Smoky Scotch & Ginger Cocktail 154

Sopapilla Cheesecake By Doug Scheiding 33

Sourdough Pizza 39

Spiced Cornish Hens With Cilantro Chutney 110

Spiced Orange Ribs 72

Spiced Pulled Pork Shoulder 63

Spiced Smoked Swordfish 88

Spicy Asian Brussels Sprouts 20

Spicy Bbq Whole Chicken 95

Spicy Beer Beef Jerky 115